Gender, Genre, and Victorian Historical Writing

LITERATURE AND SOCIETY IN VICTORIAN BRITAIN
VOLUME 5
GARLAND REFERENCE LIBRARY OF THE HUMANITIES
VOLUME 2073

LITERATURE AND SOCIETY IN VICTORIAN BRITAIN

SALLY MITCHELL, *Series Editor*

VICTORIAN URBAN SETTINGS
Essays on the Nineteenth-Century City and Its Contexts
edited by Debra N. Mancoff and D.J. Trela

THE MATERNAL VOICE IN VICTORIAN FICTION
Rewriting the Patriarchal Family
by Barbara Z. Thaden

WOMEN'S THEOLOGY IN NINETEENTH-CENTURY BRITAIN
Transfiguring the Faith of Their Fathers
edited by Julie Melnyk

A MONUMENT TO THE MEMORY OF GEORGE ELIOT
Edith J. Simcox's *Autobiography of a Shirtmaker*
edited by Constance M. Fulmer and Margaret E. Barfield

GENDER, GENRE, AND VICTORIAN HISTORICAL WRITING
by Rohan Amanda Maitzen

GENDER, GENRE, AND VICTORIAN HISTORICAL WRITING

ROHAN AMANDA MAITZEN

LONDON AND NEW YORK

First published 1998 by Garland Publishing, Inc.

2 Park Square, Milton Park, Abingdon, Oxon OX14 4RN
711 Third Avenue, New York, NY 10017, USA

Routledge is an imprint of the Taylor & Francis Group, an informa business

First issued in paperback 2016

Copyright © 1998 by Rohan Amanda Maitzen

All rights reserved. No part of this book may be reprinted or reproduced or utilised in any form or by any electronic, mechanical, or other means, now known or hereafter invented, including photocopying and recording, or in any information storage or retrieval system, without permission in writing from the publishers.

Notice:
Product or corporate names may be trademarks or registered trademarks, and are used only for identification and explanation without intent to infringe.

Library of Congress Cataloging-in-Publication Data

Maitzen, Rohan Amanda.
    Gender, genre, and Victorian historical writing / by Rohan Amanda Maitzen.
      p.   cm. — (Literature and society in Victorian Britain ; v. 5) (Garland reference library of the humanities ; vol. 2073)
    Includes bibliographical references (p.   ) and index.
    ISBN 0-8153-2897-4 (case : alk. paper)
    1. English prose literature—19th century—History and criticism.
2. Literature and history—Great Britain—History—19th century.
3. Women and literature—Great Britain—History—19th century.
4. Historiography—Great Britain—History—19th century. 5. Historical Fiction, English—History and criticism. 6. Eliot, George, 1819–1880—Knowledge—History. 7. Women—Great Britain—Intellectual life.
8. Women historians—Great Britain. 9. Literary form.   I. Title.
II. Series.   III. Series: Garland reference library of the humanities. Literature and society in Victorian Britain ; v. 5.
PR788.H57M35   1998
828'.08099287—dc21   98-29566
                                                                                         CIP

Cover illustration of *Lady Jane Grey and Robert Ascham* (1853) engraved by L. Stocks after John Callcott Horsley. Permission granted by Courtauld Institute of Art.

ISBN 978-0-8153-2897-1 (hbk)
ISBN 978-1-138-97496-8 (pbk)

for Steve

Contents

Acknowledgments ix
Introduction xi

Chapter 1
   The Victorian Discourse of History: Problems of Gender
      and Genre 3
Chapter 2
   "A Clique of Living Clios": Nineteenth-Century Women
      Historians 33
Chapter 3
   Stitches in Time: Needlework and Victorian
      Historiography 61
Chapter 4
   Gender and Historiography in *Romola* 103
Chapter 5
   "'Not At All Like Being A Queen'"? Historicizing
      Female Sovereignty in *Middlemarch* 135
Chapter 6
   Mary and Elizabeth: Reconfiguring Gender and Power 161
Conclusion 199

Bibliography 207
Index 223

Acknowledgments

This book began as a doctoral dissertation at Cornell University under the guidance of Harry E. Shaw, Dorothy Mermin, Mary Jacobus, and Paul Sawyer, from whose wisdom, expertise, and patience I have benefited immensely. I am grateful to my colleagues at Dalhousie University for support and advice as I revised and extended the manuscript; in particular, without Christy Luckyj's encouragement it might never have become a book at all. As always, I owe my greatest debt to my husband, Steve Maitzen, who continues to model for me the dedication, rigor, and insight of a true scholar. He and our wonderful new son, Owen, fill my life with the love that makes all of my projects, both academic and personal, worth doing.

Much of Chapter Two originally appeared as "'This Feminine Preserve': Historical Biographies by Victorian Women," in *Victorian Studies*, Vol. 38, No. 3 (Spring 1995). This material is reprinted here by permission of the trustees of Indiana University.

Introduction

In his well-known work *What is History*, E. H. Carr makes an important distinction between "basic facts" and "historical facts." He gives the following example:

> At Stalybridge Wakes in 1850, a vendor of ginger-bread, as the result of some petty dispute, was deliberately kicked to death by an angry mob. Is this a fact of history? . . . A year ago Dr. Kitson Clark cited it in his Ford lectures in Oxford. Does this make it into a historical fact? Not, I think, yet. Its present status, I suggest, is that it has been proposed for membership of the select club of historical facts. It now awaits a seconder and sponsors. . . . [I]n twenty or thirty years' time it may be a well established historical fact. Alternatively, nobody may take it up, in which case it will relapse into the limbo of unhistorical facts about the past. . . . Its status as a historical fact will turn on a question of interpretation.[1]

The gingerbread vendor's existence is not in dispute, nor is his demise at the hands (or, literally, the feet) of the mob. The question is whether this fact, or accumulation of facts, bears historical significance—whether it deserves or perhaps even requires a part in our re-telling of the past.

Accepting Carr's distinction between "facts" and "historical facts" as an accurate model of the inevitable, if always problematic, decisions historians make as they construct their stories of the past, this study argues that during the nineteenth century a new category of facts entered the running for membership in history's exclusive club: facts about women and the circumstances of their lives. Like the gingerbread man, women were there all along, and they had even made guest appearances as "unhistorical facts," adding color or breadth to the historical panorama but not affecting its essential form or design. In the Victorian period, however, new interpretive possibilities emerged, in part responding to and in part furthering an explosion of information about women in the past. The change was not sudden or distinct; no single text marks the beginning of a new, universally dominant model of historiographical priorities. Rather, the ebb and flow of Victorian debates over gender, genre, and historical writing—debates which frequently and significantly overlapped—gradually and unevenly altered the horizons of possibility for historical writing about women and, ultimately, made women's history as we know it today conceptually possible.

In a limited sense, mine is a structuralist argument, a revision and extension of the insight that "what meaning you [are] able to articulate depend[s] on what script or speech you [share] in the first place."[2] Making a similar point, though in a different idiom, philosopher Louis Mink explains that "narrative is the form in which we make comprehensible the many successive interrelationships that are comprised by a career"; "[p]articular narratives express their own conceptual presuppositions."[3] Both of these claims helpfully articulate an important truth about both historical and fictional narratives: their intelligibility relies on the standards of coherence and meaning accepted by the culture to which they belong. Readers invoke these standards whenever they ask of a given story whether it makes sense; this question really means "does this story conform to a pattern or model, to a plot, that I recognize?" These standards are not immutable or static, and narratives often test or question them as much as they reinforce them. Indeed, challenging the limited range of available scripts or plots can be a vitally important part of any movement for social and cultural reform. For instance, as Carolyn Heilbrun points out, revising narrative forms is crucial to feminist activism:

> [L]ives do not serve as models; only stories do that. And it is a hard thing to make up stories to live by. We can only retell and live by the stories we have read or heard. We live our lives through texts. They may be read, or chanted, or experienced electronically, or come to us, like the murmurings of our mothers, telling us what conventions

Introduction xiii

demand. Whatever their form or medium, these stories have formed us all; they are what we must use to make new fictions, new narratives.[4]

As her comments imply, narrative is never a purely literary concern. Rather, it is, in Mink's phrase, "a primary and irreducible form of human comprehension," something that affects the range of our imaginations and hence of our actions, for it is hard to pursue a plan or a plot which we have no means of expressing or understanding.[5]

This study examines Victorian historical writing in light of these concepts of the structure and implications of literary form. I examine the ways in which a variety of nineteenth-century texts interact with the scripts or plots available for making experience, especially women's experience, intelligible and meaningful within the confines of Victorian presuppositions about history, about gender, and about narrative. My fundamental claim is that during this period writers from Agnes Strickland to George Eliot take advantage of instabilities in existing models of history—instabilities brought on by generic competition with the novel and by gender confusion due to the feminization of historical practice and subject matter—to broaden the range of meanings that could be articulated. As these formulations suggest, I intend this project as a contribution to literary history. Thanks to the wide-ranging and sophisticated work of critics such as Gillian Beer, Jerome McGann, Alexander Welsh, and Dorothy Mermin, I use this term with almost no anxiety that it will be understood as implying either naïve positivism or tired antiquarianism. Today, literary history at its best reflects the influence of feminism and cultural studies in the variety and complexity of its questions and the legacy of New Criticism as well as post-structuralism in the rich textual detail of its answers.[6] It also reflects the conviction (usually implicit) of its practitioners that the theoretical questions about narrative historiography currently so topical in the academy have not been settled in favor of skepticism, a conviction which I share but which I will not endeavor to defend here.[7] Like the Victorian historians whose writings I examine in this essay, today's literary historians do not despair because writing history turns out to be something other than transcribing a single, unified story told in one dominant voice. Rather, they—and I—make it a priority to recover lost stories and disregarded voices and bring them into dialogue with our own present concerns, while always respecting their distance, their difference, and their own words.[8]

In my first chapter I argue that history as both subject and practice was a site of contestation and anxiety throughout the nineteenth century. Examining articles and reviews in a wide range of Victorian periodicals, I show that concerns about both gender and genre inflected debates about the style, form, and content of historiography. These aesthetic and historiographical problems intersected with contemporary social and political concerns, transforming the debate into something of interest and relevance to a much wider audience than simply those scholars, antiquarians, and intellectuals directly involved in producing overtly historical works.

Chapter Two focuses on gender issues more narrowly. Although, as Chapter One shows, gender in Victorian historiography is a problem, rather than a fixed category, associated with the stylistic, formal, and substantive choices of an author aspiring to produce historical texts—that is, writers of either sex could manifest "manly" or "womanly" qualities in various aspects of their work and with varying effects—literal gender did play a role in changing definitions of history because of the increasing number of women writing historical works and the increasing attention paid to the lives and circumstances of women in the past. This chapter surveys many of the multitude of historical works by Victorian women, reading them as experiments in writing women into history and focusing on the kinds of stories they tell, the model of women's history they present, and what answers or alternatives they offer to the general problems discussed in Chapter One. I argue that these writers draw on gender ideologies that allowed women a particular kind of power—influence—and on new historiographical theories that replaced the public sphere with the private as the site of historical significance, to develop a distinct model of women's history as well as a wider theory of history in which women for once played an important part. These models, I contend, have both conservative and subversive potential: they comport with restrictive patriarchal ideas, but they also foster a revisionary and in some senses feminist approach to history.

The next chapter takes a closer look at two particular historical works by women, Agnes Strickland's *Lives of the Queens of England* and Elizabeth Stone's *Art of Needlework*, placing them in the context of a widespread preoccupation with needlework's role as the paradigmatic

Introduction xv

marker of Victorian femininity as well as an equally widespread concern about women's substituting the pen for the needle. In both works, the authors strangely literalize these debates by explicitly and conspicuously importing needles into their historical prose. Strickland never misses an opportunity to describe needlework done by any of her subjects; doing so cements her own gender credentials as well as those of the queen in question, while also upholding her avowed intention to bring previously neglected material into the historical record. Stone's work encapsulates every aspect of the debates already discussed about gender and historiography. Her history of needlework, which begins with a spirited denunciation of traditional historians for preferring the sword to the needle, challenges old notions of historical significance and advances a new, feminized historiographical theory of influence and undercurrents. These works, I suggest, exemplify the possibilities of this approach to women's history, but this chapter also highlights a limitation of this approach easily overlooked when focusing on it simply as an alternative form of biographical writing: its reinforcement of class hierarchies and boundaries. Needlework was in fact a common part of almost all nineteenth-century women's lives, whether they were poor, working class, bourgeois, or aristocratic, but Strickland and Stone rely on its ladylike associations to bolster their claims for women's inherent nobility and civilizing influence. Nowhere in their volumes is there even a hint that, for some women, the needle was an obligation rather than an option—a means to a subsistence income earned at the expense of health, even life—and in this absence, most striking in Stone's text, we find a reminder that the whole discourse of history which they are creating in opposition to masculine norms is itself founded on exclusionary presuppositions.

My next two chapters read two of George Eliot's novels as contributions to the effort to redefine women's place in historiography. *Romola*, I argue, uncovers a fatal flaw in the theory of women's history propagated in the works by women historians: because this theory relies heavily on a notion of woman's nature as universal, essential, and ahistorical, ultimately it cannot sustain a realistic, fully historicized narrative. If you adopt, as Eliot does in *Romola* and her other novels, a model in which contextual detail and historical difference are crucial, essentializing women leaves them once again out of the historical narrative. Romola is a misfit in her novel, and the novel abandons realism for symbolism and myth, for just this reason. Here we see two of Eliot's intellectual commitments—fully-realized historical representation, in the mode of Sir Walter Scott, and gender essentialism—clashing; although the contest may not have been deliberately staged, the lesson is there for us once we read the novel in the context of the Victorian discourse of history. Eliot's own subsequent projects, *Middlemarch* in particular, suggest that she too recognized, if only intuitively, the incompatibility of the "queenly ideal" promulgated in the women historians' volumes with her historical and realist vision.

Chapter Five reads *Middlemarch* as Eliot's attempt to reconcile femininity and historicism. Like Romola, Dorothea Brooke resembles the queens of the women's books, but her aspirations are frustrated, her grandeur is undermined by ironic commentary as well as by her failures and errors, and her character is clearly embedded in a specific historical moment and a carefully realistic narrative—not for her any mythic apotheosis. Not, then, a figure of universal or idealized sovereignty, Dorothea is queenly only metaphorically. I argue that Eliot's characterization of Dorothea participates in a redefinition of female sovereignty as bourgeois femininity similar to that found in texts such as Ruskin's "Of Queens' Gardens," which adapted queenliness to the private sphere, or in the real world where Queen Victoria's overwhelming domesticity further entangled middle-class ideals with regal images. Dorothea's ardent desire to do concrete social good through beneficent influence links her directly to the tradition of queenly influence she herself admires, a tradition persistently summoned up in the novel. Aware of the limitations of this tradition but unwilling to abandon it completely, Eliot adapts it, constructing a queenly identity suitable for historical representation by shaping the ideal to the possible, turning from the essential and universal to the individual, and yet preserving a vision of potential greatness of a distinctly feminine kind.

My final chapter looks at Froude's *Reign of Elizabeth*, Strickland's *Life of Mary Queen of Scots*, and Strickland's volume on Elizabeth I from her *Lives of the Queens of England*. In their opposing religious and political allegiances, Elizabeth I and Mary, Queen of Scots, embodied central ideological controversies of the Victorian age. But their most problematic identity was one they shared: both were politically powerful women for whom marriage, for the Victorians

Introduction xvii

perhaps the defining relationship of the private sphere, was a matter of state. Froude and Strickland struggle to produce coherent narratives of these problematic lives compatible with their divergent views of women and history and comprehensible within the imaginative limits of their culture. Though their accounts differ significantly, together they clarify the otherwise rather mysterious appeal of Mary Stuart to the Victorians: despite the many ways in which she affronted nineteenth-century prejudices, she proved easier to narrate, to account for within the range of available historical plots, than her royal cousin. Even so, however, both historians work hard and conspicuously to reconcile conflicts between facts and formulas in their texts; the results highlight once again the impossibility of considering Victorian historical writing without considering both gender and genre.

NOTES

1. E. H. Carr, *What is History*. 2nd edition, ed. R. W. Davies (London: MacMillan, 1961), pp. 6-7.

2. Terry Eagleton, *Literary Theory: An Introduction* (Minneapolis: U of Minnesota P, 1983), p. 107.

3. Louis O. Mink, "Narrative Form as Cognitive Instrument," in *Historical Understanding,* ed. Brian Fay, Eugene Golob, and Richard Vann (Ithaca: Cornell UP, 1987), pp. 182-203; pp. 185-6.

4. Carolyn Heilbrun, *Writing a Woman's Life* (New York: Ballantine, 1988), p. 37.

5. Mink, "Narrative Form as Cognitive Instrument," p. 186.

6. Robert Weimann, in "Past Significance and Present Meaning in Literary History," *New Directions in Literary History,* ed. Ralph Cohen (Baltimore: Johns Hopkins UP, 1974), pp.43-61, gives a useful overview of challenges to and changes in literary historical approaches.

7. In *Is Literary History Possible?* (Baltimore: Johns Hopkins UP, 1992), David Perkins applies these debates to literary history; his conclusion is more pessimistic than my own.

8. For further discussion of literary history as a dialogic exchange with the past, see Gillian Beer, *Arguing with the Past: Essays In Narrative from Woolf to Sydney* (London: Routledge, 1989), Jerome McGann, *The Beauty of Inflections: Literary Investigations in Historical Method and Theory* (Oxford: Clarendon, 1985), or Weimann, "Past Significance and Present Meaning in Literary History."

Gender, Genre,
and Victorian Historical Writing

CHAPTER ONE

The Victorian Discourse of History
Problems of Gender and Genre

*Are means to the end, themselves in part the end?
Is fiction which makes fact alive, fact too?*[1]

"The perfect historian," Macaulay wrote in 1828, "... gives to truth those attractions which have been usurped by fiction."[2] Today, "usurped" seems a strong and even strange word in this context; its unexpected force alerts us to the intense competition between history and fiction during the nineteenth century. They competed to dominate the historical field, an influential jurisdiction in an age coming, as much recent scholarship has confirmed, to place more and more faith in the past's explanatory power.[3] Reviewing Froude's history of Tudor England in 1864, Charles Kingsley remarked that

> [t]his generation is getting a wholesome philosophical instinct, that only by knowing the past can one guess at the future; that the future is contained in the past, and the child father to the man; that one generation reaps what its forefathers have sown.... [I]t desires more and more to know what manner of men they were, these ancestors of ours....[4]

As the metaphors in this passage suggest, the Victorian historical sense was generational and evolutionary; the relationship between past and present—and thus between present and future—was one of organic process and development. Existing conditions resulted from previous events and actions; today's choices would in their turn determine tomorrow's aspect. Historical interpretation was therefore of vital present-day importance: historical description easily could, and often did, become political prescription. If the past was not dead but lived on in contemporary problems (or successes), the historian might be not a dusty antiquarian, but a sage, a teacher, or even a prophet.

History's seemingly sudden appeal itself grew out of historical circumstances. In a time of dramatic technological, social, and political transformation, and of profound challenges from science and scholarship to the belief systems that had ordered the world in earlier centuries, historical explanations were, potentially, secularized theodicies; they replaced chaos and tumult with order fixed not in abstractions but in the lives of real human beings in a real social environment. "[T]he reading public," as T. W. Heyck explains, "wanted to establish continuities with the past, to be assured that English institutions were sound, to use the past as a guide through perilous times, and to secure a basis for hope that continuing change would be beneficial."[5] Peter Allan Dale draws a similar conclusion: "the intellectual history of the nineteenth century," he submits, "may fairly be described as a search for an adequate replacement for the lost Christian totality."[6] In the right historical context, change could appear grounds for optimism rather than anxiety, and as these remarks suggest, historical knowledge was one way of easing the sensation of displacement and loss under which the Victorian consciousness suffered. In the words of Archibald Alison, a prominent Victorian historian, after the cataclysm of the French Revolution the public sought a history

> which should bring the experience of the past to bear on the visions of the present, and tell men, from the recorded events of history, what they had to hope, and what to fear, from the passion for innovation which had seized possession of so large a portion of the active part of mankind.[7]

For all of these reasons, the Victorian public's "appetite for history [was] a great and increasing one," and books flooded from the presses to feed it.[8]

Vital present-day political and social concerns thus made the territory over which historiography and fiction struggled highly significant. In this contest for representational ascendancy, conventional historiography had the advantage of tradition, centuries of authority backing its claims. But fiction, although lacking in overtly scholarly credentials, had other advantages: novelists had imaginative access to the interior states of history's characters, as well as freedom to describe and embellish so as to present individual actions and circumstances with greater immediacy. A fictional account could be more evocative, more colorful, and more emotionally gripping than a conventional historical one, while still depicting undeniably historical events. The usurper Macaulay had particularly in mind in his essay was Sir Walter Scott, who with the 1814 publication of *Waverley* had issued an unprecedented challenge to historiography, combining historical detail with fictional interest "in a manner," to quote Macaulay again, "that might well provoke [the historian's] envy."[9] Scott's novels, exemplifying the possibilities of a fictional historiography, powerfully stimulated the generic rivalry. "Without one word of direct precept," wrote one early reviewer, "[the Waverley novels] have made us feel more than any essays or lectures ever did, to what end history should be read, and in what manner it should be written."[10] Not everyone was equally appreciative, but everyone recognized that, for good or ill, his novels had changed the terms of the historiographical debate. He had, in the words of one contemporary, "laid the muse of History under contribution to the nymph of fiction."[11]

This image of fiction as a graceful young maiden highlights a key implication of history's indebtedness to and competition with the novel: because the novel, from its earliest days, was an artistic medium accessible to and widely associated with women, the contest over genre was inevitably gendered. As the representational vehicle for private life, for instance, the novel focused on traditionally feminine topics: courtship, marriage, domestic life, manners, morals. Though most women were barred from the classical education considered necessary for other literary projects, "[n]o educational restrictions can shut women out from the materials of fiction," as George Eliot wrote in 1856, "and there is no species of art which is so free from rigid requirements."[12] Further, the female mind, considered unfit for the rigors of philosophy or science, could, it was supposed, exert itself with facility in these lighter endeavors and produce narratives praiseworthy for such appropriately womanly qualities as liveliness, affect, insight into character, attentiveness to social milieu, and ingenuity in plotting. Many, perhaps most, would have agreed with M. A. Stodart, who wrote in 1842 that "[women's] powers of delicate observation, joined to their instinctive penetration into the movements of the human heart," gave them "peculiar advantages" as novelists.[13]

Historiography, by contrast, traditionally treated the major events of the public world: courts, not hearths; wars, not romances; treaties, not engagements; the births and deaths of empires, not of children. And it proceeded according to rules of form and content quite unlike the rules for fiction, or so at least many writers contended: it was impersonal, grave, serious, methodical, strictly impartial, and concerned with large transformations and philosophical abstractions rather than with concrete, personal details. "The task of an historian," wrote W. R. Greg in the *Edinburgh Review* in 1853, "is a grand and noble one. . . . He sits in the judgment-seat of an august tribunal"; it is a "post of high dignity and solemn obligation."[14] Just as many qualities of fiction fall easily under the rubric "traditionally feminine," these qualities are "traditionally masculine," and the oppositions established are completely unsurprising, even mundane, typifying as they do well-known Victorian presuppositions about the differences between women and men. History, then, is to fiction as male is to female: a simple formula, it seems, for this intersection of gender and genre.

Not only explicit statements or manifestos from a variety of nineteenth-century writers on history but also twentieth-century studies of Victorian historiography tend to uphold this tidy model, simply by the total absence of any evidence to the contrary. John Kenyon's 1983 volume called simply *The History Men* is one striking example, but G. P. Gooch's classic survey *History and Historians in the Nineteenth-Century* (1913), Thomas Preston Peardon's *The Transition in English Historical Writing 1760-1830* (1933), J. W. Burrow's 1981 study *A Liberal Descent: Victorian Historians and the English Past*, Rosemary Jann's *The Art and Science of Victorian History* (1985), and Joseph M. Levine's *Humanism and History: Origins of Modern English Historiography* (1987) similarly perpetuate the notion that, in this period, men and their concerns completely dominate the historical field. Literary critics, too, typically accept that historiography was a masculine preserve. Christina Crosby's provocative book *The Ends of History: Victorians and 'the Woman Question'* depends on this assumption, as her thesis is that women were the necessarily excluded "other" against which history (both as experience and as practice) was defined in the Victorian period. Carol Christ, in her turn, argues that nonfiction prose in general was aggressively masculinized during the nineteenth century, while the "discursive space that women could claim was that of the novel, and, to a much slighter extent, poetry." Even Ina Ferris, in her sophisticated analysis of the ways the Waverley novels rearranged Victorian notions of history and fiction, accepts that Victorian historiography was an essentially masculine discourse. Scott, she maintains, appropriated history's (male) authority for his fictions, thereby forging, if only temporarily, a new, *masculine*, model of novel-writing and reading; once he had brought about this transformation, the struggle was to establish just which forms of this masculine discourse would be preeminent, what would qualify for membership in history's once-exclusive club.[15]

This study will assert, however, that this tidy model of the Victorian discourse of history treats as stable standards and oppositions which were, in fact, profoundly in question at the time. One can't read for long in the periodical literature without finding that writing of and about history in the period was not, for the Victorians, a unified, unproblematically masculine enterprise. Not only were numerous women claiming discursive space for themselves as well as representational space for women of the past, but also writers of both sexes were engaging in projects challenging the rigid and exclusionary standards of conventional historiography—both its form and its content—in ways that inevitably challenged its masculinist biases as well. Articles and reviews reveal a pervasive interest, enthusiastic or uneasy, in these developments. At stake, these essays make clear, was the nature of the historical project as a whole: What should be included? How should material be selected and organized? What formal constraints should be operative? Given the extraordinary importance of historical understanding and interpretation in Victorian culture and society, these questions were clearly more than academic, and the answers with which the Victorians experimented are intricately related to both gender and genre.

I

In an 1855 review of Dr. Doran's *Queens of England of the House of Hanover* in *Fraser's Magazine*, J. M. Kemble finds the author guilty of faults "essentially womanish," and, while warning the unworthy doctor away from "the *man's* work, for which he is not fitted," he takes the opportunity to object to a larger trend of which he takes Dr. Doran's efforts to be merely symptomatic:

> We do assuredly lament that people should be found to write history who ought to be writing novels; and that the public require history to be written like novels in order to read it.... [W]e must plead guilty to a great dislike for the growing tendency among women to become writers of history. These authoresses, often gifted as they are with a certain insight into character, a vivid appreciation of individual facts and a great facility of narration, have in our opinion no historical grasp—no powerful comprehension of events; and what they produce is at the best but a pretty phantasmagoria of coloured figures.[16]

Kemble's primary targets are women who, in his view, overstep the bounds of their gender by switching genres, and his composure is disturbed by a sense that their numbers are increasing. He was right in the latter respect at least: the only extended study of any Victorian women historians calls this "growing tendency among women to become writers of history" "a minor phenomenon of nineteenth-century book-making."[17] A reviewer in 1855 might have been aware of, for example, the work of Agnes Strickland, the most prominent, though not the first, of the "lady historians." She published her twelve-volume series *Lives of the Queens of England* between 1840 and 1848 and followed up her considerable success with *Lives of the Queens of Scotland* (1850-1859), *Lives of the Bachelor Kings* (1861), *Lives of the Tudor Princesses* (1867), and *Lives of the Last Four Princesses of the House of Stuart* (1872).[18] Among the many others were Lucy Aikin, who wrote *Memoirs of the Court of Queen Elizabeth* (1818) and *Memoirs of the Court of King Charles the First* (1833); Elizabeth Ogilvy Benger, whose works include memoirs of Anne Boleyn (1821) and Mary Queen of Scots (1823); Hannah Lawrance, whose *Historical Memoirs of the Queens of England* appeared in 1838 and 1840 and who also wrote *A History of Woman in England* (1843); Julia Kavanagh, who published *Woman in France During the Eighteenth Century* in 1850; Annie Forbes Bush, whose *Memoirs of the Queens of France* appeared in 1843; Martha Walker Freer, among whose productions were biographies of Jeanne d'Albret, Queen of Navarre (1855),

Marguerite d'Angoulême (1854), and Henry III of France (1858); Mrs. Matthew Hall, whose *Queens Before the Conquest* (1854) filled the gap in Strickland's coverage; and Mary Ann Everett Green, whose volumes included *Lives of the Princesses of England* (1849-1855).[19] The particular criticisms Kemble directs at what obviously seemed to him a flood of transgressive works typify the Victorian discourse of history in a variety of ways. In the first place, he lodges a complaint much like Macaulay's about the encroachment of fiction on historical territory. Unlike Macaulay's remarks, however, Kemble's are gender-specific, and the characteristics he enumerates as the gifts found among aspiring women historians coincide with the features widely considered to specially fit women for writing fiction. His rhetoric belittles rather than appreciates these gifts: he opposes insight, facility of narration and appreciation for details to the more effective and important skills of the historian, namely, a firm "grasp" of, or control over, broad historical issues and patterns. By rejecting the women's admitted talents as sufficient qualifications for historical writing, Kemble locates himself in a wider discussion about historiographical priorities.

At least since the publication of *Waverley*, critics had debated the merits of greater affect and color in historical narration. Scott's reviewers praise his turning away from abstractions and towards concrete details that made the past come alive as never before. Thomas Carlyle, for example, himself always suspicious of fiction's power to misrepresent, famously declared that Scott's novels had

> taught all men this truth, which looks like a truism, and yet was as good as unknown to writers of history and others, till so taught: that the bygone ages of the world were actually filled by living men, not by protocols, state-papers, controversies and abstractions of men.[20]

This achievement was valuable in part because it made history's lessons more vivid and thus more memorable; as a reviewer wrote in *Fraser's* in 1857, "no history can be really instructive if it be not also amusing":

> when the narrative descends into particulars, and brings the reader into connexion with the private life, the hopes, the fears, the misfortunes, and the triumphs of real men and women, it holds on by so many fibres, ramifying into so many human affections, that it will

not be eradicated from the memory.[21]

If the historians could only learn Scott's stylistic lesson well enough, they might be able to compete with him and so dispel their own anxieties about his usurpation of their territory. Macaulay himself certainly saw the situation in this way. Reviewing Sir James Mackintosh's *History of the Revolution in England in 1688* in 1835, he admires Mackintosh's rare combination of scholarship and liveliness: "A history of England, written throughout in this manner, would be the most fascinating book in the language. It would be more in request at the circulating libraries than the last novel."[22] Conscious as he obviously was of fiction's special power to please (and to sell), Macaulay would no doubt have been gratified, had he lived, to hear James Moncrieff's description of his own *History* as uniting "the rarest accuracy of an historian to the charms and witchery of a romance."[23]

On the opposing side were those who preferred history to retain its special dignity. Like Kemble, this party considered truth all but incompatible with lightness of touch or of tone, and affect far less important than seriousness and ostentatious impartiality. Reviewers of this persuasion typically set up hierarchical oppositions between works erring on the side of color and liveliness and "real" historical writing. In the *Edinburgh Review* in 1842, for example, C. S. M. Phillipps deplores Archibald Alison's use of the present tense, a not uncommon device for increasing the pace and immediacy of a narrative, as "utterly inconsistent with the sober dignity of the historical style," while G. W. Abraham, writing in the *Dublin Review* in 1855, finds Agnes Strickland's style "rather more chatty and familiar than quite beseems an historian."[24] In *Fraser's Magazine* in 1857, T. C. Sandars complains that there is a "want of dignity and repose" in Buckle's *History of Civilization in England* which makes it "a great falling off from the level of modern English historians" whose tone, Sandars declares, "is almost always that of men sensible of the dignity of their subject."[25] Kemble, in his 1855 review of Dr. Doran, similarly holds up the qualities of a "serious" historian as a contrast to the work of the women historians; although he allows their "pretty phantasmagorias" aesthetic advantages, this juxtaposition diminishes their claims to be producing an authoritative discourse, a result reinforced by his pejorative linking of them with novelists.

Macaulay's comment about appealing to the market of the circulating libraries hints at the larger stakes in a debate that might otherwise seem an oddly inflated dispute over literary taste. Macaulay's biographer, John Clive, comments that Macaulay wanted his own *History* to be "instructive, entertaining, and universally intelligible";[26] those who argue, as Macaulay does, for more readable, memorable, historical books seem to want historical knowledge disseminated more widely, to be accessible to a range of audiences, and to be effective, as they often say explicitly, morally and pedagogically. In a time in which looking back was believed to tell people how to interpret what they saw around them as well as what to look forward to, however, such an approach potentially destabilized both political and gender structures.

In the background of the controversy over historical writing was the reaction against increasing literacy sparked by the French Revolution; in the late eighteenth century a mass reading public appeared to be a potential threat to social order—if the wrong sorts of books fell into its hands.[27] Indeed, as Alexander Welsh has observed, resistance to the spread of literacy tends to be linked to a more general hostility to the wider dissemination of knowledge.[28] The early and mid-Victorians recognized print's power as an agent of socialization (J. F. C. Harris notes that "[t]he process of assimilation [to middle-class values] was closely related to the spread of literacy"[29]), but as Richard Altick emphasizes, increased literacy also fostered political awareness and activism.[30] Given the widespread view of history as the genealogy of the present and the harbinger of the future, and the historian's accepted role as teacher and prophet, the message and audience of historical publications were of special concern. Extensive historical study and understanding had previously been the domain of the privileged few. The newly readable, popular histories, by contrast, offered information about past and present to a wide range of readers: as Margaret Oliphant remarked, for instance, "the country *en masse* read [Macaulay's *History*] as it never had read anything before, except, perhaps, the Waverley novels."[31] Moreover, as I discuss more fully below, specific characteristics of nineteenth-century history books, such as their increasing awareness of and emphasis on everyday life and the private sphere, potentially underwrote a radical, or at the least a progressive, political agenda. Discomfort at works descending below the "dignity of history," then, reflects an uneasiness about loss of control over what had become one of the nation's most important cultural properties as well as about the lessons the newly fashionable works might be teaching their expanding audience.

A further source of anxiety was the possibility that its growing resemblance to fiction and its changed tone would emasculate historical writing. The qualities for which Scott and then Macaulay were praised included grace and liveliness of narration, attention to detail, and emotional affectiveness—qualities which were, as already noted, supposed to be women's special gifts; indeed, as Dorothy Mermin points out, "elements conventionally coded as feminine" give much canonical Victorian non-fiction prose its "distinctive flavour." [32] These stylistic features are precisely those Kemble dismisses in the work of the "lady historians." In response to such allegations of effeminacy, Macaulay's supportive reviewers frequently and, I suspect, defensively, characterize his *History* as masculine: James Moncrieff in the *Edinburgh Review*, for example, praised Macaulay for his "*manly* determination to pass at once beyond the line of the established topics to which it has been the fashion for historians to confine themselves" in his third chapter on the condition of England in 1685.[33] Critics often applaud other male historians, including Archibald Alison, J. A. Froude, and Henry Hallam, for manliness explicitly or for displaying masculine qualities: penetration, strength, and vigor in inquiry or style, or impartiality and gravity of judgment. As a rule, little prestige or cultural status attached either to women writers or to novelists, and the majority of critics labor to dissociate "the history men" (to borrow John Kenyon's label) from these lesser forms and secure them an appropriately higher standing.

II

The formal and organizational aspects of historical texts were as controversial as their style and tone. Again, Kemble's remarks lead into the larger debate. Among the pleasing but ultimately inferior gifts of the historical "authoresses," he notes "a vivid appreciation of individual facts"; they lack, however, "historical grasp" and "powerful comprehension of events." The problem of the proper relationship between details and broader logical, philosophical, or narrative structures surfaces repeatedly in nineteenth-century discussions of history.[34] Most writers acknowledge that the age of sweeping philosophic history, of, for example, Montesquieu, is past; both public taste and the standards of the historical community had changed, and readers desired greater minuteness and particularity. "[Froude] writes," Goldwin Smith reported in the *Edinburgh Review* in 1858, "under the auspices of a new school of historical composition, which requires effect to be produced not by brilliant rhetoric and imposing generalisation, but by minute accuracy of detail."[35] This model suited what Carol Christ has identified as the "growing conviction of the subjectivity of experience and the demand for scientific standards of truth."[36]

One desirable effect of the accumulation of "decorative detail," as R. H. Patterson says about Macaulay's *History*, is that it "serve[s] to bring the past times more vividly before us."[37] But most reviewers still demanded that the historian subordinate details to a larger conceptual whole, that particulars illustrate, not supersede, the narrative. The information explosion led Victorians to value "synthesis, generalization, and evaluation," T. W. Heyck observes, so that "[f]or the man of letters, the ability to assimilate and interpret rated as a higher quality than the ability to report special knowledge."[38] Reviews of historical work consistently reflect just this priority placed on control over information; the historian's success or failure at achieving an appropriate balance between the forest and the trees is a central formal concern in almost every case. In *Blackwood's* in 1860, for example, a reviewer praises Archibald Alison for "massing details, and bringing them to bear upon the general stream of events" in his depiction of the Greek Revolution, while another, writing in 1866, considers Alison's *History* a model of "writing a narrative which shall embrace every point of importance without wearying the reader by faulty arrangement or wearisome detail."[39] In the *Edinburgh Review* in 1858, Goldwin Smith notes approvingly that in Froude's account of the Pilgrimage of Grace "details are selected with judgment and taste, and thrown into a vivid and striking form by the powers of a fine imagination."[40] In a review of Macaulay's *History* in 1856, J. M. Kemble argues that producing a historical work such as Macaulay's requires both a "most extensive knowledge of facts" and "a coup-d'oeil, capable of arranging and co-ordinating such facts."[41] James Moncrieff, writing in the *Edinburgh Review* in 1857, admires Macaulay's ability to "[grasp] with the eye of a statesman the bearing of details on the great consequences of the time," and in *Fraser's Magazine* in 1856 W. B. Donne comments that "the researches of the antiquary are often tedious and trivial; but where ... they furnish materials for a master-builder, the studies of Dryasdust deserve our thanks and assume the dignity of labour."[42] All of these reviewers emphasize proportion; ideally, providing the minute details, signs of a microscopic eye, completes and perfects the historian's work—but does not constitute it.

When the details seemed to overrun the page, the historian might be, and usually was, accused of failing to discriminate between the trivial and the significant, of falling below the dignity of history by allowing the formal ordering of the text to be overrun by clutter. "Macaulay's pages," Archibald Alison comments uneasily in *Blackwood's* in 1849,

> often remind us of the paintings of Bassano, in which warriors and pilgrims, horses and mules, dromedaries and camels, sheep and lambs, Arabs and Ethiopians, shining armour and glistening pans, spears and pruning-hooks, scimitars and sheperds' crooks, baskets, tents, and precious stuffs, are crammed together without mercy, and with an equal light thrown on the most insignificant as the most important parts of the piece.[43]

Alison does not deny that these details are facts about the past, but he resists categorizing them all as what Carr would call "historical facts" and resents Macaulay's apparent abdication of the historian's responsibility to draw this distinction. Also drawing his metaphor from the visual arts, Walter Bagehot, in the *National Review* in 1856, wishes Macaulay had not expended his narrative powers on "the superficies of circumstance, the scum of events," but rather had produced essays "solely on great men and great things":

> The diffuseness of the style would have been then in place; we could have borne to hear the smallest minutiae of magnificent epochs. If an inferior hand had executed the connection-links, our notions would have acquired an insensible perspective; the best works of the great artist, the best themes, would have stood out from the canvas. They are now confused by the equal brilliancy of the adjacent inferiorities.[44]

Over and over critics make the same complaint: the important facts of

The Victorian Discourse of History

history are getting buried in a mass of inferior, insignificant particulars; the historians are failing in their task of sorting out what really matters from miscellaneous matter. J. L. Sanford objects that Froude has "trodden almost too closely in the footsteps of the general chronicler, and not preserved the due proportion between the space allotted to important and trivial incidents."[45] T. E. May fears that Froude may be "beguiled" into the "fault" of giving such prominence to newly discovered primary sources that "the higher philosophy of history is in danger of being lost in a multiplicity of secondary events."[46] And W. F. Pollock, though often admiring Carlyle's colorful illustrative material, fears that "this power in minute parts is attained by the sacrifice of the subject considered as a whole."[47] "There is a want of proportion," he says, "... leading him to an apparently capricious omission of really important details in some places, while they are without mercy or evident reason accumulated in others."[48]

Like the controversy over affectivity in historical writing, the overwhelming concern with the relationship of details to larger conceptual wholes signifies more than conflicting aesthetic preferences. In the first place, the same aspects of the Victorian world that made the study of history so attractive also contributed to a widespread anxiety about the apparent fragmentation of a world once seen as a coherent whole. Carol Christ argues persuasively that the explosion of knowledge in the form of minute, discrete facts defying containment within old typologies and systems of categorization had made it frighteningly difficult for the Victorians to sustain any holistic view of their world: "sensitivity to the microscopic," she says, "comes to imply a particularistic conception of the universe, according to which each individual is a law only unto itself. The particular understood as the minute comes to connote the particular as the absolutely individual."[49] It is a vision of increasing isolation, arbitrariness, and separation, as knowledge comes to seem increasingly subjective and dispersed. The disorganization and indiscriminate mingling that seemed to typify some historiographical works, with broad outlines lost in a vivid but bewildering mass of individual bits of information, exemplified the disorder coming to characterize the world in general, and scholarship in particular, and it was especially troubling as a feature of historical writing because history was being invoked precisely as a solution to the absence of other unifying principles.

A tendency to valorize specifics over generalizations is a

potentially unsettling aesthetic principle for other reasons as well. Martin Meisel's description of Victorian historical painting as bringing about an "affective refamiliarization" of history by portraying historical scenes as "readable human situation[s]," thus "reconnecting the past to the present," provides a pertinent and useful analogy for the changes taking place in historical narration.[50] Historical books, too, increasingly emphasized "human situation[s]" and appealed to "natural" sentiments such as pity, fear, sorrow, or pleasure with their evocative, personal details. Insofar as they realize this model, historical works, because their effects are "felt instantly on the pulses," promise that a life, "for all its apparent arbitrariness and obscurity, might indeed work in some sense very like a rational law."[51] But the overabundant details creating this "affective refamiliarization" might be threatening in their resistance to categorization and reimposition of order, rather than comforting in their appeal to sensibility.[52] Certainly abstractions and theories tend to lose their persuasive force and interest when individual cases appear in intimate and attentive detail; the more singular the example, the harder it is to sustain the generalization. Naomi Schor, citing Baudelaire, notes the association of an indiscriminate "riot of details" with a revolutionary mob; Carlyle's *French Revolution* (1837) exemplifies the ways such an aesthetic principle could evoke and replicate social and political chaos.[53]

But the most disturbing implication of the growing valorization of details was that, as Naomi Schor shows, attention to detail is an aesthetic principle historically associated with women: on the one hand details are aspects of ornamentation, a feminine (or effeminate) preoccupation; on the other, they are aspects of the everyday, the domestic, a category overdetermined as feminine by the mid-Victorian period. Thus, as she says, "the detail is gendered and doubly gendered as feminine."[54] Further, women were understood to have a particularly keen eye for details coupled with an innate inability to rise to universals—a distribution of qualities assumed to make them good novelists, if indifferent historians, and also to fit them for certain kinds of scientific work involving acute perception rather than abstract conceptualizing—while men, with their eyes on higher things, were less minutely observant.[55] A telling moment in Macaulay's essay "History" illustrates how the seemingly complimentary observation that women have a special facility with particulars in fact reduces them to second-class citizens in the historical domain. Macaulay notes that "the talent of deciding on the circumstances of a particular case is often possessed in the highest perfection by persons destitute of the power of generalization." "Women," he goes on, "have more of this dexterity [with particulars] than men," but "the species of discipline by which this dexterity is acquired tends to contract the mind, and to render it incapable of abstract reasoning."[56] Male historians whose work failed to maintain a judicious balance between general principles and minutiae, like those whose writing fell below the "dignity of history," thus fell on the wrong side of a fine line between appropriating feminine qualities for masculine ends and themselves seeming unmanly and out of control, even uncivilized, no better, by Victorian standards, than the Mohawks and thieves who are Macaulay's other examples. May's remark that Froude's tendency to let "secondary events" overwhelm his narrative leads him close to the "voluminousness" of a "memoir-writer" is thus, clearly, a gender-specific warning.[57]

Not surprisingly, then, reviews of women historians are especially dismissive of their accumulation of particulars, as if to guarantee the difference between their formal practices and those of the "serious" historians whose works might superficially resemble theirs. The *Spectator*'s review of the fourth volume of Strickland's *Queens of England* is typical: Strickland displays, says the critic, damning with faint praise, "a great though not a very discriminative industry in the collection of authorities and materials."[58] Throughout its reviews of Strickland's later volumes, the *Spectator* raises similar objections: Volume V, for example, is executed with "minute diffuseness" and its chief defect is "a deficiency in critical acumen, that prevents her from selecting what is necessary to her subject and rejecting all the rest"; it is a "readable but trifling olla podrida of characteristic anecdotes, minute information, curious facts [and] questionable conjectures."[59] (An "olla podrida," from the Spanish for "rotten pot," the *Oxford English Dictionary* tells us, is literally a stew of various meats and vegetables; figuratively, then, it means a medley or miscellaneous assortment—for all the descriptive appropriateness of this metaphor, the association of Strickland's historical work with the lesser but more womanly work of cookery is surely not innocent.) Reviewing Martha Walker Freer's biography of Henry III of France, the *Spectator*'s critic makes the more general observation that in biographical writing of this type "[g]reat events seem to fare the worst . . . because their accounts, compared with the artistic narratives and broad effects of eminent historians, are lost in the prosaic accumulation of minute particulars."[60] Here, clearly, the "eminent historians" are men, and their work is characterized by the masculine quality of "broad" and "artistic" mastery of their material— the same "powerful comprehension of events" and "historical grasp" J. M. Kemble claims to find lacking in the work of the lady-historians.

III

As important and controversial as stylistic and formal changes, and indeed often hard to separate from them, was the question of the content of historical works, of the subjects of historical inquiry and the kinds of details appropriate to include. Reviewers who criticize historians for failing to discriminate between important and trivial material invoke standards of significance that were increasingly contested during the Victorian period. "The time is approaching," Thomas Carlyle wrote in 1832, "when History will be attempted on quite other principles [than it is today]; when the Court, the Senate and the Battlefield, receding more and more into the background, the Temple, the Workshop and Social Hearth will advance more and more into the foreground."[61] This prophesied turn to the everyday has in fact been the great revolution in contemporary historiography, the invention of social history, today among the profession's most respected fields. In the early nineteenth century, however, people were just beginning to recognize the historical importance of the commonplace. One reason for this development was a post-Malthusian consciousness that the smallest domestic details—such as eating habits or sexual habits— could affect the development and prosperity of nations. Malthus himself, in his *Essay on the Principle of Population* (1798), had lamented the absence of historians studying marriage, mortality, and customs among what he called the "lower classes of society," "that part of mankind" where the "oscillations" of happiness caused by changes in the ratio between population and food supply are felt most directly.[62] In his own historical overview, he claims that

> Want was the goad that drove the Scythian shepherds from their native haunts, like so many famished wolves in search of prey. Set in motion by all this powerful cause, clouds of Barbarians seemed to collect from all points of the northern hemisphere. Gathering fresh

darkness and terror as they rolled on, the congregated bodies at length obscured the sun of Italy and sunk the whole world in universal night.[63]

Empty cupboards (or the Scythian shepherd equivalent) have, it turns out, far-reaching consequences.

The new sensitivity to quotidian matters was also a result of the Romantic reaction to Enlightenment historiography, characterized by a demand for less attention to 'man in general' and more to historical particularity.[64] "Historians have sometimes been laughed at for their almost exclusive affection for heroes, kings, and demi-gods," wrote J. S. Brewer in 1871, "[but] [i]t has become a fashion of late to insist upon social and economical questions, the rate of wages, the prices of food, the distribution of wealth."[65] His words register the realization of Carlyle's hopeful vision: over the century, the subjects and social groups considered worthy of historical scrutiny had expanded dramatically, as had the kinds of sources mined for information about the past.

Finally, like other changes in historical practice, the turn to social history was inspired by the novel and, more particularly, by Scott. The lesson of the Waverley novels, as T. H. Lister wrote in the *Edinburgh Review* in 1832, was that

> dates and names,—nay, even the articles of a treaty, or the issue of a battle, although desirable pieces of knowledge, are yet trivial, compared with the importance and utility of being able to penetrate below that surface on which float the great events and stately pageants of the time.... Great changes in the condition and opinions of a people will silently and gradually take place, unmarked by any signal event; whilst events the most striking, and apparently important, will glitter and vanish like bubbles in the sun, and leave no visible trace of their effect. History has been hitherto too prone to note with eagerness only the latter;—avoiding, as if with disdain, the more difficult, honourable, and useful task, of tracing the progress of the former.[66]

Historical works that attended to more than "great events and stately pageants" were easily seen as carrying on Scott's legacy, a genealogy not necessarily to their advantage, as the case of Macaulay's *History of*

England illustrates.

Macaulay and Carlyle were among the most eminent advocates of the shift in historiographical priorities. Both emphasize in their theoretical essays on history that unnoticed or seemingly trivial events may have far-reaching implications. "When the oak-tree is felled, the whole forest echoes with it," says Carlyle;

> but a hundred acorns are planted silently by some unnoticed breeze.... Well may we say that of our History the more important part is lost without recovery, and ... look with reverence into the dark untenanted places of the Past, where, in formless oblivion, our chief benefactors, with all their sedulous endeavours, but not with the fruit of these, lie entombed.[67]

"The circumstances which have most influence on the happiness of mankind," Macaulay says in his turn,

> the changes of manners and morals, the transition of communities from poverty to wealth, from knowledge to ignorance, from ferocity to humanity—these are, for the most part, noiseless revolutions. Their progress is rarely indicated by what historians are pleased to call important events. They are not achieved by armies, or enacted by senates. They are sanctioned by no treaties, and recorded in no archives. They are carried on in every school, in every church, behind ten thousand counters, at ten thousand firesides.[68]

The agents of these "noiseless revolutions" have, like Dorothea Brooke in *Middlemarch*, an "incalculably diffusive" effect on the world, even though their lives are made up of "unhistoric acts" and they remain among "the number who lived faithfully a hidden life, and rest in unvisited tombs."[69]

Macaulay was explicit about his intention to widen the scope of historical inquiry in his *History of England*, regretting the usual historical preoccupation with courts and kings and stating that his own design was to speak, not just of battles or governments, but of the people and their arts, religion, manners, and customs: "I should very imperfectly execute the task which I have undertaken," he declares, "if I were merely to treat of battles and sieges, of the rise and fall of

The Victorian Discourse of History

administrations, of intrigues in the palace, and of debates in the parliament. It will be my endeavour," he goes on,

> to relate the history of the people as well as the history of the government, to trace the progress of useful and ornamental arts, to describe the rise of religious sects and the changes of literary taste, to portray the manners of successive generations, and not to pass by with neglect even the revolutions which have taken place in dress, furniture, repasts, and public amusements.[70]

"I shall cheerfully bear the reproach of having descended below the dignity of history," he asserts, "if I can succeed in placing before the English of the nineteenth century a true picture of the life of their ancestors."[71] The little word "even" in this passage may signal a lingering anxiety about how such a descent below history's proper dignity will be received, but it also invites admiration at his courage in pursuing in such an unorthodox enterprise.

Despite these bold proclamations, Macaulay in fact spends the greater part of his long volumes on accounts of political affairs and conventional historical events, obedient to traditional historiographical priorities. He approaches a new kind of historical practice most closely in what one reviewer called "that delightful chapter": the third chapter of Volume I, "The State of England in 1685."[72] Here, as Jane Millgate puts it, "the muse of history turned—as Macaulay had continually advocated that she should—to matters which were normally beneath her gaze."[73] Macaulay undertakes a full description of English society at a particular moment in history, ranging over population, taxation, agriculture, mining, urbanization, transportation, communication, education, literature, science, art, architecture, and more. Twentieth-century historians are quick to point out the importance of his project to the development of their discipline. "[Chapter 3] is not complete, and [is] far from adequately analytical" by modern standards, Peter Gay admits, but, as he goes on, "[w]ith all its failings, Chapter 3 permitted social history to become a serious discipline."[74] "The wonder of the thing," says Owen Dudley Edwards, "is to see what one man could do at the dawn of modern historiography."[75] John Clive's claim that Chapter 3 "must be called, by friend or foe, a pioneering piece of social history" seems hardly overstated.[76]

Chapter 3 was widely acknowledged as novel when the *History* first appeared as well, but then it provoked both praise and criticism. James Moncrieff in the *Edinburgh Review* waxes enthusiastic:

> A few great battles, a few much debated political events, and one or two notorious crimes, have generally formed the staple of most of our historical works; while events far more operative and influential on the people, and far more important in their social and political progress, are wholly overlooked.... In the chapter we speak of, Mr. Macaulay has made a courageous and very successful endeavour to lead history into a deeper and wider channel; and has brought all his great descriptive powers to bear on the attempt to convey to his reader an impression of the domestic and every-day life of those times, in comparison with that of our own.[77]

Moncrieff has clearly picked up on Macaulay's cues; his praise for the historian's courage deflects anticipated criticisms of his descent below the dignity of history by emphasizing, as Macaulay himself does in the introductory pages of his History, that he is bravely defying, not overlooking, this conventional standard. But J. W. Croker, in the *Quarterly Review*, is not won over to this radical agenda; he attacks Macaulay for including "a heap of small facts, worthless in themselves—having no special relation to either the times or the events treated of" and compares Chapter 3 to "an old curiosity-shop, into which ... the knick-knacks of a couple of centuries are promiscuously jumbled."[78] Croker's criticisms are of just the sort Macaulay presumably expected and hoped to preempt by his defensive remarks, as they not only insist on the historiographical hierarchy Macaulay explicitly discards but also accuse him, with the use of gender-laden terms such as "knick-knacks" and "promiscuously," of a distinctly feminine failure of judgment.

It is not coincidental that the most enthusiastic support for Macaulay's experiment came from the Whig *Edinburgh Review*, the most virulent opposition to it from the Tory *Quarterly Review*. Even aside from the obvious political bias of Macaulay's *History*, the new emphasis on the "undercurrents" of history had ideological implications, for it meant acknowledging as historical agents groups previously held to be outside or below such important national consideration: farmers, artisans, factory workers, teachers, low-ranking clergymen, the shop-keepers behind Macaulay's "ten thousand counters." Every private individual participated in the "noiseless revolutions" Macaulay and like-minded writers celebrate as much as did the public figures to whom the label "historical" more commonly attaches. But if all members of society contribute to the nation's history, it becomes harder to justify the concentration of political power in the hands of a few. Further, knowing the history of the social group with which one identifies is potentially empowering: it clarifies and solidifies that group identity and helps formulate shared goals. In our own century, historical articulation consistently accompanies demands for a share in political power or for fully equal participation in society—thus historical studies of marginalized or disenfranchised groups are almost always considered political, however "purely" scholarly their ostensible goals, with women's history only one prominent example. In the Victorian period, when historical interpretations were widely considered guidelines for present and future conduct, histories that treated the general population of England as more than faceless supporters of political or military leaders fed easily into other developments that seemed to promise the "common man" a greater share in the governing of his country. At least potentially, a historiography valuing the everyday and the commonplace underwrites a democratic or progressive politics.

Not only the "common man" was implicated in these revisionist histories; although most discussions of the expanding field of historical study never mention women explicitly, the turn to the domestic and the everyday dramatically historicized women's lives. For centuries, women had been excluded, with rare exceptions, from the events of the public world previously considered the only appropriate material for historical study. Increasing attention to the "noiseless revolutions ... carried on in every school, in every church, behind ten thousand counters, at ten thousand firesides," made a historical story with women at its center at least conceptually possible—after all, the "Angel in the House" presided over the hearths of those firesides.

As if recognizing this expanded realm of possibility, women wrote innumerable volumes about women of the past, creating a pantheon of what Natalie Davis has called "women worthies."[79] Important as this development was for fostering a sense of historical inheritance and pride in women's achievements, however, it was less fundamentally significant than the gradual incorporation of information about the world of ordinary men and women brought about by the turn towards social history. Writing women into history, as scholars in this century have emphasized, requires "redefining and enlarging traditional notions of historical significance";[80] almost certainly without meaning to, Victorian historians and critics who advocated new criteria for historical relevance paved the way for just such a project. Indeed, their contributions to the development of modern women's history have been explicitly recognized by twentieth-century historians who, like Davis, acknowledge their debt to "the work of late eighteenth- and nineteenth-century writers in expanding the boundaries of social history so as to include subjects in which the activities of women, or of women and men together, could not fail to be considered explicitly." [81]

The irritable responses of some critics to historians who jumble together too many "unimportant" facts suggests that they had an unconscious or intuitive suspicion of where this revisionist historiography might lead. They almost always point to those details most obviously associated with women's sphere or concerns as the most ludicrous or objectionable lapses in a historian's work. In a typical comment, Charles Kingsley notes disparagingly that

> [some histories] have degenerated into mere inventories of old clothes, or bills of indigestible fare; and it is not important to the human race to know the exact day on which Queen Adeliza Johanna Maud wore a green boddice over a blue kirtle, or on which Abbot Helluo de Voragine cooked five porpoises whole for a single feast.[82]

A conspicuous mark of "degeneration" is including details of clothing or diet, descending from the historian's lofty height to such trivial, feminine particulars: in a familiar polemical move, the abstract and supposedly inclusive subject "the human race" somehow turns out to have masculine interests. Similarly, Margaret Oliphant observes that

> little weight can be attached to the chronicle in which a graceful individual act holds equal place with a national revolution; and the fashion of a coronation robe is of quite as much importance as the framing of a law.[83]

The Victorian Discourse of History

Like the many critics who insist on an appropriate balance between the important and the merely illustrative, she does not disallow the interest of a coronation robe but wishes it clearly subordinated to an obviously historical subject such as lawmaking. She selects not just any detail to make her point, but uses two markedly feminine examples. Like one of Strickland's reviewers, Oliphant considers such womanly things "frequently not incurious or uninteresting," but wonders "whether this inferior sort of attraction has not been cultivated at the expense of higher objects."[84] The serious historian treats, and treats only, the material Macaulay ostensibly sought to go beyond, "battles and sieges, ... the rise and fall of administrations," and does not, as Strickland does, consider Elizabeth I's silk stockings pertinent to her narrative.[85]

IV

On one side of the divide, then, one is supposed to find politics, on the other, manners; on one side should be philosophy, on the other, fashion; and a text equating or mingling the two realms represents a serious threat to a variety of political and social hierarchies, particularly when the text is aimed at a mass market and promises to explain the present by way of the past. Historiography, ideology, and gender politics cross and recross in these debates, and the intersections mark out a discursive field more complex than we often imagine when we think about the practice of history in the Victorian period. Passages such as the following quickly seem polemical and prescriptive, instead of analytic and descriptive, when seen in this context:

> The historical Muse ... has come to a new stage of development. The time has come when she has ceased to be either the garrulous gossip or the all-believing annalist of old.... The model historian of our day is an Ithurial armed with that spear which dispels all disguises. The prettiest fays of tradition disappear before its touch; long reigns, elaborate systems of legislation, entire dynasties crumble into fable under his eye—nothing is safe from his investigation.... He must pass over those picturesque incidents which seize the popular fancy, and turn aside sternly from the embroideries of romance....[86]

Here Margaret Oliphant describes the displacement of a graceful feminine muse associated with tradition, gossip, and fiction by an emphatically male figure brandishing a phallic spear with which he penetrates the mists of the past. It sounds like Macaulay's wish come true: the manly historian decisively regaining control over the feminized romancer. But not that long before Oliphant had described another transformation:

> No rustling brocades, no measured march, no solemn *avant courier* proclaims the journeys or the researches of *our* historic muse. There she is—behold her!—in the library of the British Museum, with her poke bonnet, her umbrella, her india-rubber overshoes.... [I]nstead of her triumphal car, putting up with an omnibus, and possibly carrying her notes in her little bag or basket, like any ordinary womankind who has been buying buttons or hooks-and-eyes.... In short, it is not Edward Gibbon, but Agnes Strickland....[87]

Oliphant was right both times. Along with the rise of a homely and feminine historiography came an assertion of masculine difference and prerogative that culminated in the professionalization of history as a specialized discipline. Participants in the ongoing discussion aligned themselves with or attempted to establish definitive distinctions between possible configurations of gender, genre, and history (as subject and as practice), each of which had political implications and potentially enormous significance in the contemporary world. The result was not coherence and hegemony but incoherence, discord, even some confusion—and a tremendous expansion of possibility as the definition and the face of history changed and changed again to fit different conceptions of what a story of the past should look like, aesthetically, formally, and substantially.

NOTES

1. Robert Browning, *The Ring and The Book*. Ed. Richard D. Altick. (Harmondsworth: Penguin, 1971), p. 42 (Book I, ll.704-5).

2. "History," in *The Lays of Ancient Rome & Miscellaneous Essays and Poems* (London: J. M. Dent & Sons, 1910; rpt. 1963), pp. 1-39; p. 36.

3. Useful discussions include Richard A. E. Brooks, "The Development of the Historical Mind," in Joseph E. Baker, ed., *The Reinterpretation of Victorian Literature* (Princeton: Princeton UP, 1950), pp. 130-152; Jerome Hamilton Buckley, *The Triumph of Time: A Study of the Victorian Concepts of*

Time, History, Progress, and Decadence (Cambridge MA: Harvard UP, 1966); Raymond Chapman, *The Sense of the Past in Victorian Literature* (London: Croom Helm, 1986); A. Dwight Culler, *The Victorian Mirror of History* (New Haven: Yale UP, 1985); Peter Allan Dale, *The Victorian Critic and the Idea of History: Carlyle, Arnold, Pater* (Cambridge MA: Harvard UP, 1977); T. W. Heyck, *The Transformation of Intellectual Life in Victorian England* (New York: St. Martin's, 1982); Walter E. Houghton, *The Victorian Frame of Mind 1830-1870* (New Haven: Yale UP, 1957).

4. Charles Kingsley, Review of Froude's *History of England from the Fall of Wolsey to the Death of Elizabeth* Vols. 7 & 8, *Macmillan's Magazine* Vol. 9 (January 1864), pp. 211-24; p. 212.

5. *The Transformation of Intellectual Life in Victorian England*, p. 122.

6. *In Pursuit of a Scientific Culture: Science, Art, and Society in the Victorian Age* (Madison: U of Wisconsin P, 1989), p. 5.

7. [Archibald Alison], Review of Macaulay's *History*, *Blackwood's Magazine* Vol. 65 (April 1849), pp. 383-405; p. 383.

8. [J. S. Brewer], "New Sources of English History," *Quarterly Review* Vol. 130 (April 1871), pp. 373-407; p. 407.

9. "History," p. 37.

10. [T. H. Lister], "The Waverley Novels," *Edinburgh Review* Vol. 55 (April 1832), pp. 61-79; p. 77. For explorations of this aspect of Scott's work, see Mark Phillips, "Macaulay, Scott, and the Literary Challenge to Historiography," *Journal of the History of Ideas* Vol. 50 No. 1 (Jan.-Mar. 1989), pp. 117-133; Ina Ferris, *The Achievement of Literary Authority: Gender, History, and the Waverley Novels* (Ithaca: Cornell UP, 1991); Ann Rigney, "Adapting History to the Novel," *New Comparison* Vol. 8 (1989), pp. 127-143; or Rohan Maitzen, "'By No Means an Improbable Fiction': *Redgauntlet's* Novel Historicism," *Studies in the Novel* Vol. 25 No. 2 (Summer 1993), pp. 170-183.

11. [J. A. Heraud?], "Historical Romance II," *Fraser's Magazine* Vol. 5 (March 1832), pp. 202-17; p. 207.

12. "Silly Novels by Lady Novelists," in *Selected Critical Writings*, ed. Rosemary Ashton (London: Oxford UP, 1992), pp. 296-321; p. 320. See Dorothy Mermin, *Godiva's Ride: Women of Letters in England 1830-1880* (Bloomington: Indiana UP, 1993), p. 53.

13. M. A. Stodart, *Female Writers: Thoughts on Their Proper Sphere, and on Their Powers of Usefulness* (London: Seeley and Burnside, 1842), p. 131.

14. [W. E. Greg], Review of Alison's *History of Europe 1815-1852*, *Edinburgh Review* Vol. 97 (April 1853), pp. 296-314; pp. 276-77.

15. John Kenyon, *The History Men: The Historical Profession in England Since the Renaissance* (Pittsburgh: U of Pittsburgh P, 1983); G. P. Gooch, *History and Historians in the Nineteenth-Century* (New York: Peter Smith, 1913); Thomas Preston Peardon, *The Transition in English Historical Writing 1760-1830* (New York: Columbia UP, 1933); J. W. Burrow, *A Liberal Descent: Victorian Historians and the English Past* (Cambridge: Cambridge UP, 1981); Rosemary Jann, *The Art and Science of Victorian History* (Columbus: Ohio UP, 1985); Joseph M. Levine, *Humanism and History: Origins of Modern English Historiography* (Ithaca: Cornell UP, 1987); Christina Crosby, *The Ends of History: Victorians and 'the Woman Question'* (New York: Routledge, 1991); Carol Christ, "'The Hero as Man of Letters': Masculinity and Victorian Nonfiction Prose," in Thaïs Morgan, ed., *Victorian Sages and Cultural Discourse: Renegotiating Gender and Power* (New Brunswick NJ: Rutgers UP, 1990), pp. 19-31, p. 25; Ina Ferris, *The Achievement of Literary Authority* and "Re-Positioning the Novel: *Waverley* and the Gender of Fiction," *Studies in Romanticism* Vol. 28 No. 2 (Summer 1989), pp. 291-301.

16. [J. M. Kemble], *Fraser's Magazine* Vol. 52 (August 1855), pp. 135-49; p. 149, original emphasis; p. 136.

17. Carl Ballstadt, *The Literary History of the Strickland Family* (Unpublished Ph.D. dissertation, University of London, 1965), p. 125.

18. Dame Una Pope-Hennessy, *Agnes Strickland: Biographer of the Queens of England 1796-1874* (London: Chatto & Windus, 1940).

19. I am indebted to Ballstadt's excellent bibliography for many of these titles, and to Joan Thirsk's essay "The History Women," in *Chattel, Servant or Citizen: Women's Status in Church, State and Society*, eds. M. O'Dowd and S. Wichert (Belfast: Institute of Irish Studies, the Queen's University, 1995), pp. 1-11.

20. Thomas Carlyle, "Sir Walter Scott," *Selected Essays* (N.p.: T. Nelson & Sons, n.d.), pp. 65-125; p. 116.

21. [John Mounteney Jephson], Review of Palgrave's *History of Normandy and of England*, *Fraser's Magazine* Vol. 56 (July 1857), pp. 16-32; p. 16.

22. [T. B. Macaulay], Review of Sir James Mackintosh's *History of the Revolution in England in 1688*, *Edinburgh Review* Vol. 61 (July 1835), pp. 265-322; p. 271.

23. [James Moncrieff], Review of Macaulay's *History* Vol. 5, *Edinburgh Review* Vol. 114 (October 1861), pp. 279-317; p. 284.

24. [C. S. M. Phillipps], Review of Alison's *History of Europe 1789-1815*, *Edinburgh Review* Vol. 76 (October 1842), pp. 1-60; p. 8; [G. W. Abraham], Review of Strickland's *Lives of the Queens of Scotland*, *Dublin Review* Vol. 38 (March 1855), pp. 73-97; p. 74.

25. [T. C. Sandars], Review of Buckle's *History of Civilization in England*, *Fraser's Magazine* Vol. 56 (Oct. 1857), pp. 409-424; p. 409.

26. John Clive, "Macaulay's Historical Imagination," in *Not By Fact Alone: Essays on the Writing and Reading of History* (Boston: Houghton Mifflin, 1989), pp. 66-73; p. 67.

27. See Richard Altick, *The English Common Reader: A Social History of the Mass Reading Public 1800-1900* (Chicago: U of Chicago P, 1957), especially pp. 66-77.

28. Alexander Welsh, *George Eliot and Blackmail* (Cambridge MA: Harvard UP, 1985), p. 41.

29. J. F. C. Harris, *The Early Victorians 1832-1851* (New York: Praeger, 1971), p. 136.

30. Altick explicitly attributes the spread of political power to the growing reading public. *The English Common Reader*, p. 4.

31. [Margaret Oliphant], Review of Trevelyan's *Life and Letters of Lord Macaulay*, *Blackwood's* Vol. 119 (May 1876), pp. 614-37; p. 636.

32. Dorothy Mermin, *Godiva's Ride*, p. 95.

33. [James Moncrieff], Review of Macaulay's *History*. *Edinburgh Review* Vol. 90 (July 1849), pp. 249-92; p. 253, emphasis added.

34. Scott Elledge's essay "The Background and Development in English Criticism of the Theories of Generality and Particularity" is informative about the eighteenth-century background of this aesthetic controversy. *PMLA* Vol. 62 No. 1 (March 1947), pp. 147-182.

35. [Goldwin Smith], Review of Froude's *History of England from the Fall of Wolsey to the Death of Elizabeth*, *Edinburgh Review* Vol. 108 (July 1858), pp. 206-52; p. 206.

36. Carol Christ, *The Finer Optic: The Aesthetics of Particularity in Victorian Poetry* (New Haven: Yale UP, 1975), p. 13

37. [R. H. Patterson], Review of Alison's *Histories of Europe 1789-1815 & 1815-1852*, *Blackwood's* Vol. 79 (April 1856), pp. 404-21; p. 406.

38. T. W. Heyck, *The Transformation of Intellectual Life in Victorian England*, p. 42.

39. [Archibald Alison Jr.], Review of Alison's *History of Europe 1815-1852, Blackwood's* Vol. 87 (April 1860), pp. 441-67; p. 460; [R. H. Patterson], Review of Alison's *History of Europe 1815-1852* (revised edition), *Blackwood's* Vol. 100 (Oct. 1866), pp. 475-93; p. 485.

40. [Goldwin Smith], Review of Froude's *History of England from the Fall of Wolsey to the Death of Elizabeth*, p. 207.

41. [J. M. Kemble], Review of Macaulay's *History, Fraser's Magazine* Vol. 53 (Feb. 1856), pp. 147-66; p. 148.

42. [James Moncrieff], Review of Macaulay's *History* Vols. 3 & 4, *Edinburgh Review* Vol. 105 (January 1857), pp. 142-81; p. 144; [W. B. Donne], Review of Froude's *History of England from the Fall of Wolsey to the Death of Elizabeth, Fraser's Magazine* Vol. 54 (July 1856), pp. 31-46; p. 38.

43. [Archibald Alison], Review of Macaulay's *History*, p. 390.

44. [Walter Bagehot], Review of Macaulay's *History, National Review* Vol. 2 (April 1856), pp. 357-87; pp. 386-87.

45. [J. L. Sanford], Review of Froude's *History, National Review* Vol. 3 (July 1856), pp. 102-27; p. 108.

46. [T. E. May], Review of Froude's *Reign of Elizabeth, Edinburgh Review* Vol. 124 (October 1866), pp. 476-511; p. 478.

47. [W. F. Pollock], Review of Carlyle's *Frederick the Great, Quarterly Review* Vol. 105 (April 1859), pp. 275-304; p. 277.

48. [Pollock], Review of Carlyle, p. 302.

49. Christ, *The Finer Optic*, p. 30.

50. Martin Meisel, *Realizations: Narrative, Pictorial, and Theatrical Arts in Nineteenth-Century England* (Princeton: Princeton UP, 1983), p. 229.

51. Terry Eagleton, *The Ideology of the Aesthetic* (Cambridge MA: Basil Blackwell, 1990), p. 17.

52. In *The Ideology of the Aesthetic*, Eagleton provides an explanatory model which might account for the vehemence with which the middle-class reviewers denounce the overflow of particulars. Looking at the rise of aesthetic philosophy in late eighteenth-century Germany, Eagleton argues that the increasing and multifaceted importance attached to the particular and the subjective posed a serious threat to abstract thought. History, as "a matter of determinate specificities," might "fall outside the compass of reason" and thus resist the mastery of the ruling class (p. 16). Eagleton's overall thesis is that the category of "the aesthetic," a form of cognition by which "the dense particulars of perception can be made luminous to thought, and determinate concretions assembled into historical narrative," develops precisely in response to this

The Victorian Discourse of History 31

dangerous possibility (p. 17). The trend towards more affective narrative in Victorian historiography does seem to parallel the functioning of the aesthetic as Eagleton describes it.

53. Naomi Schor, *Reading in Detail: Aesthetics and the Feminine* (New York: Methuen, 1987), p. 21. For more about Carlyle's use of overabundant detail, see Rohan Maitzen, "'When Pit Jumps On Stage': Historiography and Theatricality in Carlyle's *French Revolution,*" *Carlyle Annual* Vol. 13 (1992/93), pp. 44-54.

54. *Reading in Detail*, p. 4.

55. On women and science, see Mermin, *Godiva's Ride*.

56. "History," p. 11.

57. [May], Review of Froude's *Reign of Elizabeth*, p. 478.

58. *Spectator* No. 719 (April 9 1842), p. 353.

59. *Spectator* No. 742 (Sept. 17 1842), pp. 907-8; p. 907.

60. *Spectator* No. 1586 (Nov. 20 1858), pp. 1225-26; p. 1225.

61. "Boswell's *Life of Johnson,*" *Selected Essays* (N.p.: T. Nelson & Sons, n.d.), pp. 165-227; p. 183.

62. Thomas Malthus, *An Essay on the Principle of Population*. Ed. Antony Flew. (Harmondsworth: Penguin, 1970), p. 78.

63. Malthus, p. 83.

64. J. R. Hale notes that Gibbon was the last to win his reputation using Enlightenment methods: "Romanticism was demanding a different sort of sympathetic involvement with the past, more concern with the common man and still wider subject matter." *The Evolution of British Historiography from Bacon to Napier* (Cleveland: Meridian, 1964), p. 34. See also Joseph M. Levine, *Humanism and History*, especially pp. 192-3, or A. Dwight Culler, *The Victorian Mirror of History*, pp. 4-5.

65. [J. S. Brewer], "New Sources of English History," p. 384.

66. [T. H. Lister], "The Waverley Novels," pp. 77-78.

67. "On History," *A Carlyle Reader*, ed. G. B. Tennyson (Cambridge: Cambridge UP, 1984), pp. 55-66; p. 58.

68. "History," p. 34. For an interesting comparison of the two historians' theoretical essays see Saul Isaacson, "Carlyle and Macaulay in the Journals: Toward A New Historiography," *Carlyle Annual* Vol. 10 (1989), pp. 21-30.

69. George Eliot, *Middlemarch: A Study of Provincial Life*, ed. W. J. Harvey (Harmondsworth: Penguin, 1965), p. 896.

70. *The History of England from the Accession of James II* (London: J. M. Dent & Sons, 1913). 3 Volumes. Volume I, p. 10.

71. *History of England* Volume I, pp. 10-11.

72. [James Moncrieff], Review of Macaulay's *History*, p. 253.
73. Jane Millgate, *Macaulay* (London: Routledge & Kegan Paul, 1973), p. 136.
74. Peter Gay, *Style in History: Gibbon, Ranke, Macaulay, Burckhardt* (New York: Norton, 1974), p. 117.
75. Owen Dudley Edwards, *Macaulay* (New York: St. Martin's, 1988), p. 134.
76. *Not By Fact Alone*, p. 10.
77. [James Moncrieff], Review of Macaulay's *History*, p. 253.
78. [J. W. Croker], Review of Macaulay's *History*. *Quarterly Review* Vol. 84 (March 1849), pp. 549-630; p. 585; p. 579.
79. Natalie Zemon Davis, "'Women's History' in Transition: The European Case," *Feminist Studies* Vol. 3 No. 3/4 (Spring/Summer 1976), pp. 83-103.
80. Ann D. Gordon, Mari Jo Buhle & Nancy Schrom Dye, "The Problem of Women's History," in Berenice Carroll, ed., *Liberating Women's History: Theoretical and Critical Essays* (Urbana: U of Illinois P, 1976), pp. 75-92; p. 89.
81. Davis, "'Women's History' in Transition," p. 84. See also Joan Scott, *Gender and the Politics of History* (New York: Columbia UP, 1988), p. 21; Anna Davin, "Redressing the Balance or Transforming the Art? The British Experience," in S. Jay Kleinberg et al, eds., *Retrieving Women's History: Changing Perceptions of the Role of Women in Politics and Society* (Oxford: Berg/Unesco, 1988), pp. 60-78; Sheila Rowbotham, *Hidden From History* (New York: Pantheon, 1974), p. xviii.
82. [Charles Kingsley], Review of Froude's *History*, p. 213.
83. [Margaret Oliphant], "Modern Light Literature—History," *Blackwood's* Vol. 78 (Oct. 1855), pp. 437-51; p. 439.
84. Review of Strickland's *Queens of England*, *Spectator* No. 719, p. 353.
85. *Lives of the Queens of England*, Volume 6, p. 137.
86. [Margaret Oliphant], Review of John Hill Burton's *History of Scotland to 1688*, *Blackwood's* Vol. 101 (March 1867), pp. 317-37; p. 317.
87. [Margaret Oliphant], "Modern Light Literature—History," p. 437.

CHAPTER TWO
"A Clique of Living Clios"
Nineteenth-Century Women Historians[1]

> *Much as we regret to make any remarks which may pain an individual, we should not discharge our duty, if we abstained from pointing out to our readers the manner in which the confidence of the public is abused at present by literary ladies, who ought to be contented with marking pinafores and labelling pots of jam. . . . [B]ut we doubt, after all, if [Mrs. Forbes Bush] is worse than a fair average specimen of a whole clique, or clack, of living Clios.*[2]

For all the apparent confusion of gender issues in the discourse of history, the didactic, public role of the historian was not one easily appropriated by women; during the nineteenth century the past came to be seen as the key to the present, particularly the political present—and this was *man's* business. Although, as Chapter One shows, the scope of historiography expanded during the century, this development was controversial rather than normative, and so although it contributed in the long run to the inclusion of women in both the subject and the practice of history, there was no decisive change of attitude. Every historical work by a woman or about women (or simply not about politics, wars, and great men) was potentially a lightning rod for disputes over these contentious issues. "What share have women in the history of men?" asked Julia Kavanagh in 1851; given the deterrents, we might reasonably expect the answer to have been "not much."[3]

Women did write history in this period, however, and their works ranged from the grand sweep of politics to the minutiae of everyday life. To give just a few examples of their prodigious output, Harriet Martineau wrote a *History of England During the Thirty Years' Peace*

(1849) and Anne Marsh published *The Protestant Reformation in France and the Hugeunots* in 1847. Through such works as *Legends of the Madonna, as Represented in the Fine Arts* (1852), Anna Jameson earned a reputation as an art historian; Elizabeth Stone wrote a history of fashion (1845) and one of needlework (1840); Fanny Palliser wrote a history of lace (1865). Elizabeth Ogborne published a *History of Essex* (1817), while Hannah Lawrance and Georgiana Hill both wrote general accounts of English women through the ages, Lawrance's *History of Woman in England* appearing in 1843 and Hill's *Women in English Life* in 1896.

By far the greatest number of volumes are historical biographies, accounts of famous women of the past.[4] They appeared throughout the century but proliferated especially in the early and mid-Victorian decades, the years when the middle-class values which came to be overwhelmingly associated with "Victorianism" most conspicuously took hold. They participated in the codification and dissemination of these values, and in particular of Victorian gender ideology. More than just conduct books, however, they also engaged with central problems in Victorian historiography. Their authors, like other nineteenth-century historians, challenge conventional assumptions about historical significance, but because of their overt focus on women they uncover the gender inflections of the turn to social history. They offer their books as supplements to the historical master-narratives in which both women and woman's sphere are either invisible or marginal, and they vigorously assert a feminine presence in history, while at the same time they rely on a theoretical model that contains the disruptive potential of this revisionist practice. These volumes constitute a significant but neglected body of writing that shows us at least one way in which Victorian women claimed a "share" in a history that, as they often insist, should not be only "of men."

I

The women historians faced, even more than other nineteenth-century women writers, problems of self-presentation and self-authorization: How should they write? What voice should they use? What relationship to their readers should they cultivate? What kinds of stories should they tell? Could they fulfill their obligations as historians without violating expectations of them as women? And what exactly *were* their obligations as (women) historians, anyway? Their answers to these questions vary, but most of them begin by using a common strategy to enable or authorize their work: they differentiate themselves from "historians." Almost all of them, for instance, wrote "Lives" or "Memoirs" rather than "Histories." Memoirs and biographies exist mid-way between the public and the private, the general and the personal. They usually focus on public figures, but interpret their better-known aspects in the light of their personal experiences, sometimes to show them as exemplars, sometimes to show the "real" person behind a careful façade, perhaps to satisfy what Patricia Spacks calls "the universal hunger to penetrate other lives."[5] Biographies break down the line between public and private by showing the private aspect of public affairs, or the public manifestations of private problems, or just by making the intimate details of someone's private life public fare. These were the conventions in the nineteenth century as much as today. T. H. Lister, discussing Lucy Aikin's *Memoirs of the Court of Charles I* in the *Edinburgh Review* in 1834, describes "that wide and ill-defined place which the memoir ought to occupy" as

> a place intermediate between political history and historical romance. It should have the truth and authority of the former—the detail and lively interest of the latter. It should convey to us the graphic exhibition of those characteristic trifles which the gravity of history will not stoop to notice. It should aim at rendering us intimately acquainted with the most eminent characters of the period it embraces, and make us live in former times.[6]

Strickland's *Lives of the Queens of Scotland* are likewise "a medium between the romantic novel and the philosophic history"; they "aim at being more amusing than the one, and more instructive than the other."[7] Lister's word "stoop" makes clear the hierarchy of genres involved. According to this model, the memoir is colorful and lively instead of grave, trifling and intimate yet authoritative, and thus hovers uncomfortably, if attractively, somewhere—to use a deliberately gendered expression—in the no-man's land between politics and romance, between history and fiction.

For women culturally constrained from freely entering into public life, inhibited from claiming the kind of overt cultural authority required to write history, historical biography was thus a useful camouflage: it allowed them to treat serious historical material in what might at least appear to be an appropriately ladylike manner. In M. A. Stodart's words, "[a]lthough history is one of the most useful studies which a woman can pursue, her powers of mind are hardly fitted to enter this field for the sake of instructing others," but "the humbler walk of Biography is less unfitted to feminine power."[8] At least superficially, most of the women historians adapt their work to these cultural pressures and presuppositions, and a rhetoric of distinction and subordination pervades their volumes. One subtle manifestation of this strategic differentiation is the frequent reference to "historians," to what "they" have said or how "they" have interpreted the evidence; in typical instances, Mary Hays reports on the way "Nitocris, Queen of Egypt and Ethiopia, is spoken of by historians," and Agnes Strickland notes that the "details of [Essex's] expedition will be found in Camden, Birch, Lingard, and the other historians of Elizabeth's reign."[9] These gestures allow the women writers at once to distance themselves from "historians" and to appropriate their authority. More directly, the women writers frequently disavow any intention to poach on the historian's territory; Lucy Aikin, for example, in her early *Memoirs of the Court of Queen Elizabeth* (1826), declares "it has been the constant endeavour of the writer to preserve to her work the genuine character of Memoirs, by avoiding as much as possible all encroachments on the peculiar province of history."[10] In strikingly similar language, Hannah Lawrance asserts of her *Historical Memoirs of the Queens of England* (1838) that "it is not intended . . . to encroach upon the province of general history,"[11] and Strickland says that "the plans and limits" of her *Lives of the Queens of England* (1840-48) "will not admit of launching into the broad stream of general history."[12] Margaret Oliphant's dig at Dr. Doran, who wrote *Queens of the House of Hanover*, confirms that women were establishing for themselves a special field of authority and expertise, a distinct if marginal territory; Oliphant calls him "a male intruder . . . into this feminine preserve—a gentleman who clearly has no business here, and who ought to be incontinently expelled by the original proprietors of the domain."[13] Her territorial rhetoric ironically echoes that of male critics such as the one cited in the epigraph for this chapter. Both sides apparently saw the problem as one of defining and policing borders—borders Mary Anne Everett Wood knew she had crossed without permission with her edition of *Letters of Royal and*

Illustrious Ladies (1846), which she prefaces with "an apology for the seeming, perhaps real, presumption with which [the editor] has ventured upon a field usually occupied by the learned of the other sex."[14]

II

The historiographical territory over which women claimed proprietary rights closely resembles the sphere they supposedly ruled over in Victorian society as a whole: private life, the domestic realm, personal experience, matrimony and maternity. Their historical biographies are history "up close and personal," intimate portraits of individuals and their social conditions rather than abstract or large-scale discussions of wars or administrations. The "general" history against which these women defined their own work, then, is the history of the public sphere, of direct action, of political plots and military maneuvers, of diplomacy and religious strife. "The events which marked the following years [of John's reign] belong to the political historian," Hannah Lawrance says, making the dividing line perfectly clear, and she refers the reader who desires to know more about Magna Carta to Lingard and Turner.[15] "The great events of Elizabeth's reign, in war, in politics, in legislation, belong to the historian," Elizabeth Stone writes.[16] "The consequences of this stupendous step," says Agnes Strickland of Henry VIII's break with Rome, "fill many vast folios, devoted to the mighty questions of contending creeds and differing interests"; her "unambitious pages," however, will only "trace its effects on one faithful feminine heart, wrung with all the woes that pertain to a forsaken wife and bereaved mother."[17] And of the Northern Rebellion during Elizabeth's reign, Strickland asserts that the "details of that ill-judged and most disastrous enterprise belong to general history."[18] Of course, the usual focus on royal women made the distinction between these historical biographies and "general history" difficult to uphold, since the lives of consorts are closely bound up with those of their husbands, while the life of a queen regnant is inseparable from the public affairs of her realm; some of the disclaimers seem disingenuous. Nonetheless, the women historians generally uphold the ideologically crucial distinction in their rhetoric, if not always in their practice. Indeed, this persistent effort to maintain clear distinctions between gender-specific spheres of activity reveals the precedence taken by gender over class in these biographies and in Victorian ideology more generally: the queens' identities *as women* are clearly assumed to override the difference in their rank.

Writing about women's lives meant more than just focusing on personal experiences, however. It also led these women historians into other areas only recently becoming objects of historical inquiry, such as dress, diet, education, and manners. Seemingly irrelevant or, at most, peripheral to the concerns of traditional historians, these aspects of life loomed significantly larger in discussions of past women for the simple reason that women historically had more to do with them—or less to do with other, more conspicuously decisive, things. Like the male historians I quoted in Chapter One, who fault the historian's traditional preoccupation with great events, the "lady historians" emphasize the historical significance of the multitudes of quiet happenings that make up daily life. Hannah Lawrance, whose *Historical Memoirs of the Queens of England* includes a long chapter on "Society in England During the Middle Ages," justifies the space spent describing the workings of commerce and taxation and the style and furnishings of houses, among other digressions from her central narrative, in terms reminiscent of Macaulay's, although in language far more deferential and tentative:

> We may perhaps have lingered too long over this subject; but while battles, treaties, the strife of statesmen, and court intrigues, so often fill up the whole page of general history, it may be permitted ... to turn aside from the records of princes, to trace the progress of commerce and social improvement—to contemplate, not merely 'the damsel clad in miniver,' but the household maiden; not merely the knight, but the bold yeoman....[19]

"[H]ow necessary to the correct view of any given period," she says elsewhere, "is a knowledge of the social condition of the people."[20]

In Chapter One I pointed out some of the gender implications of expanding history's borders in this way, of the turn towards social history. Most nineteenth-century historians and reviewers respond at most indirectly to the possibility that meeting the demand for a new kind of historical study means (or at least enables) writing women into history. Even those great historiographical patriarchs Carlyle and

"A Clique of Living Clios" 39

Macaulay, however, reveal through their language a lurking consciousness that the shadowy part of the past exciting their interest is populated largely by women. Carlyle, for example, mingles images of generation and productivity with images of barrenness to produce an uncannily apt and paradoxical figure for women's contributions to historical development:

> a hundred acorns are planted silently by some unnoticed breeze.... [We] look with reverence into the dark untenanted places of the Past, where ... our chief benefactors, with all their sedulous endeavours, but not with the fruit of these, lie entombed.[21]

Agnes Strickland uses a similar image in the last volume of her *Lives of the Queens of England*:

> we labour in a high vocation, even that of enabling the lovers of truth and moral justice, to judge of our queens and their attributes—not according to conventional censure or praise, but according to the unerring test, prescribed not by 'carnal wisdom, but by heavenly wisdom coming down from above,' which has said, 'By their fruits ye shall know them.'[22]

In Strickland's explicitly feminine context, the queens' metaphorical offspring, the "fruits" of their productive lives, unproblematically reveal their historical significance and worth with the passage of time. Carlyle's version is darker and more complex: the past is a life-giving womb and "unnoticed" acts prove incalculably fertile, like women's unrecorded deeds, but womb and tomb are elided so that the "dark untenanted place" appears a place of burial, not gestation, and the world's "chief benefactors" lie in obscurity, denied the "fruit" of their efforts as women are denied credit for their part in history. Did Carlyle mean to summon up women's history with this metaphorically rich but deeply ambivalent passage? Almost certainly not, but that his imagery is so heavily gendered suggests the inevitability of associating the history of what Macaulay called "noiseless revolutions" with women's history. Indeed, the passage from Macaulay also indirectly but inevitably points to women. History's really significant transformations, he says, are not achieved by armies, or enacted by senates. They are sanctioned by no treaties, and recorded in no archives. They are carried on in every school, in every church, behind ten thousand counters, at ten thousand firesides.[23]

The world Macaulay summons up but does not name is the private sphere—parish church, local school, home and hearth—and this world is, of course, in crucial respects the world of women.

In their volumes, which insist, as Carlyle's and Macaulay's do, on the historical significance of what Eliot in *Middlemarch* calls "unhistoric acts," the women historians almost unanimously adopt a theoretical model which dovetails neatly with a pervasive strain of Victorian gender ideology, making women's history at once conceptually possible and culturally acceptable. The chief ideological stumbling block for a would-be women's historian was that Victorian gender stereotypes minimized the scope of, or even the possibility of, female agency; presenting women as historical actors, then, in the way kings or generals are, was problematic. The new historiographical emphasis on indirect agency, on effects stemming from diffuse causes rather than decisive acts, on an infinitude of tiny changes bringing about gradual revolutions, created a new model of historical explanation, one that was entirely consistent with women's accepted form of power: influence.

Throughout the century, conduct books such as Sarah Stickney Ellis's *Wives of England* (1843) emphasized that women's influence should be, "like the gentle dew, and the cheering light, more felt . . . in its softening, healing, harmonizing power; than acknowledged by any single act."[24] Ellis's words typify a pervasive rhetoric about women's influence. Compare, for instance, the words of Sarah Lewis, who in *Woman's Mission* (1840) explicitly contrasts female influence with male power: protesting against demands for equal political participation, Lewis asks why we should "disturb the beautiful simplicity of arrangement which has given to man the power, and to woman the influence, to second the plans of Almighty goodness."[25] "It is a vast and substantial influence which woman exerts," writes the author of *Woman's Worth: or, Hints to Raise the Female Character* (1847), "and not the less real because unseen."[26] This refrain echoes Macaulay's comments that the "circumstances which have most influence on the happiness of mankind ... [are] rarely indicated by what historians are pleased to call important events."[27] Agnes Strickland brings together these two lines, the feminine and the historical, to depict a new kind of historical heroine: "Mary Beatrice of Modena," she says, "played an important rather than a conspicuous part in the historic drama of the stirring times in which her lot was cast."[28] Not direct, remarkable action but oblique, pervasive, beneficent sway over circumstances is the ideal for female behavior as well as an increasingly popular conception of historical significance. The women historians made the most of this congruence between ideology and historiography, legitimizing their scholarly projects by the parallels or overlap between women's history and social history while minimizing their challenge to the patriarchy by showing that their subjects contributed to history in acceptably ladylike ways. "In pursuing the broad stream of history, how few writers take the trouble of tracing the under-currents by which the tide of events is influenced," Strickland exclaims; her aquatic metaphor paradigmatically combines an image of inferiority with an assertion of force.[29]

Almost every one of the women historians' volumes contains a similar passage. "Woman, possessing, as she ever does, an all-powerful influence over the events of her day, has thrown a bright light over the dark history of the first eleven centuries of our annals," says Mrs. Matthew Hall in *Queens Before the Conquest* (1854), crediting her subjects with just the kind of enlightening effect Sarah Ellis praises in good Victorian wives.[30] Similarly, as queen of Scotland, Mary Stuart, Strickland tells us, "employed her gentle influence, as woman should, in reconciling feuds, and teaching vindictive and hereditary foes to learn from her own example the duty of forgiveness"; her "gentle sway and refining influence had been blessed to Scotland."[31] Woman's influence is the governing theme and thesis of Julia Kavanagh's *Woman in France During the Eighteenth Century* (1850), where the distinction between visible and unseen agency that provides a theoretical model for these volumes becomes itself part of the story being told:

> It was chiefly in the eighteenth century that women exercised, to its fullest extent, the great and remarkable influence they always possessed in France. They were allowed no political rights, but society gave them the power denied by law.[32]

Often the influence women are credited with is explicitly spousal or maternal; Hannah Lawrance, for example, laments that, in an age "distinguished by a spirit of historical inquiry," so little is yet known "of our female ancestors—the women whose powerful influence moulded the characters of those to whom we owe our national greatness."[33] "Women, whose influence extended over a wide and important sphere, and whose maternal counsels so frequently impressed a character of good, or ill, on the reign of the succeeding monarch," Lawrance says elsewhere, "have been passed over with scarcely the slightest notice."[34] "There are few histories which do not present instances of the political influence of woman," asserts Hall; "the wife, the daughter, the mother, or the friend, has, in innumerable cases, become the arbitress of the destiny of an empire."[35]

These claims are at once novel and conventional. They reinforce the hierarchical structure of Victorian gender ideology by making it a historical constant, but they also open up a place in the historical narrative in which to record the real and often impressive achievements of women of the past. They summon up a historical community, a female tradition, to balance somewhat the empowering sense of historical inheritance otherwise restricted to men—an achievement of great potential significance in an age placing as much importance on history as the Victorian age. This array of female biographies was one means through which half the population could look into what A. Dwight Culler has called the Victorian "mirror of history" and see people at least somewhat like themselves.

III

Again like the ideal wives of Sarah Ellis's conduct books, the historical women are represented as exercising their influence in particular ways, towards ends consistent with what were supposed to be women's special gifts and with their accepted roles. Despite their inevitably close association with the worlds of politics and public affairs, the chief interests and accomplishments of royal consorts, as they are drawn in these volumes, are spiritual, moral, and educational. As writers as otherwise dissimilar as Ellis and John Ruskin (in, for example, "Of Queens' Gardens") proclaimed, women were at once unsuited for and far above the grubby material world in which their men perforce moved. The domestic sphere was constricting in many ways, but their confinement within it resulted from and preserved their potential for higher preoccupations than the mundane—or so the rhetoric goes. The civilized world depended on women to provide sanctuary for their men and to foster the lofty values "without which," as Ellis puts it, "[man] can enjoy nothing beyond a kind of animal existence."[36]

The women historians eulogize the majority of their subjects for their contributions to this civilizing project. In the preface to the first volume of her *Queens of England*, Strickland declares that her object is "to trace the progress of civilization, learning, and refinement in this country, and to show how greatly these were affected by queenly influence in all ages."[37] She makes similar claims for her *Queens of Scotland*, which is "the development of one purpose unswervingly pursued—that of tracing ... the progressive march of civilisation and the interior life and domestic history of our country."[38] By Strickland's account Mary, Queen of Scots, was a leader in this march, seeking "by indefatigable endeavours to induce her people to adopt the best usages of civilization."[39] Hannah Lawrance introduces her *Historical Memoirs* in similar terms:

> Many of these queens ... were pre-eminent for their princely beneficence; many were munificent patronesses of our early literature; while many adorned their high station by the mortal lustre which they shed around them.... [Memoirs of them] should aim at tracing the progress of the arts, the literature, and the social advancement of England.[40]

Introducing her *History of Woman in England* (1843), Lawrance makes bolder and more specific claims:

> Female influence gave the impulse to those doctrines which produced the Reformation,—to woman's patronage, England owes the introduction of printing,—while amid all the changes of after-times her voice was still heard.[41]

And it seems queen after queen exemplifies these virtues in her own behavior; the overwhelming chorus of praise and admiration supports Lawrance's generalization that "we seldom meet with the name of queen, or high-born woman, save as engaged in acts of charity, or in attempting, too often unavailingly, to mitigate the barbarism of the times."[42] In hard times Berengaria, Richard I's queen, "exerted her restored influence over the heart of the king, by persuading him to give all his superfluous money in bountiful alms to the poor; and through her goodness many were kept from perishing," Anna Jameson reports.[43] "[A]s a British sovereign, [Julia 'Domina'] ... certainly helped to refine the manners of the rude people amongst whom she sojourned," according to Mrs. Matthew Hall.[44] "A profound peace and a wise administration distinguished the reign of Christina [of Sweden]," Mary Hays informs her readers; "[o]f letters and the arts she was the distinguished patroness; while her liberality, character, and talents, attracted to the Swedish Court all the learning and genius of Europe."[45] Henry I's first wife, Matilda, "used her influence over the mind of her mighty lord, for the mitigation of the sufferings of the people whom he had subjugated to his yoke," says Strickland approvingly, while his second wife, Adelicia, used "her queenly influence for the establishment of good order, religion, and refinement, and the encouragement of learning and the arts."[46] "Our queens," Strickland claims in her concluding volume, "have been instruments in the hands of God, for the advancement of civilization and the exercise of a moral and religious influence."[47]

Of course, there are exceptions, women whose lives or characteristics unfit them, in one way or another, for this pantheon of "women worthies" (to use historian Natalie Davis's phrase).[48] The misfits fall into two categories, both of which reinforce rather than disrupt the basic model of ideal female behavior: masculine heroines and bad examples. The masculine heroines manifest unwomanly traits, such as ambition, strength of purpose, independence, military valor, or personal fortitude. The foremost example of such a figure is, not surprisingly, Elizabeth I. Gloriana's legendary political and military successes are generally accounted for by stressing her manly qualities; rather than proving by example that women can, in fact, succeed in these masculine arenas, in most accounts she confirms the general unfitness of women for such work by her exceptional status—she is not like other women. Agnes Strickland quotes approvingly the words of Elizabeth's tutor, Roger Ascham: "'the constitution of her mind is exempt from female weakness, and she is endued with masculine power of application.'"[49] Elizabeth was, says Louisa Costello, a "woman of wonderful and masculine spirit" whose famous vanity was a "blemish on her *manly* qualities."[50] Reports of other successful but unladylike women similarly stress their distance from the norms of their sex: Mary Hays reports, for example, that Margaret of Anjou "manifested an energy that extorts admiration and respect; and a courage surpassing her sex.... With the beauty and accomplishments of her own sex, she possessed a masculine force and dignity."[51] And Isabella of Castile, according to Anna Jameson, succeeded in her military ventures because of "her talents, her activity, and her masculine energy of mind."[52]

The second category of exceptions, the bad examples, are also set apart from the good queens, held up as models of what *not* to do. Perhaps the most striking example of such a negative construction is Strickland's account of Katharine Howard, Henry VIII's fifth wife, who at the young age of eighteen was condemned and beheaded for adultery. "The career of Katharine Howard," Strickland observes,

> affords a grand moral lesson—a lesson better calculated to illustrate the vanity of female ambition, and the fatal consequences of the first unguarded steps in guilt, than all the warning essays that have ever been written on those subjects. No female writer can venture to become the apologist of this unhappy queen; yet charity may be permitted to whisper, ere the dark page of her few and evil days is unrolled,
> 'Full gently scan thy brother, man,
> Still gentler sister, woman.'[53]

As well as registering the delicate situation of a woman writer treating an indelicate subject, this remarkable passage openly acknowledges that one goal of a historical text may be to teach a "moral lesson," in this case an ideologically crucial lesson for women: "ambition" (seeking political advancement) and "guilt" (unrestrained sexuality) are, quite literally, "fatal." This account of Katharine Howard sharply delineates the limits on female sovereignty. Page after page, volume after volume, extols the beneficent results of womanly influence exercised over an extended version of the private sphere. Betray that "home," however, by seeking a role outside it or by being unfaithful to its ideals, and pay the price.

Moments like this one make explicit the didactic nature of most of these women's volumes. While all forms of historical representation have ideological underpinnings, historians rarely show their hand in this way; Macaulay may have been widely identified as a Whig, but he does not introduce his *History* with instructions on how to vote in the next election, and for all that he obviously admires William of Orange, he never instructs his male readers to emulate him. In most cases the women historians also are not so blunt, but they leave little doubt that their heroines are role models and exemplars as much as (and sometimes more than) historical personages. Thus their books have a dual role. In the first place, they accomplish, in their own way, the goal of restoring at least some women to the body of historical knowledge and, as I have discussed, of arguing for new ways of understanding historical significance so as to include women's concerns and the details of everyday life and the private sphere. This historiographical project has ideological implications of its own, as I discussed in Chapter One. In the second place, however, these volumes have a crucial pedagogical role. Sarah Lewis, in her influential volume *Woman's Mission*, complains that woman's education does not fit her for the important duties she must fulfill:

> Have the duties of maternity,—the nature of moral influence,—been pointed out to her? Has she ever been enlightened as to the consequent unspeakable importance of personal character as the source of influence? In a word, have any means, direct or indirect, prepared her for her duties? No! but she is a linguist, a pianist, graceful, admired. What is that to the purpose?[54]

What could be more "to the purpose" than the real-life examples provided by these abundant volumes of historical biography? Indeed, the author of *Woman's Worth: or, Hints to Raise the Female Character* explicitly directs women to "make themselves familiar with the lives of those of their own sex who have adorned the different countries of the globe":

> The record of their trials and temptations—their misgivings and doubtings, though finally triumphant, seems to speak with an affecting earnestness to those now alive, urging to the performance of good actions, and assuring that though there may be much to

discourage and perplex, at last victory will crown present efforts, as it did the past.[55]

The goal of exposing young women to such tales was clearly, as Carl Ballstadt suggests, "to encourage women readers to pursue similar activities," to expand along specific lines the range of plots they saw as possible and desirable for themselves.[56] As Mary Roberts observes in her *Select Female Biography*, "reviv[ing] examples of the illustrious dead" reminds the living of their "duty" and excites them "to higher attainments by the contemplation of superior merit."[57]

Unsurprisingly, then, the authors of these volumes often show some self-consciousness about the importance of role models for women. Elizabeth I, according to Louisa Costello, bestowed "great benefits on her fellow females by proving of what importance they could be," and Victoria, Empress Queen of Gaul, "inspired the women of her time with high projects and haughty daring," says Hall.[58] But the women they hold up as exemplary for *their* time demonstrate not "importance" or "haughty daring" but all the domestic virtues. George II's consort Caroline was

> in private life social and exemplary, attached to her husband and the attentive instructress of her children. She loved letters, of which she was the patroness; and of the unhappy and oppressed she was the protectress and benefactress.[59]

And "Royal Females who have played distinguished parts in the history of a country" provide "the most touching examples of all that is lovely, holy, and endearing in womanhood."[60] The Victorians widely assumed that women identified with the subjects of their reading; these texts direct their readers' sympathetic energies towards female figures whose virtues match those most valued by Victorian bourgeois society. As Kate Flint has argued, biographical compilations indeed seem particularly indicative of the belief that "reading could powerfully instill and confirm desirable moral and social qualities."[61]

IV

This pervasive rhetoric of exemplarity strongly indicates that, however these women perceived their role as women historians, it was not simply as disseminators of factual information to the general public. The nature of their work in fact suggests a lot about their target audience, the readership for which their volumes were intended. Henry Colburn, for instance, who published Agnes Strickland's *Lives of the Queens of England* as well as a multitude of similar texts, specialized in works aimed at middle-class women. In addition to *The Court Journal*, which stressed fashion and incidents in aristocratic circles, he published so-called "silver fork" novels and books on royalty and people in "high life." Presumably he expected historical biographies of royal women to appeal to the same market.[62]

The texts themselves give us reason to think they were aimed primarily at a female audience. In the first place, as we have already seen, the authors take considerable trouble to distinguish themselves from "general" history, and this distinction still, throughout the century, meant distinguishing themselves from a masculine norm. While that does not necessarily prevent their works from being of interest to male readers, it does create a historiographical separate sphere likely to seem marginal to those easily accommodated within the central, dominant discourse. Moreover, moments like this one from the concluding volume of Strickland's *Queens of England* directly associate "our Queens" with a community of women: she expresses her "satisfaction" that she has

> been able to afford mingled pleasure and instruction to so extensive a circle of friends—friends who though personally unknown to us, have loved us, confided in our integrity, brought our Queens into their domestic circles, associated them with the sacred joys of home, and sent them as pledges of affection to their dear ones far away, even to the remotest corners of the world.[63]

The circle is complete: Strickland and others like her have brought "the sacred joys of home" into the historical record, which in its turn is accepted back into "domestic circles" as a pledge and affirmation of the female values it has adopted as a historical theory. In a similar passage from the introduction to her edition of Mary Queen of Scots's letters (1843), Strickland observes that contemporary readers

> desire to have [history] so written . . . that they may read it with their children, and that the whole family party shall be eager to resume the book when they gather round the work-table during the long winter evenings.[64]

Again, history is to be part of the "family party," comfortably assimilated into the domestic sphere; the feminity of Strickland's volumes is guaranteed here by their location at the work-table, alongside the sewing that made up the most recognizable and acceptable form of women's "work."

In the second place, there was pervasive concern that women's histories meet standards of modesty and propriety suitable for women readers, especially young women. The women historians knew that the truth is not always decorous, and they struggled to bring their obligations to the facts in line with their audience's expectations of them as "ladies," sometimes raising the issue quite explicitly. For instance, Strickland assures her readers in the preface to her fourth volume that "[d]ue care has been taken to present facts in such a form as to render the Memoirs of *all* the queens of Henry VIII available for the perusal of other ladies."[65] Reviews of women historians show how necessary such assurances were. Frances Palgrave takes Annie Forbes Bush to task for her *Memoirs of the Queens of France*, for example, which spends too much time on "the lives of those unfortunate women, by Mrs. Bush kindly styled 'royal favourites,' who might be more properly designated by an emphatic monosyllable. . . . [I]t may be sufficient to ask," he continues irately, "whether any wife or mother can have too scanty a knowledge of the sports of the Parc aux Cerfs, or the double adulteries of 'La Belle Gabrielle,' or Madame de Pompadour?"[66] In contrast, but just as revealingly, Edward Cheney praises Julia Kavanagh for her delicacy in handling dangerous material: "Her volumes . . . may lie on any drawing-room table without scandal, and may be read by all but her youngest countrywomen without risk."[67] This emphasis on safe reading suggests that the expected audience for women's history was the same female audience that read novels, women who were considered especially vulnerable to corruption from their reading. They were not—indeed, women in general were not—the intended audience for "general historians," who in their emphasis on politics, wars, and other such manly pursuits often had to treat material considered unsuitable for female eyes. Macaulay makes this expectation perfectly clear in a letter responding to a criticism of his *History*:

> I open a school for men: I teach the causes of national prosperity and decay: and the particular time about which I write is a time when profligacy ... had just thrown [its] mask away ... How is it possible to treat a subject like mine without inserting a few paragraphs,—perhaps there may be, in my two thick volumes, two pages,—which it would be better that a young lady should not read aloud?[68]

Macaulay acknowledges here the tension between facts and conventions, both social and literary, that made historical endeavours difficult for both men and women but especially so for the latter, who as readers as well as writers always risked condemnation and scandal—hence Strickland's frank admission that that "[n]o female writer can venture to become the apologist of" the tragic but wanton Katharine Howard.

V

The reviewers also code as female the audience for the history books by or about women through their constant references to these works as forms of gossip. Critics refer, for example, to Strickland's "sometimes amusing sometimes twaddling gossip," her "style of elevated gossip," some details being "tittle-tattle rather than gossip," and her "easy and gossipping style."[69] In a review of Mrs. Matthew Hall's *Queens Before the Conquest*, the *Spectator* invokes Strickland's "readable not to say ... gossipy manner" as a standard to which Mrs. Hall's volumes fail to measure up.[70] Dr. Doran's *Queens of England of the House of Hanover* is "an extraordinary repository of facts and anecdotes," and though Caroline of Brunswick's life contains "nothing either lofty or attractive, there is much over which the moralist may ponder, and the lover of gossip revel."[71] And Julia Pardoe's work on Louis XIV and his court "is a popular, taking, and circulating library selection of fact and anecdote; gossipping, minute, and circumstantial .... an amusing, gossiping, sketchy publication"[72]—the reference to the circulating libraries raises the specter of popular fiction, thus strengthening the implication that Pardoe's audience includes a large proportion of not very discriminating women readers.

Gossip is, of course, gendered in the feminine by traditional association, and the array of gender-specific terms in these examples reinforces this correlation: "minute," "trifling," "twaddling," "amusing," "tittle-tattle," "easy"—they read like a catalogue of negative stereotypes of women's conversation. Tracing the long association of women with gossip, Patricia Spacks points out that Eve brought about the Fall by listening and speaking inappropriately; from such foundational myths as this comes the tradition of considering women's unrestrained talk as a symptom of weak minds, trivial concerns, and even loose morals, not least because the subject of gossip frequently is, or is generally assumed to be, sexual escapades.[73]

The pejorative implications of gossip connect this strain of criticism with one of the major issues in the general discourse of history: discriminating between significant and insignificant details and subordinating particulars to a suitable overarching pattern. Historical work overflowing with arguably inconsequential details was often characterized as feminine; to call historical texts "gossip," which by definition is material indiscriminately selected and haphazardly presented, is to accuse it of representing just such a feminine failure of discernment and control. "[G]lancing over [Strickland's] pages," one reviewer says, "is like listening to a back-stairs narrative of queenly doings and court-scandal, where great events are but the accessories to petty circumstances."[74] Not only has Strickland, according to this reader, lowered herself to the level of servants' chit-chat and rumor, but also, and relatedly, she has produced her historical snapshot in negative, so that which should be in shadow is illuminated while that which should predominate is obscured. Almost every woman historian is accused of a similar dereliction of historical duty, and almost every one is also, often in the same sentence, labelled a "gossip."

In their identification of these books with this discursive practice the reviewers may, however, have been more perspicacious (and less pejorative) than they seem (or intended). According to Patricia Spacks, serious gossip, which she distinguishes from malicious gossip, is much more than casual conversation: it is an exchange of information and point of view that creates or fosters a sense of community and allegiance, a feeling of common interests and causes. It "embodies an alternative discourse to that of public life, and a discourse potentially challenging to public assumptions; it provides language for an alternative culture."[75]

Strickland's picture of an extensive circle of friends bonded through their reading of her *Lives of the Queens of England*, "friends who ... have loved us, confided in our integrity, brought our Queens into their domestic circles, [and] associated them with the sacred joys of home," summons up just such a close community.[76] And for all their obvious compatibility, if not complicity, with the patriarchal ideologies of the age, the volumes emphasizing women's presence throughout history and asserting female influence do fit Spacks's category of an "alternative discourse." Like gossip, and like the novel, they depend "on the assumed importance of the concrete personal particular in all its revelatory power."[77] They assume the interest of details of dress, diet, education, and manners, sometimes of men, but most often of women; they presuppose that this information matters to historical understanding, perhaps not in quite the same way that more conventional historical subjects matter, but as much. They express, in fact, a position closely akin to what today would be called "cultural feminism," still a vital and controversial theoretical view.[78] Exemplified in its early days by Margaret Fuller's *Woman in the Nineteenth Century* (1845), cultural feminism explains and interprets its data, in Joan Scott's words,

> within the terms of the female sphere: by examinations of personal experience, familial and domestic structures, collective (female) reinterpretations of social definitions of women's role, and networks of female friendship that provided emotional as well as physical sustenance.[79]

Rather than emphasizing women's victimization and exclusion from the male world of political, economic and military power, cultural feminism provides a counter-tradition; rather than seeking places for women within a man's world, it challenges conventional valuations of men's activities and seeks to gain higher status for activities and priorities historically common to women.[80]

To make this connection between these historical biographies and cultural feminism is not to claim that either the works or their authors subscribe to any particular feminist agenda, although clearly, in the broadest sense of a term that has come to mean so many things today, all works promoting better understanding of women's lives contribute to a feminist project. There is, in fact, both biographical and textual evidence of self-conscious advocacy for women's causes in some instances; Mary Hays, for example, declares that she writes her *Memoirs of Queens*, as she wrote other works,

> in the cause, and for the honour and advantage of my sex; and [having] deeply at heart, as connected with the welfare of the human species, and of society at large, the moral rights and intellectual advancement of *woman*.[81]

But this kind of explicit political avowal is rare. I would argue that all of these works make a less direct contribution: by telling stories about women in history, they expand the range of narrative possibilities for talking about women's lives. They do not provide what Carolyn Heilbrun calls a "quest plot" for women, but they recognize and respond to the absence of women in most historical accounts and work to make up for that absence.[82] "[P]erhaps," Heilbrun suggests,

> women have not told stories because there were no stories to tell. There was only the dailiness of life, the attention to food, clothing, shelter, the endless replication of motherhood.[83]

Heilbrun's remarks reflect the difficulty we have recognizing the mundane, the repetitive, the particular, as stories worth narrating. What was really missing for these writers, of course, was not in fact stories, which abounded even in the scanty and little-known records of women's historical experiences, but a culturally recognized and respected plot within which to frame these stories. In the grand narrative of the advance of civilization through the enlightened and beneficent influence of women, these historians found such a plot. As the continuing controversy over cultural feminism attests, this plot is in itself only arguably emancipatory. But, as I argue in more detail in subsequent chapters, it is an experiment—a conceptual breakthrough—that provides an important touchstone for the more profound questioning of women's relationships to historical narratives found in other works of the period with a much firmer place in the literary canon, such as the novels of George Eliot.

VI

Finally, the Victorian critics do not, it seems, always intend the label "gossipy" to be pejorative—or, not strictly. For these reviewers, the term implies easy readability, graceful narrative, colorful details, an anecdotal approach, and a light, rather than serious, attitude towards the material. Like the overtly negative uses of "gossipy," this more innocent-seeming use belittles and diminishes the works to which it is applied. But it also sounds familiar—like a recipe for successful novel-writing. As we saw in Chapter One, there was considerable anxiety about the breakdown of gender barriers attendant on shifts in conventions of genre. Because of the association between women and novel writing, women's historical writing inevitably became part of this debate.

What praise the women historians get is for their lively style, their evocative use of personal details, or the dramatic interest of their narratives—that is, for their success in making history read like fiction. They themselves clearly recognize that their chief competitor is the historical novel, not Froude or Lingard; Strickland remarks, for instance, that "[t]he tastes of those who were the rising generation when the Waverley romances were the absorbing theme of interest in the literary world, have become matured. They require to have history rendered as agreeable without the mixture of fiction as with it."[84] Somewhat unexpectedly, these women market themselves by claiming, not that their true stories are morally or educationally superior, but that they are more entertaining. "History ... like real life so often puts to flight the visions of romance," says Hannah Lawrance; Strickland introduces her volume on Henry VIII's wives with the promise that "[w]e know of no tale of romance that offers circumstances of tragic interest like those which are to be traced in the lives of these unhappy ladies."[85] "The record of the political progress of nations," says Anna Jameson,

> is a wonderful romance, where truth and fable are combined in presenting to generation after generation, an entertaining volume for amusement and instruction; and, doubtless, Byron was not wide of the mark, when he denominated all history, 'a splendid fiction.'[86]

"Perhaps no novel that was ever written," declares Emily Sarah Holt, "has equalled in romantic incident, in absorbing interest, in pathetic beauty, the story of the long and eventful life of Ela the Beautiful, Countess of Salisbury."[87] "The romance of real life is often not less replete than the page of fiction with poetical material and extraordinary vicissitude," says Mary Hays in her turn.[88] These writers claim not so much that they differ from novelists but that they *exceed* them in affect, drama, and romance.

In the terms of the ongoing debates about gender, genre, and historiography, then, one thing these "lady historians" do *not* do is attempt to masquerade as masculine. In every aspect of their work they emphasize their difference, their separation, from the history men, and they display no particular concern to distance themselves in sobriety of tone or gravity of subject matter from the questionable genre of historical fiction. Their books are unapologetically by, about, and for women, and they resist the masculinist dominance in historiography on every front. It seems sensible to infer that they drew some of their confidence—itself indicated by their prolific output—from women's successes as novelists over the century. But it also seems that they themselves, by vigorously pursuing their own historiographical goals, created and sustained an intellectual climate in which it was possible to take seriously both claims about women's importance in history and historical narratives, fiction or nonfiction, in which women's history is unambiguously the subject or theme. The generally scornful and dismissive reviews they received in the major journals tell one side of their story. The serious treatment of historiographical issues in women's fiction in the nineteenth century, however, and the continuation of a tradition of women's history, despite women's exclusion from the professional practice of history for much of this century, tell another.

NOTES

1. A shorter version of this chapter has appeared in *Victorian Studies*, Volume 38 No. 3 (Spring 1995), under the title "'This Feminine Preserve': Historical Biographies by Victorian Women." This material is reprinted by permission of the trustees of Indiana University. Two other recent articles explore similar territory, though from different perspectives. Rosemary Mitchell's essay "The Busy Daughters of Clio: Women Writers of History

between 1820 and 1880," forthcoming in the *Women's History Review* (Spring 1998), focuses especially on the difficulties women historians encountered in their research and publishing. Joan Thirsk's "The History Women," in *Chattel, Servant, or Citizen: Women's Status in Church, State and Society*, eds. M. O'Dowd and S. Wichert (Belfast: Institute of Irish Studies, the Queen's University, 1995), pp. 1-11, emphasizes the women historians' work on primary documents. I am grateful to Dr. Mitchell and Dr. Thirsk for sharing early, unpublished versions of these papers with me. Daniel Woolf's "A Feminine Past? Gender, Genre, and Historical Knowledge in England, 1500-1800," *American Historical Review* Vol. 102 No. 3 (June 1997), is a thorough examination of women's involvement in historical practices prior to the Victorian period.

2. [Francis Palgrave], Review of Annie Forbes Bush, *Memoirs of the Queens of France*, *Quarterly Review* Vol. 71 (1843), pp. 411-16; p. 416.

3. Julia Kavanagh, *Women of Christianity, Exemplary for Acts of Piety and Charity* (New York: D. Appleton & Co., 1869, first published London, 1851), p. 10.

4. In "The History Women," Thirsk also cites almost exclusively biographical studies.

5. Patricia Meyer Spacks, *Gossip* (New York: Knopf, 1985), p. 93.

6. [T. H. Lister?], *Edinburgh Review* Vol. 58 (1834), pp. 398-422; p. 399.

7. [John Hosack?], "Miss Strickland's *Queens of Scotland*," *Tait's Edinburgh Magazine* Vol. XVIII (April 1851), pp. 238-45; p. 238.

8. M. A. Stodart, *Female Writers: Thoughts on Their Proper Sphere, and on Their Powers of Usefulness* (London: Seeley and Burnside, 1842), pp. 124, 128.

9. Mary Hays, *Memoirs of Queens, Illustrious and Celebrated* (London: T. & J. Allman, 1821), p. 450; Agnes Strickland, *Life of QueenElizabeth* (London: J. M. Dent & Sons, 1910), p. 608.

10. Lucy Aikin, *Memoirs of the Court of Queen Elizabeth* (London: Longman, Hurst, Rees, et al., 1826). 2 Volumes. Vol. I, p. vii.

11. Hannah Lawrance, *Historical Memoirs of the Queens of England, from the Commencement of the Twelfth Century* (London: Edward Moxon, 1838). 2 Volumes. Vol. I, p. 60.

12. Agnes Strickland, *Lives of the Queens of England, from the Norman Conquest* (Philadelphia: Lee and Blanchard, 1848). 12 Volumes. Vol. 6, pp. 131-2.

13. [Margaret Oliphant], "Modern Light Literature—History," *Blackwood's Magazine* Vol. 78 (Oct. 1855), pp. 437-51; p. 443.

14. Mary Ann Everett Wood, *Letters of Royal and Illustrious Ladies of Great Britain, from the Commencement of the Twelfth Century to the Close of the Reign of Queen Mary*. (London: Henry Colburn, 1846). 3 Volumes. Vol. I, p. xi.

15. *Historical Memoirs of the Queens of England*. Vol. 1, p. 318.

16. Elizabeth Stone, *The Art of Needlework from the Earliest Ages; including some notices of the Ancient Historical Tapestries*. 3rd edition. (London: Henry Colburn, 1841), p. 299.

17. *Lives of the Queens of England*. Vol. 4, p. 106.

18. *Life of Mary Queen of Scots*. (London: George Bell & Sons, 1888.) 2 Volumes. Vol. 2, p. 240.

19. Hannah Lawrance, *Historical Memoirs of the Queens of England*. Vol. 2, p. 156.

20. Lawrance, *Historical Memoirs of the Queens of England*. Vol. 2, p. 2.

21. "On History," *A Carlyle Reader*, ed. G. B. Tennyson (Cambridge: Cambridge UP, 1984), pp. 55-66; p. 58.

22. *Lives of the Queens of England*, Vol. 12, p. x.

23. "History," *The Lays of Ancient Rome & Miscellaneous Essays and Poems* (London: J. M. Dent & Sons, 1910, rpt. 1963), pp. 1-39; p. 34.

24. Sarah Stickney Ellis, *The Wives of England, Their Relative Duties, Domestic Influences, & Social Obligations* (London: Fisher, Son & Co., 1843), p. 109.

25. Sarah Lewis, *Woman's Mission* (Boston, W. Crosby & Co., 1840), pp. 45-6.

26. Anonymous, *Women's Worth; or, Hints to Raise the Female Character* (London: Steves & Co., 1847), p. 26.

27. "History," p. 34.

28. *Lives of the Queens of England*. Vol. 9, p. viii.

29. *Lives of the Queens of England*. Vol. 1, p. 25.

30. Mrs. Matthew Hall, *The Queens Before the Conquest* (London: Henry Colburn, 1854). 2 Volumes. Vol. 1, p. iv.

31. Strickland, *Life of Mary Queen of Scots*. Vol. 2, p. 26; Vol. 1, p. 201..

32. Kavanagh, *Woman in France During the Eighteenth Century* (London: G. P. Putnam's Sons, 1893, originally published London: Smith & Elder, 1850). 2 Volumes. Vol. I, p. 4.

33. Hannah Lawrance, *The History of Woman in England, and Her Influence on Society and Literature from the Earliest Period* (London: Henry

Colburn, 1843). 2 Volumes. Vol. 1, pp. iii-iv.

34. *Historical Memoirs of the Queens of England*. Vol. 1, p. iii.

35. Hall, *Queens Before the Conquest*. Vol. 1 pp. 85.

36. *The Women of England, Their Social Duties, and Domestic Habits*, (London: Fisher, Son & Co., 1839), p. 58.

37. *Lives of the Queens of England*. Vol. 1, p. xiv.

38. *Lives of the Queens of Scotland and English Princesses Connected with the Regal Succession of Great Britain* (London: Blackwood, 1852). 8 Volumes. Vol. 8, p. 2.

39. *Life of Mary Queen of Scots*. Vol. I, p. 173.

40. *Historical Memoirs of the Queens of England*. Vol. 1, p. iv.

41. *History of Woman in England*. Vol. 1, p. vi.

42. *History of Woman in England*. Vol. 1, p. 138.

43. Anna Jameson, *Lives of Celebrated Female Sovereigns and Illustrious Women*, ed. Mary E. Hewitt (Philadelphia: Porter and Coates, 1870, originally published London, Henry Colburn, 1831), p. 67.

44. Mrs. Matthew Hall, *Queens Before the Conquest*. Vol. 1, p. 101.

45. Mary Hays, *Memoirs of Queens*, p. 249.

46. Strickland, *Lives of the Queens of England*. Vol. 1, p. 73; Vol. 1, p. 124.

47. *Lives of the Queens of England*. Vol. 12, p. viii.

48. Natalie Zemon Davis, "'Women's History' in Transition: The European Case," *Feminist Studies* Vol. 3 No. 3/4 (Spring/Summer 1976), pp. 83-103.

49. *Lives of the Queens of England*. Vol. 6, p. 41.

50. *Memoirs of Eminent Englishwomen* (London: Bentley, 1844). 2 Volumes. Vol. 1, p. iii, original emphasis.

51. Mary Hays, *Memoirs of Queens*, p. 367.

52. Jameson, *Celebrated Female Sovereigns*, p. 134.

53. *Lives of the Queens of England*. Vol. IV, pp. 279-80. The lines are slightly misquoted from Robert Burns's "Address to the Unco Guid"; I am indebted to the expertise of scholars on the VICTORIA e-mail list for this reference.

54. Sarah Lewis, *Woman's Mission*, p. 63.

55. *Woman's Worth*, p. 82.

56. *The Literary History of the Strickland Family*. (Unpublished Ph.D. dissertation, University of London, 1965), p. 117.

57. Mary Roberts, *Select Female Biography, Comprising Memoirs of Eminent British Ladies* (London: Harvey & Darton, 1829), p. v.

58. *Memoirs of Eminent Englishwomen.* Vol. 1, pp. v-vi; *Queens Before the Conquest.* Vol. 1, p. 133.

59. Mary Hays, *Memoirs of Queens*, p. 93.

60. Agnes Strickland, *Lives of the Queens of Scotland and English Princesses Connected with the Regal Succession of Great Britain* (New York: Harper & Bros., 1851). Vol. 1, p. v.

61. Kate Flint, *The Woman Reader 1837-1914* (Oxford: Clarendon, 1993), p. 36.

62. Ballstadt, *Literary History of the Strickland Family*, pp. 128-133.

63. *Lives of the Queens of England.* Vol. 12, p. xii.

64. *Letters of Mary Queen of Scots* (London: Henry Colburn, 1843), Vol. 1, p. xv.

65. *Lives of the Queens of England.* Vol. 4, p. ix, original emphasis.

66. [Palgrave], Review, p. 416.

67. [Edward Cheney], Review of Julia Kavanagh's *Woman in France During the Eighteenth Century. Quarterly Review* Vol. 88 (1851), pp. 352-85; p. 352.

68. [To unidentified recipient, 31 March 1849]. *Selected Letters of Thomas Babington Macaulay*, ed. Thomas Pinney (Cambridge: Cambridge UP, 1982), p. 234.

69. *Spectator* No. 742 (Sept. 17 1842), p. 907; No. 885 (June 14 1845), p. 569; No 947 (Aug. 22 1846), p. 808; No. 611 (March 14 1840), p. 258.

70. *Spectator* No. 1369 (Sept. 23 1854), p. 1006.

71. *Spectator* No. 1415 (Aug. 11 1855), p. 837.

72. [A. V. Kirwan?], Review of Pardoe's *Louis XIV, and the Court of France in the Seventeenth Century. Fraser's Magazine* Vol. 35 (June 1847), pp. 694 & 699.

73. Patricia Spacks, *Gossip*, pp. 38ff.

74. *Spectator* No. 611, p. 258.

75. *Gossip*, p. 46.

76. *Lives of the Queens of England.* Vol. 12, p. xii.

77. *Gossip*, p. 19.

78. See, for example, Josephine Donovan, *Feminist Theory: The Intellectual Traditions of American Feminism*, New Expanded Edition (New York: Continuum, 1992), especially Chapter Two, "Cultural Feminism."

79. Joan Scott, *Gender and the Politics of History* (New York: Columbia UP, 1988), p. 20. Scott is referring specifically to historical work governed by these assumptions.

80. For more about the debate over cultural feminism, particularly in historiography, see Cécile Dauphin, Anette Farge, et al., "Women's Culture and Women's Power: An Attempt at Historiography," *Journal of Women's History* Vol. 1 No. 1 (Spring 1989), pp. 63-88; Ellen Dubois, Gerda Lerner, Carroll Smith-Rosenberg, et al., "Politics and Culture in Women's History," *Feminist Studies* Vol. 6 No. 1 (Spring 1980), pp. 26-64; Hilda L. Smith, "Female Bonds and the Family: Recent Directions in Women's History," in Paula A. Treichler, Cheris Kramarae and Beth Stafford, eds., *For Alma Mater: Theory and Practice in Feminist Scholarship* (Chicago: U of Illinois P, 1985), pp. 272-291; or Sarah Stage, "Women's History and 'Woman's Sphere': Major Works of the 1970s," *Socialist Review* Nos. 50/51 (March-June 1980), pp. 245-53.

81. *Memoirs of Queens*, p. v, original emphasis.

82. Carolyn Heilbrun, *Writing A Woman's Life* (New York: Ballantine, 1988).

83. Carolyn Heilbrun, *Reinventing Womanhood* (New York: Norton, 1979), pp. 210-11.

84. *Letters of Mary Queen of Scots*. Vol. 1, p. xv.

85. Lawrance, *Historical Memoirs of the Queens of England*. Vol. 1, p. 136; Strickland, *Lives of the Queens of England*. Vol. 4, p. ix.

86. Anna Jameson, *Celebrated Female Sovereigns*, p. 42.

87. Emily Sarah Holt, *Memoirs of Royal Ladies* (London: Hurst & Blackett, 1861). 2 Volumes. Vol. 1, p. 4.

88. Mary Hays, *Memoirs of Queens*, p. 48.

CHAPTER THREE
Stitches in Time
Needlework and Victorian Historiography[1]

> *That this should prove*
> *More than the personal episode, more than all*
> *The little lives sketched on the teeming loom*
> *Was then withheld from you*. . . . [2]

"Never, perhaps," wrote John Collingwood Bruce in 1856,

> was so important a document written in worsted. It is a full and faithful chronicle of an event on which the modern history of the world has turned. It is referred to as an historical authority by nearly every writer who discusses the period. . . . It is, however, a double memorial; it is a record of the love and duty of William's consort, as well as of the skill and valour of the great hero himself. . . . Matilda could not bestride the war-horse, and do battle in the field by her husband's side; but she could commit his exploits to the Tapestry.[3]

Bruce was writing, of course, about the Bayeux Tapestry, which, as he indicates, resonated with special significance for the Victorians. This phenomenon can be accounted for partly by the generally increasing interest in antiquities, but Bruce's and others' interest in the Bayeux Tapestry also indicates the unexpected intersection of two discourses during the period: needlework and historiography. In the first place, as an embroidered narrative, a story "written in worsted," the Tapestry presents an unusual twist on the age-old debate over women and writing in which, traditionally, the needle is held up as the appropriate womanly alternative to the pen. This debate intensified during the nineteenth century as needlework became more and more closely associated with proper middle-class femininity while, simultaneously, more and more middle-class women began to write. In the second place, study of the Tapestry itself as an artefact represents the changes taking place in standards of historical significance which made such everyday female activities as embroidery worthy of serious study. This chapter examines the interplay between needlework and historiography encapsulated, symbolically and literally, in the Bayeux Tapestry. I argue that needlework, the quintessentially feminine art, furnished at once a metaphorical, a formal, and a substantive alternative to traditional conceptions of history, in the process fixing gender as a constant and conspicuous component of the debate. Focusing on needlework also exposes a limitation of the feminized historiography writers such as Strickland and Stone advocate: the female community and traditions they and the other historical biographers summon up is class-specific. Their emphasis on needlework as a ladylike, aristocratic, ennobling occupation overlooks its widespread importance as a means of survival for poor and working-class women. Their assumption that its universality as women's work overrides these differences in its applications obscures and thus reinforces class hierarchies and boundaries, just as the general rhetoric of essentialized femininity does throughout the volumes of women's biographies.

I

"If the pen is a metaphorical penis," Sandra Gilbert and Susan Gubar wrote in a pivotal essay on women and authorship, "with what organ can females generate texts?"[4] Had they asked "with what implement?" the question might not have been simply rhetorical. Historically, writing has demanded a level of education unusual, unsuitable, or often simply impossible for a woman; further, if intended for public consumption it bespeaks an unladylike degree of self-assertion, even self-aggrandizement. Anne Finch's complaint that "a woman who attempts the pen" is considered "an intruder on the rights of men" indicates the simple but powerful form this general prejudice had taken by the late seventeenth century: she echoes the territorial rhetoric of men anxious to establish separate and gendered spheres of authority and expertise, with literary production securely within the masculine domain.[5]

Stitches in Time 63

Hindered by both education and convention from wielding the pen, women were urged instead to devote their energies to the needle, which by the time of Finch's writing functioned as a crucial and indelibly gendered cultural symbol. Since Roman times, a girl's education had consistently included instruction in some form of needlework, but associations between sewing or embroidery and particular, class-specific definitions of femininity accreted gradually between the Middle Ages and the eighteenth century and hardened into dogma during the Victorian period.[6] In the Middle Ages, needlework was a respected art and craft practiced by both sexes; elaborate embroidery signalled the wealth and power of church, state, or family. In the Elizabethan period, as changes in social and economic structures removed many women from productive labor and isolated them in the home, amateur needlework began to carry connotations of leisured, well-bred femininity which were intensified by prominent examples of royal or aristocratic women who excelled at it. By the seventeenth century, when Finch wrote, needlework was one of the primary means by which every girl was trained in her society's ideology of womanhood. Samplers in particular measured progress not only in specific stitching skills but also in self-discipline, patience, and industry; often their texts—biblical verses, homilies, or moralizing epigrams—reinforced other desirable virtues such as piety, obedience, submission, and resignation. As the separation of the world into masculine and feminine spheres continued in the eighteenth century, amateur needlework became unambiguously and inextricably linked with women and domesticity and thus opposed to the masculine world of public affairs, high culture, and, of course, literary production. Thus, when another woman poet irately asked in 1754, "Why are the needle and the pen / Thought incompatible by men?" her rhetorical question addressed a complex array of cultural presuppositions about writing, sewing, and gender.[7]

In the nineteenth century, thanks to the ideological and cultural legacy of the previous three hundred years, every girl learned to sew, and to lack this skill was to appear not just ill-trained but unfeminine. As Deborah Gorham reports, quoting in her turn from an 1879 volume called *The Mother's Home Book*,

> Sewing and needlework were considered to be the most essential of [the] domestic skills [that mothers should teach their daughters], and

right through the Victorian period, it was advised that training in sewing should begin early in a girl's life. ... A girl who could not sew was considered not only to lack a useful skill, but to lack one that was essential to her *as a female*: 'Nothing can be more pitiable than to see a female ... unable to ply her needle, her case being somewhat similar to that of a male ... who does not know how to read.'[8]

Technological changes over the century, such as the invention of sewing machines and the availability of ready-made patterns and clothes, reduced the practical necessity of much hand-sewing but left intact its ideological implications. Gorham comments that "the continued emphasis placed on this skill [of needlework] indicates that its importance was not solely practical: it had, as well, a symbolic connection with femininity"—clearly an understatement.[9] The particular skills each girl was expected to perfect, however, and the use to which she was expected to put them, varied with her class. For a working-class girl, sewing was a practical skill, a form of vocational training for either work within the home or paid employment.[10] By this time professional needlework had fallen dramatically in status and, not coincidentally, become almost entirely women's work—an 1841 census found that only 563 of the 106,801 people who were dressmakers or milliners were men.[11] Below I address the ways in which the plight of seamstresses and milliners and the intense public debate about it complicate the discourse I lay out here by raising the spectre of class which most discussions of needlework's feminine virtues ignore. To begin with, however, I will focus on the social and symbolic significance of amateur needlework, needlework done by middle-class women in their homes, perhaps for a practical purpose but never for a profit.

A woman's activities in the middle-class or upwardly mobile Victorian home indicated and reinforced her family's social standing. Indeed, as Elizabeth Langland has recently argued, women's economic and political importance in this arena has often been underestimated.[12] For one thing, although few middle-class families could afford enough domestic help to render their wives and daughters completely idle, women had to maintain as much as possible an appearance of leisure as evidence of economic prosperity. They needed to know enough about domestic chores to supervise them, but, to avoid any taint of vulgarity, their own hands had to be occupied with genteel and primarily ornamental pursuits. Needlework was just such an elegant, ladylike accomplishment. As Joan Burstyn comments, "[a] woman who could lounge on a sofa all day reading or embroidering was obviously wealthy. Her husband or father had provided servants to cook and clean; *he* was a success economically and consequently *she* was a success socially."[13] Although some stitchery projects might produce something useful, such as slippers, handkerchiefs, or cushions, these items were not essential contributions to the household but rather decorative extras indicating their maker's freedom from other demands. Or, from a somewhat different angle, since middle-class women were generally prohibited from pursuing an education or a career, they needed something to fill their hours of obligatory inactivity; because of its historical association with well-bred femininity, needlework provided an acceptable outlet for energy otherwise arrested at every turn.[14]

Not surprisingly, then, because of its ubiquity and its rich ideological significance, needlework figured largely in nineteenth-century discussions of woman's role. To proponents of the ideal of 'true womanhood,' needlework played an important part in inculcating desirable feminine attributes. In a story from an 1855 volume called *Treasures in Needlework*, for example, Mary's mother chastises her daughter for her carelessness about needlework:

> '[I]n itself, Mary, needlework is an elegant amusement, giving exercise to some of the best qualities of a woman. Diligence, patience, perseverance, and a great many other virtues are brought into exercise, and taste and refinement are cultivated.'[15]

Her admonition draws Mary's attention away from the actual product of her stitching to the intangible and heavily class-inflected traits putatively fostered by rigorous application to this difficult and tedious technical skill: elegance, taste, and refinement indicate affluence united with good breeding.

This and other similar representations of needlework as bringing a higher level of distinction to the middle-class home rely on the popular Victorian image of embroidery as a favorite activity of noble and royal women of past ages. In the medieval noblewoman, in particular, many Victorians saw a "blueprint for the middle-class Victorian wife: pious, secluded, faithful and dutiful"—and sedulously embroidering.[16] "Shut up in her lofty chamber," wrote Charles Henry Hartshorne in 1848,

> within the massive walls of a castle, or immured in the restricted limits of a convent, the needle alone supplied an unceasing source of amusement; with this [the medieval English gentlewoman] might enliven her tedious hours, and depicting the heroic deeds of her absent lord, as it were, visibly hasten his return; or on the other hand, softened by the subdued influences of pious contemplation, she might use this pliant instrument to bring vividly before her mind the mysteries of that faith to which in her solitude she fondly clung.[17]

Historical and fictional literature provided specific examples of virtuous and high-born women who expressed their love for their husbands or their God in painstaking stitches. At least in theory, the Victorian embroideress replicated this ideal of wifely and Christian devotion, and these elevated precedents gave her labors with her own "pliant instrument" an aristocratic air.

These historical antecedents also link needlework to the more general phenomenon of Victorian medievalism, which manifested itself in everything from poetry to architecture. Widespread interest in the Middle Ages as a historical period fuelled rather than dispelled myths about this phase of England's past as a time of social and religious order and harmony that contrasted favorably with the chaos and conflict of the modern period. Medievalism, as Alice Chandler explains,

> satisfied the nation's needs. It brought to an increasingly urbanized, industrialized, and atomistic society, the vision of a more stable and harmonious social order, substituting the paternal benevolence of manor and guild for the harshness of city and factory and offering the clear air and open fields of the medieval past in place of the blackening skies of England.[18]

It was a fantasy, as Chandler's word "vision" suggests, of a world in which interactions were governed by relationships of kin or loyalty rather than by money, in which everyone knew his place in a rigid but unifying social hierarchy. The Victorian middle-class embroideress, working by hand, not machine, and for love, not wages, evoked this idealized past in a form perfectly suited for her time and role. In her image, the class stratifications of the Middle Ages shade into the gender divisions of the nineteenth-century middle class; the Lady of the court becomes the lady of the house, and through this symbolic appropriation the supposedly natural social disposition of the earlier age lends credibility to the very different configuration of the later one—one myth in the service of another.

In the ongoing drama of pen versus needle, then, the Victorians continued the centuries-old project of construing needlework as the proper feminine alternative to the masculine implement, imbuing it with properties both intrinsic and extrinsic, material and symbolic, so as to cement its identification with genteel middle-class womanhood. Predictably, needlework therefore attracted substantial criticism from those who found this definition of femininity inadequate and confining—needlework's symbolic richness made it a natural target. The most common objection was that women could never develop their mental powers as long as they devoted their best energies to stitching. In an essay published in the *British Lady's Magazine* in 1815, Mary Lamb asserted that "[n]eedlework and intellectual improvement are naturally in a state of warfare"; twenty-five years later, a writer in the *Athenaeum* spoke out still more strongly:

> It is impossible . . . to conceive any mode of getting rid of time more stultifying, and more calculated to unfit the parties for becoming meet associates for men of intellect and of business, than that eternal embroidering and finical needlework. . . . We readily admit, that what may be called fancy needlework is an elegant amusement, when called in to relieve the tedium of more serious labours; but as an all-engrossing pursuit, such as at present it is too often made, we hold that it is as injurious to mind as it is to bodily health.[19]

Criticism of needlework generally follows the same lines: time spent mastering this skill is time stolen from other, more worthwhile, enriching, and intellectual work. The indictment is explicitly directed at middle-class women who misjudge the amount of time and energy appropriate to expend on such an "elegant amusement," but the implications for those forced by economic circumstances to make it an "all-engrossing pursuit" are unmistakable: in a nice example of the way this supposedly universal feminine skill highlights rather than diminishes class differences, their professional preoccupation with their needles deepens the chasm between them and their more privileged sisters.

While the writer from the *Athenaeum* mostly stresses the unfitness of needlework devotees for intelligent masculine companionship, others emphasize stitching's deleterious effects on women themselves. Women writers particularly tend to depict needlework as undisguised drawing-room drudgery, a tedious chore absorbing energy and skill while yielding neither pleasure nor utility in return. Their harsh view of one of their culture's most cherished symbols of femininity speaks volumes about the difficulties they faced in realizing their literary ambitions; for them, the debate about pens and needles was anything but abstract. A brilliant tongue-in-cheek passage by G. H. Lewes sums up the hostile attitude they faced:

> Wherever we [men] carry our skilful pens, we find the place preoccupied by a woman.... Does it never occur to them that they are doing us a serious injury, and that we need 'protection'? Woman's proper sphere of activity is elsewhere. Are there no husbands, lovers, brothers, friends to coddle and console? Are there no stockings to darn, no purses to make, no braces to broider? *My* idea of a perfect woman is of one who can write but won't.... To knit a purse or work an ottoman is a graceful and useful devotion of female energies.... *This* is what I call something like woman's mission! Women of England! listen to my words: Your path is the path of perdition, your literary impulses are the impulses of Satan. Burn your pens, and purchase wool.[20]

In her *Autobiography*, Margaret Oliphant makes clear her awareness that she participated in a tradition of female authorship founded on putting aside the needle:

> I had no table even to myself, much less a room to work in, but sat at the corner of the family table with my writing-book, with everything going on as if I had been making a shirt instead of writing a book.... Miss Austen, I believe, wrote in the same way.... The family were

half ashamed to have it known that she was not just a young lady like the others, doing her embroidery.[21]

In her biography of her most successful and famous literary sister, Jane Margaret Strickland repeatedly mentions Agnes's fondness for needlework. "We must . . . remember," she asserts at one point,

> that Agnes Strickland was really more of the woman than the author. She had a feminine love of dress and female employments, was fond of fine needlework, and did not despise the more useful handicrafts to which the needle is applied. . . . [Both] the authors of the Queens were as familiar with the use of the needle as with that of the pen.[22]

By thus protesting too much, she makes obvious how problematic a woman writer's situation was, how profoundly her vocation challenged her gender identity.

References to needlework abound in Victorian women's writing, where characters sometimes seem to be acting out their authors' undoubtedly fraught relationships with needlework. In George Eliot's *Felix Holt*, for instance, the narrator acidly comments,

> A little daily embroidery had been a constant element in Mrs. Transome's life; that soothing occupation of taking stitches to produce what neither she nor any one else wanted, was then the resource of many a well-born and unhappy woman.[23]

Here embroidery is the opiate of the well-bred; Mrs. Transome's perfunctory stitches "soothe" her though they are a depressingly inadequate substitute for intellectual enrichment or social autonomy. The saddest aspect of Mrs. Transome's "daily embroidery" is that it produces nothing of value, nothing "she [or] any one else wanted." Elizabeth Barrett Browning's Aurora Leigh, an aspiring writer explicitly confronting the conventional alternative to her chosen implement, similarly emphasizes the oppressive futility of her exercises in needlework:

> By the way,
> The works of women are symbolical.
> We sew, sew, prick our fingers, dull our sight,
> Producing what? A pair of slippers, sir,
> To put on when you're weary—or a stool
> To tumble over and vex you . . 'curse that stool!'
> Or else at best, a cushion where you lean
> And sleep, and dream of something we are not,
> But would be for your sake. Alas, alas!
> This hurts most, this . . that, after all, we are paid
> The worth of our work, perhaps.[24]

The pink-eyed shepherdess Aurora produces when she mistakes the colors of her silks epitomizes the terrible waste of her effort and blood on projects with neither aesthetic nor utilitarian value. In these examples needlework represents the enforced and stifling leisure, the unrewarding but inviolable tedium, of a middle-class woman's life—what Eliot in *Middlemarch* calls "the gentlewoman's oppressive liberty."[25]

These dismissive characterizations of amateur needlework accept that in the contest between pen and needle the best possible outcome involves women's repudiating the feminine implement in favor of the masculine. According to this model, stitching is a bad alternative to other forms of expression or other skills; all the fine-sounding rhetoric about noblewomen and women's special excellences merely puts a pretty face on the harsh truths of women's exclusion from education, from economic independence, and from full participation in life outside the cloistered realm of the middle-class home. Indeed, the writer in the *Athenaeum* makes this point explicitly, bluntly accusing Stone's *Art of Needlework* of being "a 'conservative' production, intended to seduce the sex from revolutionary reading and writing, and to subdue their natures to a servile drudgery."[26] Ironically, although this account accurately exposes the constraining agenda of the Victorian ideal of womanhood, it also accepts a masculinist view of the world by failing to find any value in an activity engaged in, if only by default, by almost every woman in history—by assuming the intrinsic superiority of the pen to the needle.[27] A further element in Victorian discussions of needlework suggests an alternative to both the idealizing and the excoriating analysis by emphasizing needlework as part of a distinct women's culture, marginal perhaps, but nonetheless important, interesting, and sometimes even empowering.[28]

The Victorian needlewoman would have seen herself as participating in a special feminine tradition. "The art of Needlework in every form," as the authors of *Treasures in Needlework* write,

> is well known to be as old as the hills; but in past ages the higher or picturesque gradations of [needlework] were confined to the delicate fingers of Queens and Court ladies. . . . In our own times much has been done to raise the art of picturesque and useful Needlework in popular estimation; and it is gratifying to think that a spirit of emulation has been aroused, which must, sooner or later, render the knowledge of this art necessary to the perfection of womanly education.[29]

Inverting Hartshorne's image of "confined" women finding solace in their needles, they depict embroidery as a captive now liberated by its nineteenth-century practitioners as they pick up the thread left by their medieval foremothers.

As well as emphasizing needlework's antiquity, Victorian writers on the topic stress its universality: its practice, they like to suggest, transcends not only historical but also class boundaries, providing a common denominator between contemporary women. In the introduction to her *Art of Needlework*, Elizabeth Stone makes this point explicitly:

> If there be one mechanical art of more universal application than all others, and therefore of more universal interest, it is that which is practised with the NEEDLE. From the stateliest denizen of the proudest palace, to the humblest dweller in the poorest cottage, all more or less ply the busy needle; from the crying infant of a span long and an hour's life, to the silent tenant of 'the narrow house,' all need its practical services.[30]

Stone chooses not to dwell on the important differences between uses of the needle in palaces and in cottages; her only concern is to justify her extended historical treatment of needlework by its undeniable prevalence. For others, this ubiquity becomes part of an argument for reevaluating needlework, for recognizing its traditional and continuing importance as both a practical and an artistic endeavor. In her *Hand-Book of Needlework*, Miss Lambert points out that

> [i]f we consult the earliest writings, abundant proof will be found of the high estimation in which this,—one of the most elegant and useful of the imitative arts,—has been held in all ages, and in every country.[31]

Later she expresses her hope that needlework will regain its high standing. More emphatically, Christian Johnstone, reviewing Stone's *Art of Needlework* in *Tait's Edinburgh Magazine*, insists that

> needlework is entitled to consideration as an art which has contributed essentially to the comfort and grace of life, and to the enjoyment of the sex, whose amusements and pleasures have ever been strictly circumscribed by their position in the social scale, and the lordly will of their masters. . . . Whether, therefore, we look to the comfort or the elegances of life; to the cottage matron . . . or to the royal lady, gracefully bending over her embroidery frame, we must respect the little implement, which to women holds the place of the pen, the pencil, the lancet, the gun, the oar, the fishing-rod, the axe, the hammer, and many more ingenious implements of amusement or industry than we need here put on record.[32]

Although portraying women's proficiency with "the little implement" as a symptom of their oppression, of the social and artistic constraints within which they live, Johnstone rejects the masculinist prejudice against it, again emphasizing its twofold contribution as both a practical and a graceful skill.

Such references to needlework's double aspect sustain the rhetoric of universality by supplying a bridge between upper- or middle-class and working-class applications. While all women stitched, they did so to ends dictated by their station and circumstances, but even the fanciest embroidery bears a generic resemblance to simple hemming or mending, and writers bring out this similarity in order to create a gender bond that transcends class. Mrs. Warren and Mrs. Pullan, for instance, announce that their volume is suitable to all ranks; its instructions can be carried out by all capacities. Therefore let us hope, that while the work may grace the Boudoir of the Peeress, it shall also penetrate into the Cottage of the Peasant; that while it can become a source of useful recreation to the rich, it may also prove a reliable aid to the industrious effort of the poor.[33]

Women widely separated by social standing will have these patterns in common. Their differences will not thereby be erased, but these writers clearly assume that they can be made insignificant or even invisible.

Less abstract than the desire to forge bonds between women otherwise sharing very little is the fact that needlework figured in women's lives in concrete ways that contributed to a strong sense of female community and culture. In the first place, women learned to sew from other women, usually their mothers. Further, women sewed when they were together, often while enjoying a gossip or listening to one of their party read aloud; the frequent depictions in historical literature of queens sewing with their ladies again provided an elevating historical precedent. Such gatherings brought women together to share expertise as well as friendship and bound them together through the interests and priorities reflected in the common occupation of their fingers.[34]

The authors of books about needlework recognize that women constitute a community, a well-defined audience for their writings. Stone offers her book "to you, my countrywomen," and the American edition of Miss Lambert's *Hand-Book of Needlework* is dedicated to "the Ladies of the United States."[35] Hartshorne's work on medieval embroidery concludes with "A Practical Chapter, by another hand"—a woman's—offering "practical assistance to those of our countrywomen, who in the present day may be emulous of the pious works of their ancestors."[36] Johnstone admits that "captious or masculine criticism may cavil" at Stone's work but predicts that "all those whom needlework more immediately concerns will admire and value [it]"; it will furnish "an agreeable accessory to every work-table."[37] Such embracing gestures counter the widespread attacks on needlework as intellectually and creatively stifling: these books appeal to women who find meaning and community in the practise of this traditional female skill.

II

In the Victorian period, then, the opposition between pen and needle was complicated by varied and often contradictory views of needlework, which might be revered or reviled depending on the viewer's attitude towards conventional femininity and women's traditions. The range of responses needlework evoked as well as its indelible gender markings make it particularly resonant when it surfaces as a metaphor, as it frequently does in Victorian discussions of history Sometimes the references are only implicit. For instance, just as the finer kinds of stitchery ornament or supplement clothing or furniture, adding to their appeal but not to their utility, so, too, the works of the women historians, or works sharing their most typical features, were, as we have seen, characterized by authors and reviewers alike as occasionally attractive but extraneous additions to conventional history. The *Dublin Review*, for example, praises the "rich colouring" which the fourth volume of Strickland's *Queens of England* "gives to general history."[38] Just as suggestively if less positively, a reviewer in Blackwood's notes that Archibald Alison's pages are "loaded with anecdotes and decorative detail" which are "interesting" but redundant and "unimportant."[39] "A dissertation of this kind," protests the *North British Review* about Macaulay's Chapter 3, "is an unnecessary appendage to a work of history."[40]

In other cases, needlework is quite explicitly invoked to further the aims or criticisms of a reviewer. Its negative connotations make it a useful image of frivolity and idleness. Margaret Oliphant, for instance, reviewing Burton's *History of Scotland to 1688*, proclaims that the "historical Muse" faces new demands: "[h]e must pass over those picturesque incidents which seize the popular fancy, and turn aside sternly from the embroideries of romance."[41] Not only does she warn the Muse away from romance, associated with the worst kinds of female literary indulgence, but her central metaphor fixes as a gender difference the distinction between "picturesque incidents" and the "sterner" stuff history is now to be made of: quite literally, this Muse does not embroider.

Still more strikingly, in the single most hostile review of Macaulay's *History of England* references to women's work recur. J. W. Croker, writing in the Tory *Quarterly Review*, saw in Scott's success the roots of Macaulay's faults:

Mr. Macaulay ... saw ... that history itself would be much more popular with a large embroidery of personal, social, and even topographical anecdote and illustration, instead of the sober garb in which we have been in the habit of seeing it.[42]

To reinforce the association between Macaulay's approach to history and the feminized genre of fiction, Croker, like Oliphant, invokes the figure of embroidery—extraneous, inconsequential, and also intractably feminine. Later in the same review, Croker uses a similar tactic to discredit Chapter III; it is, he says,

> as entertaining as ... any of the many scrap-book histories which have been recently fabricated from those old materials ... [Anecdotes, etc.] should be ... woven into the narrative, and not, as Mr. Macaulay generally treats them, stitched on like patches.[43]

The implication that Macaulay is merely piecing together odds and ends undeserving of serious historical attention is damning enough, but the metaphor of patchwork guarantees that he appears not only trivial but unmanly—the price of venturing into the feminized field of social history.

Using the same metaphor to a more positive end, Johnstone calls Stone's *Art of Needlework*

> just such an affair of 'shreds and patches,' snips of gorgeous golden and silken tissues, and odds and ends of all manner of gay or rich fabrics, as Lady Morgan or Miss Lawrance might have thrown into a 'piece basket,' while engaged—the former with her splendid and hitherto ill-appreciated work, 'Woman and her Master,' and the latter while composing her 'Memoirs of the English Queens.'[44]

Johnstone appreciates the variety and vibrancy of Stone's book despite its patch-work quality, its lack of unity and coherent order. Further, she depicts a remarkable inversion of a conventional sewing circle: at this literary quilting bee, a community of women writers share "scraps" of information rather than actual "materials" or "fabrics." The result is no imposing tome but a "pleasant patch-work of brilliant odds and ends," a testament to an alternative vision of historical priorities and writing.[45]

Like needlework in its literal manifestations, metaphors of needlework thus had both positive and negative associations which came into play in the discourse of history to buttress opposing perspectives on the new, feminized historiography. On the one hand, the figure of needlework suggests richness of detail and color filling in the broad outlines of what the women historians so often call "general history." On the other hand, needlework provides a perfect metaphor for unnecessary clutter distracting from history's central narrative. For all their differences, however, both views share a basic conception of embroidery, or the sort of history it represents, as inessential, a supplement—whether to good or bad ends—to the fundamental fabric or pattern of history. Croker accuses Macaulay of taking "history, strictly so called" and "adding to it such lace and trimmings as he could collect";[46] while there might be some disagreement over the quality of the result, neither side would dispute either the basic premise of this description or the strong imputation that the end result suggests a woman's touch.

This strategy of portraying social or women's history as an ornamental border on the essential stuff of history relies on the associations of needlework with domestic femininity to contain the unsettling possibilities of the new historical discourse: like the women who do it, needlework impinges on but does not participate fully in the public, historical world. What does it mean, though, to introduce such a supplement to a history aspiring to, or even laying claim to, completion? A supplement serves as a stop-gap, a temporary measure, but its very presence is a constant reminder of the need for substantial revision, of the inadequacy of the main text, which might explain why the concern about new kinds of historiography was so widespread.[47] The volumes by the women historians contain innumerable assurances that their authors do not intend to interfere with "general history," but the logic of the supplement means that their presence on the margins challenges that neat distinction. And what if needlework, seemingly such an ideal metaphor for keeping the supplement in its place, itself moved from the margins to the main text of history? The works I turn to now give this disturbing possibility concrete form. In *Lives of the Queens of England* and *The Art of Needlework*, Agnes Strickland and Elizabeth Stone defy the unwritten law polarizing pen and needle. They incorporate needlework into their historical narratives—indeed, in

Stone's text, needlework is the whole subject of the narrative—and thus define at once their primary audience, their own gender identifications, and their allegiance to controversial new standards of historical significance. In many respects, the treatment of needlework in these two texts exemplifies both the changing nature and the shifting gender of nineteenth-century historical writing.

III

Most of the abundant references to needlework in Strickland's *Lives of the Queens of England* add to the already overwhelming impression that the queens exemplify the virtues of Victorian middle-class womanhood: patience, industry, selflessness, benevolence, and piety. Demonstrating these qualities through a culturally loaded symbol such as needlework helps guarantee that these heroines of historical texts do not, despite their public roles, appear unwomanly and thus unfit subjects for either female readers or, just as crucially, female writers: showing the queens plying their needles made it easier for Strickland to ply her trade. Because Strickland's subjects *are* queens, though, her emphasis on their similarities to ordinary Victorian women also contributes to the identification of the latter's domestic confinement and occupations with an aristocratic tradition. In an ideologically tidy circle, needlework both domesticates and ennobles; in these volumes, the needle confirms the gender and the class fitness of both past and present women otherwise, potentially at least, seen as outside their proper sphere.

Throughout her series, Strickland gives frequent examples of royal women's hand-stitched offerings. Queen Editha, wife of Edward the Confessor, for example, was "not only an amiable, but a learned lady," Strickland reports; in addition to her interest in Latin grammar, she was "skilful in the works of the needle, and with her own hands she embroidered the garments of her royal husband."[48] In another instance of wifely devotion, Mary Beatrice of Modena commissioned a work of embroidery to decorate the spot in Chaillot "where the heart of her deceased consort, king James, was enshrined" (X:24). While still a princess, Mary I "embroidered a cushion with her own hands as an offering for the queen"; another time, she and her attendants "worked" a chair for her father Henry VIII.[49] Even Elizabeth I, the problematic heroine, provides an example:

78   *Gender, Genre, and Victorian Historical Writing*

> On the second anniversary of [her brother] Edward's birth, when the nobles of England presented gifts of silver and gold, and jewels, to the infant heir of the realm, the lady Elizabeth's grace gave the simple offering of a shirt of cambric worked by her own hands. She was then six years old. Thus early was this illustrious lady instructed in the feminine accomplishment of needle-work, and directed to turn her labours in that way to a pleasing account. (VI:13)

The contrast between Elizabeth's "simple offering" and the precious stones and metals of the lords highlights the desired transcendence of gender over class distinctions in this Victorian ideology of femininity: although she is "illustrious," Elizabeth must learn "feminine accomplishments," and she demonstrates her fealty with an offering indicating her skill at these rather than her rank. And, like all the women in these examples, Elizabeth is shown to be, in this respect if in no other, a good Victorian woman, dedicating time and energy to attractive but non-essential contributions to her family.

Other examples similarly show historical women doing needlework in contexts or to ends resonant with the nineteenth-century discourse. Henry VIII's cast-off queen, Katharine of Aragon, spent the dreary years following the Divorce

> in much prayer, great alms, and abstinence; and when she was not this way occupied, then was she, and her gentlewomen, working with their own hands, something wrought in needlework, costly and artificially, which she intended, to the honour of God, to bestow on some of the churches. (IV:109)

This picture of the exiled queen recalls Hartshorne's depiction of the medieval gentlewoman immured in her lonely tower with only her needle to comfort her, turning her efforts to pious ends; it also shows needlework as part of a female community, a shared project for an aristocratic sewing circle. Katharine's rival, Anne Boleyn, frightened by her failure to produce the heir Henry wanted, repented of her earlier frivolity and ambition during her second pregnancy and turned to her ladies and her needle:

she became grave and composed in manner, and, ceasing to occupy herself in the gay pursuits of pleasure, or the boisterous excitement of the chase, spent her hours of domestic retirement with her ladies, as her royal mistress Katharine had formerly done before her, in needlework and discreet communication. (IV:183)

In an effort to save her reputation, her child, and her marriage, Anne retreats to a quiet, feminine world; her needlework is the outward sign of her resolution to lead a life of piety and virtue, of "discreet" rather than promiscuous intercourse. In keeping with the Victorian view of needlework as a continuing tradition, Katharine becomes a model for her successor; Anne's reformation is in turn exemplary for Strickland's readers.[50]

That many, if not most, of those readers are women is implied by all of the minute details about examples, patterns, and costs of needlework projects. Who besides other embroiderers, after all, could be expected to take much interest in the fact that Richard II's queen, Isabella, had chamber-hangings of "red and white satin, embroidered with figures of vintages and sheperdesses" (III:15), or that "curious original portraits of Henry VI and Margaret of Anjou, wrought in tapestry, [are] still preserved in St. Mary's Hall at Coventry" (III:163)? Particulars such as that Elizabeth of York's household accounts include "[e]ightpence ... charged for an ell of linen cloth 'for the queen's samplar [sic],' perhaps a pattern piece for her embroidery" (IV:55), that the chair Princess Mary worked for Henry VIII "was of such ample dimensions that the materials cost twenty pounds," and that Mary "paid John Hayes handsomely for drawing her work-patterns"—"seven and sixpence" once for "devising the pattern" for a cushion she embroidered for the queen—create an impression of kinship and familiarity with these remote figures for Strickland's Victorian audience.[51] These remarkably specific references foster the sense of a female tradition, an ongoing community of women linked by shared interests, that was so important to nineteenth-century discussions of needlework. As Strickland says, "the ornamental labors of the needle have become once more a source of domestic recreation to the ladies of England"; this remark, her justification for over a page spent describing "the magnificent counterpane and toilette cover" embroidered by Katharine Parr, could just as easily be her defense for dozens of other such passages connecting subject, author, and audience by a common thread. [52]

These details about a mundane domestic activity also mark Strickland's participation in the revisionist historical practices discussed in Chapter One: the turn away from accounts of great events in the public sphere and the activities of great men to histories of the "noiseless revolutions" and "unhistoric acts" of the private sphere. Because of its powerful ideological association with domesticity and femininity, the needle is perhaps the ultimate example of something that could not previously have been considered historically significant. Strickland controverts this conventional assumption in two ways. The first, of which we have already seen examples, is to incorporate information about needlework into her historical narrative with little or no metacommentary, simply placing it on the level of other pieces of information worthy of record. Here the crucial opposition is not so much between pen and needle but between needle and sword, the latter symbolizing the traditional historian's preoccupation with events political and military. A nice illustration of Strickland's quietly revisionist practice: she says twice about Edward I's wife, Eleanora of Castile, that she "introduced the use of tapestry as hangings for walls" (II:98, 106). Even to the champions of nineteenth-century domesticity, this would have been no great claim to fame, but to Strickland it is not just a fact but, to use Carr's distinction, a "historical" fact and as such deserves a place in the story.[53]

Strickland further disregards custom by treating works of embroidery as historical evidence, most expansively in her discussion of that "great work, the Bayeux tapestry" (I:18).[54] Here once again the needle's alternative is the pen—but here the former literally substitutes for the latter. Although allowing "for the exaggeration of feminine reminiscences" in some of its scenes (I:31), Strickland declares the tapestry

> a most important historical document, in which the events and costume of that momentous period have been faithfully preserved to us, by the indefatigable fingers of the first of our Norman queens. (I:46)

It is "a pictorial chronicle of the conquest of England" (I:18), "wherein [Matilda] has wrought the epic of her husband's exploits, from Harold's first landing in Normandy to his fall at Hastings" (I:46). Without hesitation or debate, Strickland assigns the tapestry the status of a historical text.

A certain "knightly figure" in the tapestry, Strickland notes, is "generally believed" to be a faithful portrait of "the redoubtable conqueror of this realm," or at least, she adds, with a touch of humor, "as correct a resemblance of him as his loving spouse Matilda could produce in cross-stitch" (I:37)—an inside joke for those familiar with the difficulties of depicting human features using only square stitches. (The joke, as it turns out, is ultimately on Strickland, as for all her purported skill at and fondness for embroidery she does not recognize that the Bayeux Tapestry is not done in cross-stitch.) Like Hartshorne's medieval lady, who, "depicting the heroic deeds of her absent lord" with her needle, consoles herself for his absence and "visibly hasten[s] his return," Strickland's Matilda appropriately devotes her hours to commemorating William's historic quest.[55] But Matilda's compensation for such seeming self-effacement is historical authority: *her* record of his deeds remains, in what one reviewer of Strickland called "an epic poem done in needlework."[56]

In fact, credit for the Bayeux tapestry may not belong to Matilda. Today most experts believe that the work was commissioned by the French and done in an English workshop. (Roszika Parker observes that if "Matilda [had] stitched all 270 feet by 20 inches of embroidered linen ... it would have been truly a Herculean task."[57]) Scholars debated this question in the nineteenth century, too: in particular, an extended controversy about the "antiquity" of the tapestry was carried on in the journal *Archaeologia*.[58] Strickland knew her claims might be challenged; in a remarkable footnote, she defies those "who are determined to deprive Matilda of her traditionary [sic] fame, as the person from whom this specimen of female skill and industry emanated":

> with due deference to the judgment of the lords of the creation, on all subjects connected with policy and science, we venture to think our learned friends, the archaeologists and antiquaries, would do well to direct their intellectual powers to more masculine objects of inquiry, and leave the question of the Bayeux tapestry, (with all other matters

allied to needle-craft,) to the decision of the ladies, to whose province it peculiarly belongs. It is a matter of doubt to us whether one out of the many gentlemen who have disputed Matilda's claims to that work, if called upon to execute a copy of either of the figures on canvas, would know how to put in the first stitch. (I:46 n.1)

In a variation on the territorial rhetoric so many of the women historians employ, in which they promise not to trespass on the masculine turf of "general history," Strickland warns male intruders off women's turf. Her disingenuous argument that men's inexperience in "matters allied to needle-craft" ought to disqualify them as judges in the dispute turns the tables on men who oppose women's writing history on the grounds that women either could not or should not have sufficient knowledge of the world to do the job. Recall Francis Palgrave's disapproving remarks about Annie Forbes Bush's *Memoirs of the Queens of France*: "[I]t may be sufficient to ask," he proclaims, "whether any wife or mother can have too scanty a knowledge" of the various liaisons her book discusses.[59] Not just adultery, though, but also politics, wars, or indeed almost any of the usual subjects of historical narratives were widely considered unsuitable for women to know, much less write, about. Strickland is thus simply turning the tables, in a manner which prompted at least one aggrieved response. In *The Bayeux Tapestry Elucidated*, John Collingwood Bruce wrote,

> Perhaps, however, we have acted rashly in having ventured even thus cursorily to touch upon the antiquity of the Tapestry. Miss Agnes Strickland, who, in her *Lives of the Queens of England*, shows how vigorously she can wield the pen, is rather indignant that anyone who is not learned in cross-stitch, should venture to discuss the subject. Before we argue, she wants to know if we can sew.... Few of the rougher sex would like to be put to the *experimentum acus*, and therefore it may be as well at once to exercise the best part of valour, and beat a hasty retreat.[60]

His snideness suggests the justice with which the women historians could have objected to being themselves subjected to such silly requirements. In any case, that Matilda be believed the creator of the Bayeux tapestry mattered to Strickland because she could then be a special kind of heroine, one whose historic act was carried out with a needle, not a sword. That men be emphatically warned off the subject mattered for a different reason: because doing so showed men that women's historical "province" was not to be easily overrun. They had to confront the possibility articulated some years later by Margaret Oliphant:

> let us state our conviction—which conviction we cast boldly a glove of defiance in the face of Sir A. Alison, Mr Macaulay, Mr Hallam, Earl Stanhope—all and sundry the historians of the day. They do very well in their own way, and within their own standing-ground, these accomplished gentlemen, but your true domestic chronicler, your real historian of homes and manners—let nobody deny it—is a woman.[61]

IV

Elizabeth Stone's *Art of Needlework* resembles Strickland's *Lives of the Queens of England* in many ways. Both works were published by Henry Colburn, Stone's single volume appearing the same year as the first volume of Strickland's series, 1840. Like Strickland's, Stone's book reaches out to a female readership; indeed, Stone is even more explicit than Strickland about her intended audience. "Fair reader!" she exclaims in her introduction; "you see that this gentle dame NEEDLEWORK is of ancient lineage, of high descent, of courtly habits: will you not permit me to make you somewhat better acquainted?"[62] She hopes to make her book "an acceptable accessory to every work-table—a fitting tenant of every boudoir" (vi), and in her concluding paragraphs she declares, "To you, my countrywomen, I offer the book" (405).

Also like Strickland, Stone devotes many of her pages to examples of historical women skilled in the use of the needle; like Strickland's, Stone's examples guarantee the association of sewing and embroidery with all the feminine virtues. The "Jewish maidens" of biblical times, for instance, had a "perfectness of finish in embroidery," learned from the Egyptians, which was "displayed so worthily in the service of the Tabernacle" (32). Cloths "delicately and beautifully embroidered" have been found with Egyptian mummies which Stone supposes to be "the result of feminine solicitude and undying affection" (36). The Bayeux tapestry "has a halo of deep interest thrown round it, from the circumstance of its being the proud tribute of a fond and affectionate wife, glorying in her husband's glory, and proud of emblazoning his deeds" (85); as well as "an historical memento [sic]," it is "a pledge of feminine affection [and] a token of housewifely industry" (86). As with Strickland's queens, these women manifest their piety and selfless devotion through their stitchery. Other royal women too are featured in Stone's catalog. Elizabeth I "was an accomplished needlewoman" (289); Mary, Queen of Scots had a "predilection for needlework [which] never forsook her, but proved a beguilement and a solace during the weary years of her subsequent imprisonment" (384); and Adelaide, the Dowager Queen, to whom Stone's volume is dedicated, "allured Needlework from her long seclusion, and reinstated her in her once familiar place among the great and noble" (10)—"it was hers . . . to weave a wreath of domestic virtues, social charities, and beguiling though simple occupations, round the stately majesty of England's throne" (394). Both authors reinforce widespread assumptions that needlework done, not for personal amusement or vanity but for the honor or pleasure of another, as a sign of wifely love or piety, is, in Stone's words, "a graceful, an elegant, and a truly feminine occupation" (317).

Both authors also write about needlework in defiance of norms of historical significance. In Strickland, the challenge is largely implicit; she does it without talking about it. Stone, however, flaunts her unconventionality. Not satisfied with literalizing the shift from military to domestic history by treating the needle instead of the sword, she includes a strongly-worded defense of her venture, which she acknowledges to be "a maiden topic," playing on the dual meaning of "maiden" to indicate both her subject's novelty and its femininity (vi). The long passages in which she justifies her project touch upon all the elements in the discourse of history discussed in Chapters One and Two. Indeed, her work takes to their logical extreme the new historical ideas in circulation; it both articulates and exemplifies the possibilities they create.

"If there be one mechanical art of more universal application than all others," Stone begins, "and therefore of more universal interest, it is that which is practised with the NEEDLE." "Yet," she continues, have the NEEDLE and its beautiful and useful creations hitherto remained without their due meed of praise and record, either in sober prose or sounding rhyme,—while their glittering antithesis, the scathing and destroying sword, has been the theme of admiring and exulting record, without limit and without end! The progress of real civilization is rapidly putting an end to this false *prestige* in favor of the 'Destructive' weapon, and as rapidly raising the 'Conservative' one in public estimation; and the time seems at length arrived when that triumph of female ingenuity and industry, 'THE ART OF NEEDLEWORK' may be treated as a fitting subject of historical and social record—fitting at least for a female hand. (v-vi)

In each of the oppositions Stone sets up—creative versus destructive, beautiful versus scathing, obscure versus admired and exulted—she praises the qualities attributed to the feminine implement and belittles the masculine. More pointedly still, she identifies "real" civilization with the triumph of the feminine and, in particular, with the rise of a feminized historiography. The changes that have taken place in historical focus authorize her project, licensing "female hands" to take up the historian's pen; indeed, the closing words of this passage might be read either as a modest disclaimer of her more radical remarks (domestic history is not really weighty enough for men to trouble themselves about) or as an assertion of female supremacy in this new domain (domestic history is *not* a "fitting subject" for a *male* hand).

Stone makes clear that she aims to "admire" and "exult" women for womanly virtues, that, for her, making them and their "ingenuity and industry" the subject of history means, not shaping them to fit conventional standards of historical significance, but revising historical standards to include feminine traits and accomplishments. "In all ages," she comments,

> woman may lament the ungallant silence of the historian. His pen is the record of sterner actions than are usually the vocation of the gentler sex, and it is only when fair individuals have been by extraneous circumstances thrown out, as it were, on the canvas of human affairs—when they have been forced into a publicity little consistent with their natural sphere—that they have become his theme. (1-2)

The women thus brought into history's foreground are out of their element; they are not active agents but are acted upon, "thrown out" and "forced into" a narrative not really their own. Sadly, only these displaced women usually occupy the historian:

> those domestic virtues which are woman's greatest pride, those retiring characteristics which are her most becoming ornament, those gentle occupations which are her best employment, find no record on pages whose chief aim and end is the blazoning of manly heroism, of royal disputations, or of trumpet-stirring records. (2)

Women must not seek a place in the historical record on these terms: "Woe to that nation whose women, as a habit, as a custom, as a matter of course . . . forget the distinguishing, the high, the noble, the lofty, the pure and *unearthly* vocation of their sex" (4). Rather, history, and historians, must change:

> [Men's] own pursuits—public, are the theme of the historian— private, of the biographer; nay, the every-day circumstances of life— their dinners—their speeches—their toasts . . . are noted down for immortality: whilst a woman with as much sense, with more eloquence, with lofty principles, enthusiastic feelings, and pure conduct—with sterling virtue to command respect, and the self-denying conduct of a martyr—steals noiselessly through her appointed path in life; and if she excite a passing comment during her pilgrimage, is quickly lost in oblivion when that pilgrimage hath reached its appointed goal. (3-4)

Stone's word "noiselessly" indicates a crucial intersection between her theory and the wider discourse of history: she built on the new-found significance of what Macaulay had called "noiseless revolutions." In language very like Carlyle's, she asserts her desire to peer into the dark places of the past in search of unnoticed but important contributors to history:

> Over those memorials of the past which chance and mischance have left us, time hath drawn a thick curtain, obliterating all soft and gentle touches, which connected harmoniously the bolder features of the

landscape, and leaving these but as landmarks to intimate what had been there. We would fain linger on those times, and call up the gentle spirits of the long departed to describe scenes of quiet but useful retirement at which we now only dimly guess. (64)

As we have seen, recognizing the historical importance of "unhistoric acts" paved the way for writing women's history, as Victorian gender ideology restricted women's actions to just the kinds of deeds these terms describe; like Carlyle's, Stone's language summons up a feminine presence, "soft," "gentle," "quiet," and "harmonious," among the "bolder landmarks" of the past. "It is entirely of insignificant details that the sum of human life is made up," Stone declares (5), and from this claim she moves smoothly into a defense of a history focusing, not on great events, but on "a system of minor actions and of occupations, *individually* insignificant in their appearance, and noiseless in their approach" (4-5). "It is not," she says,

> the independent intrinsic worth of each isolated action of woman which stamps its value—it is their bearing and effect on the mass. It is the daily and hourly accumulation of minute particles which form the vast amount. (5)

Women perform no heroic deeds suitable for "trumpet-stirring records," but their pervasive and beneficent influence has "splendid results" (4) worth more, ultimately, than all the flourishes of men.

This theme is familiar from the other volumes by women historians. Stone has her own peculiar variation on it, however:

> The hemming of a pocket-handkerchief is a trivial thing in itself, yet it is a branch of an art which furnishes a useful, a graceful, and an agreeable occupation to one-half of the human race, and adds very materially to the comforts of the other half. (5)

Thus she brings the narrative around again to her particular topic, defining needlework as the exemplary "unhistoric" occupation which, for all its seeming triviality, contributes importantly to the well-being of the world. Her entire volume thus epitomizes the new historical world opened up by the theory she expounds in her introduction, according to which the domestic, the obscure, the mundane, the feminine, *are* the details which make up "the sum of human life."

As Stone moves needlework from the margins to the mainstream of history, then, the figure of embroidery that for the male critics captured the combination of triviality and femininity characteristic of the new historiography becomes a symbol of true historical significance. The "hemming of a pocket-handkerchief" is an act resonant with meaning, a simple domestic occupation that nonetheless links past and present because, as she says, "it is impossible to suppose any state of society in which [needlework] has not existed" (56), a private task that not only gives the sewer "much internal satisfaction ... a definite vocation, an important function" (324) but also contributes to what George Eliot in *Middlemarch* calls "the growing good of the world."[63] Needlework, Stone concludes, "has in all ages been deemed too trifling to obtain more than a passing notice from the historical pen" (404). Her pioneering work will, she hopes, inspire others to "pursue this subject with loftier aims, with more abundant leisure and greater facilities of research" (405)—she hopes she will find "a seconder and sponsors," as Carr says, for her nominee to history's "select club."[64] Her ambition literalizes the possibility for which embroidery, for other writers, was only a metaphor: social history, history openly committed to women's concerns, history unproblematically suitable for a "female hand."

In its own form and content, *The Art of Needlework* suggests what such a feminized history might look like in practice. Stone's written account of needlework across cultures and through the ages accomplishes many of the same ends needlework itself furthered, particularly establishing or invoking a community of women whose common interests and skills unite them despite their many differences—urging a gender bond that transcends class barriers, historical distance, and ethnic variation. "Needlework is an art so indissolubly connected with the convenience and comfort of mankind at large," Stone remarks early in the book, "that it is impossible to suppose any state of society in which it has not existed" (56). Her historical survey goes on to establish the truth of her supposition: from Eve to the present Queen Dowager, she documents, women have occupied themselves with stitching of some kind, and their needles have been the companions of their solitude as well as integral parts of

Stitches in Time 89

their social and cultural world. In the Dark Ages, for instance, embroidery featured in the routines of convent life

> when the severer duties of the cloister gave place to the cheerful one of companionship; and the 'pale votary' quitted the lonely cell and the solitary vigil, to instruct the blooming novice in the art of embroidery, or ply her own accustomed and accomplished fingers in its fairy creations. The younger ones would be ecstatic in their commendations, and eager in their exertions to rival the fair sempstress; whilst a gratified though sad smile would brighten her own pale cheek as the lady abbess . . . , holding the work towards the casement, so that the bright slanting rays of the setting sun . . . might illumine the varied tints of the stitchery, . . . would utter some kind and encouraging words of admiration and praise. (64-5)

Stone shows a community of women sharing standards and values, getting gratification from and being rewarded for accomplishment at a specialized skill. She holds up the mirror of history to her female contemporaries, who would have seen in that medieval sewing circle an idealized image of themselves.

Needlework's continuity across the centuries would have surprised few, if any, of Stone's readers. Less commonplace would have been her frequent leaps across national borders for supporting examples or illustrations, as in this passage:

> It has been a favourite practice of all antiquity to work with the needle representations of those subjects in which the imagination and the feelings were most interested. . . . [This] mode of giving permanency to the actions of illustrious individuals was not confined to the classical nations. The ancient islanders used to [do so] . . . and the same thing is recorded of the old Persians; and this furniture is still in high request among many Oriental nations, especially in Japan and China. (165)

Here Stone extends her implicit parallel between contemporary Englishwomen and their classical counterparts to include women of modern Japan and China; by associating "Oriental" embroideresses (and consumers of embroidery) with an earlier phase of European culture, she stresses the universal human appeal of such work. Near the end of her volume, she insists more explicitly on needlework as a common denominator for women, despite the widely different forms it may take:

> Could we now take a more extended view of modern needlework, how wide the range to which we might refer,—from the jewelled and golden-wrought slippers of the East to the grass-embroidered mocassins of the West; from the gorgeous and glittering raiment of the courtly Persian, the voluptuous Turk, or the luxurious Indian, to the simple, unattractive, yet exquisitely wrought garment made by the Californian from the entrails of the whale: a range as wide as the Antipodes asunder in every point except one! that is—the equal though very differently displayed skill, ingenuity, and industry of the needlewoman in almost every corner of the earth from the burning equator to the freezing Pole. (402)

Although their work may display sensuality or ostentation, the embroideresses themselves seem exempt from these rather unladylike qualities: Stone dissociates them from the cultural stereotypes she finds manifest in their styles of stitching and turns them all into good Victorian women—skillful, ingenious, and industrious, making the most of the resources available.

Stone herself establishes a distinct community of female expertise through her many references to other women writers. While, as we have seen, writers such as Agnes Strickland or Hannah Lawrance defer or yield to the authority of those they call "historians," they in their turn are Stone's authorities, cited without deprecation or apology. When speaking of Eleanor of Aquitaine, for instance, Stone quotes "her accomplished biographer, Miss Agnes Strickland" (152); Strickland is explicitly her source for information about Berangaria as well (200-202). She cites Lawrance on convent education (60-61) as well as on the responsibilities of a "good housewife" in the Middle Ages (117-19). Christian Johnstone, who in *Tait's* described *The Art of Needlework* as a patchwork composed of odds and ends such as Lady Sydney Morgan or Hannah Lawrance "might have thrown into a 'piece basket'," had no doubt registered just these references and recognized Stone's indebtedness to other women for both actual information and a particular and gendered kind of historical authority.

Most of Stone's other explicit intertextual references are, not to historians, but to poets—from John Taylor, whose seventeenth-century work "The Praise of the Needle" she quotes extensively, to Chaucer and Milton. She justifies this practice, in the specific context of her reliance on chivalric romances for details about the Middle Ages, by an analogy to the novel, a comparison resonant with meaning and implications because of the contested and gendered nature of fiction in this period:

> [Needlework] is, naturally, too insignificant a subject to task the attention of those whose energies are devoted to describing the warfare and welfare of kingdoms and thrones. Thus did we look only to professed historians . . . our evidence would be meagre indeed as to the minuter details: but as the 'novel' now describes those minutiae of every day life which we should think it ridiculous to look for in the writings of the politician or historian, so the romances of chivalry present us with descriptions which, if they be somewhat redundant in ornament, are still correct in groundwork. . . . (119-20)

Unflinchingly asserting the novel's authority to represent everyday realities, she proposes that other literary forms ought, in the absence of perhaps more efficient alternatives, to invite the same respect. With her word "professed," she also undercuts the authority of the "general" historian. Like many other writers on these subjects, she suggests that their preoccupation with courts and battlefields blinds them to other important matters; the irony of her comment that their priorities are "natural" is hardly subtle, especially after the eloquence of her opening defense of a history with quite opposite values.

Johnstone's metaphor of patchwork, apt, as we have already noted, in so many ways, turns out also to describe accurately the unusual design of Stone's book. Its structure—or relative lack thereof—suggests that, for Stone at least, a history fit for a female hand will not only contain different material than a traditional history but will also proceed by different rules. The single organizing principle common to almost all historical narratives is that they are linear: they start at the beginning and continue chronologically through to the end. One might expect Stone's narrative, then, to begin with the earliest known examples of needlework and trace the art's development through the ages, ending with the present day—indeed, that methodical progression is just what Stone's full title, *The Art of Needlework from the Earliest Ages*, promises. And for about a third of *The Art of Needlework* Stone delivers just that. She starts with Eve, who, she supposes, used thorns to construct the very first sewn garments out of fig leaves. Then she presents examples of biblical sempstresses, noting along the way the indebtedness of Jewish women to the skills of the Egyptians. Then she addresses needlework of the classical period—then of the Dark Ages.

The first break in this orderly pattern is not so much a deviation as a digression: two chapters solely devoted to the Bayeux Tapestry. To elaborate on Johnstone's patchwork metaphor, these sections resemble a special appliquéd addition to the surface of Stone's text. Stone's pen becomes a surrogate needle, replicating the tapestry with a detailed rendition of its fabric, its threads and colors, and many of its individual scenes. Later in the volume she gives equally concrete and specific descriptions of other examples of needlework, from the tapestries displayed at Hampton Court to the State Pall of the Fishmongers Company. She makes similar digressions to explicate unusual details, such as her five-page analysis of the social and symbolic significance of peacocks (73-77). Each such digression, while it enriches her text for an audience interested in needlework as a constant, a still-current preoccupation and amusement, impedes the forward movement of her narrative—its historical direction.

After the chapters on the Bayeux Tapestry, Stone returns to her historical survey with a chapter on the Middle Ages. She never regains her forward momentum, however: topical or thematic associations increasingly replace chronology as the logic of her sequence. The next chapter, with the general heading "Tapestry," is initially motivated by the prevalence of tapestry work in the Middle Ages, but it ranges from the fourteenth to the seventeenth century; its successor, "Romances Worked in Tapestry," looks back to classical times before returning once more to the Middle Ages. The two subsequent chapters on "Needlework in Costume" range from Chaucer to the Empress Josephine and discuss every aspect of fashion from hairstyles to sumptuary laws, with actual examples of needlework far from prominent. The chapter that follows, on the Field of the Cloth of Gold, seems to return chronological order to the narrative, but then Stone offers a section giving a social history of "The Needle." Chapter XVIII, "The Days of Good Queen Bess," is the last chapter focused on one particular historical time, with the exception of the final chapter, "Modern Needlework," which addresses the current state of the art. "On Stitchery" dwells on women's special aptitude for stitching and the many uses and pleasures it affords; in "Embroidery," Stone turns from historical observations to comments on needlework as practised in other cultures. "Needlework on Books" and "Needlework of Royal Ladies" both give her a chance to revisit with a narrower focus most of the historical ground she covered in the earlier chapters.

In its form—or formlessness—as much as in its content, then, Stone's volume exhibits just the features critics of other works lamented. Stone emphasizes color and interesting detail at the expense of overarching design; she digresses, embellishes, and moves sideways or even backwards rather than following a coherent, chronological path. Such deviations from the expected form of historical writing were, as we have seen, frequently considered signs of typically feminine deficiencies in concentration and vision. With a work as conspicuously gendered as Stone's, about perhaps the most indelibly feminine subject in her world, openly addressed to a female audience and just as openly in defiance of norms she herself identifies as masculine, it is hard not to suppose that she deliberately adopted a narrative strategy which the general discourse of history would inevitably identify as itself unmistakably feminine. In any event, one effect of this nonlinear approach is to reinforce needlework's role as a common bond between women: a developmental narrative would insist on change and dissimilarity in what Stone's version presents as continuity and correspondence. Hers is not a story of progress but of kinship, and her shifts from topic to topic, her accumulation of like examples and related incidents, reproduce in her pages the fellowship between women across the ages and across geographical and cultural divides fostered by the art of needlework and celebrated in her book.

V

Towards the end of her review of *The Art of Needlework*, Johnstone's tone changes abruptly from appreciative to acerbic:

> We sincerely wish that the author of this pleasant patch-work of brilliant odds and ends could have taken some notice of the thousands and tens of thousands of young women who lose their health, and

poke out their eyes, embroidering muslin for incredibly small payments . . . but [of these] we discover no trace.[65]

The picture of impoverished and suffering women blinded by the same needles which have, as the writer earlier emphasized, contributed so much to "the comfort or the elegances of life," provides a shocking and unsettling contrast to the images of graceful, pretty femininity which until this moment have dominated the review. Johnstone raises the dark specter of the professional needlewoman, the shadowy other of the leisured amateurs stitching for pleasure and relaxation; in doing so she reveals the limitations of the discourse of needlework as I have developed it so far. For all its pretense of universality, the model of needlework as an extraneous and ornamental preoccupation takes as normative middle-class values and structures. Needlework had an alternative aspect in the nineteenth century, however, attention to which exposes the class specificity of this model and, by extension, of the historiographical models it reinforces.

Class already figures implicitly in the debate about pens and needles with which I opened this chapter, for only those not dependent on their needles for economic survival would be likely to consider them beneficent outlets for creative energy, and only those with sufficient time and money for an education could protest the expectation that they produces stitches rather than script. For many in the nineteenth century, needles literally rather than symbolically caused suffering and oppression. No one who read or wrote about needlework in the 1840s and beyond, especially after the publication of Thomas Hood's "The Song of the Shirt" in *Punch* in 1843, could have been unaware that, as well as being the hobby of choice for gentlewomen and aristocrats, it was the profession, sometimes of choice but often of necessity, of thousands of young women whose plight became the focus of intense public discussion and agitation during this period.

Victorian women who needed to support themselves faced limited career options if they wanted to achieve or maintain respectability. One alternative was to go out as a teacher or governess, but this work required more education than most lower-class girls possessed and too closely resembled domestic servitude to suit some middle-class women. Needlework's association with middle-class gentility made working in a dress-shop seem like a step up the social ladder for the former, and only a small step down for the latter. Furthermore, since girls of all classes learned to sew they were in a sense already trained. The absence of other alternatives and the notorious "surplus" of women in the period, which meant fierce competition for what jobs there were, explain why despite the horrific conditions and poor pay seamstresses and milliners experienced, the pool of available labor did not simply dry up.[66]

And conditions *were* horrific. One writer observed in *Fraser's Magazine* in 1846 that "there has been discovered to exist a class of persons whose sufferings far exceed those of the poor mechanic or the factory-girl. I allude to the young women employed by the milliners and dress-makers."[67] He was led to this conclusion by reports such as the one R. D. Grainger made in 1842 to the Children's Employment Commission. Grainger reported that professional needlewomen in London generally worked a minimum of eighteen hours a day and often put in twenty hours a day or more during the three months of the fashionable season. Sewing for such long periods caused innumerable physical problems, from headaches, fainting, and even total blindness from eye strain, to ulcers, spinal problems, and dysmenorrhea. Crowded conditions, bad lighting, poor ventilation, generally unsanitary surroundings, and inadequate diet exacerbated the situation, and illness and even death were not uncommon.[68]

The most famous attempt to raise public awareness was Thomas Hood's poem "The Song of the Shirt," published in *Punch* in 1843: "With fingers weary and worn," it begins,

> With eyelids heavy and red,
> A woman sat in unwomanly rags,
> Plying her needle and thread —
> Stitch! stitch! stitch!
> In poverty, hunger and dirt,
> And still with a voice of dolorous pitch
> She sang the 'Song of the Shirt.'[69]

At least two paintings took their titles, and others their inspiration, from Hood's poem: George Frederic Watt's "The Song of the Shirt" was painted between 1848 and 1850, and Anna Blunden's "The Song of the Shirt," also known as "The Seamstress," in 1854. Richard Redgrave painted "The Sempstress" in 1846, and John Everett Millais painted

"Virtue and Vice," representing the temptation prostitution presented to poor needlewomen, in 1853.[70] Literary works too featured girls and women sewing for a living, most famously Elizabeth Gaskell's *Ruth*, but also *Mary Barton, Little Dorrit, Alton Locke, David Copperfield,* and *Nicholas Nickleby*, among others. Public attention was further drawn to needlewomen by the founding of the Association for the Aid and Benefit of Dressmakers and Milliners in 1843 and of the Distressed Needlewoman's Society in 1847. Stone's dedicatee, the Dowager Queen Adelaide, was the Patroness of the latter organization.[71]

The handbooks and histories of needlework I have cited invoke a universal, timeless sisterhood of seamstresses and embroiderers, but what links Hartshorne's medieval noblewoman or Matilda of Normandy to the thousands of women going blind or dying as they bent their wasted bodies over their needles? The superficial similarities reveal genuine commonalities at the same time as they conceal—or at least minimize—the drastic differences of motivation and experience between amateurs and professionals, between those for whom needlework was part of an elaborate construction of femininity and those for whom it was simply drudgery and toil. The books stress taste, refinement, elegance, pious benevolence, and wifely devotion as essential feminine virtues promoted by and reflected in needlework, but this account in fact takes as an ostensibly universal standard an exclusive, class-specific set, not just of values, but of possibilities.

Still, class differences do not necessarily preclude gender alliances. Contemporary commentators sought to awaken sympathy in middle-class women for their suffering sisters:

> Surely, O ladies of England—ye women that are at ease, you have some part or lot in this matter—the cry of the poor dress-maker appealing to you for assistance to alleviate her condition will not be heard in vain? Will you continue to require your orders to be executed in an unreasonably short time, when you know that many a poor girl must be deprived of rest, of health, of strength, nay perhaps of life, for the satisfaction of your fashionable caprice[?][72]

The writer appeals to a community of women with shared interests and patterns of behavior, a rhetorical strategy I already pointed out in the needlework books and the other volumes by women historians. Here, though, particular women are coldly lumped, rather than affectionately drawn, together, and the effect is to emphasize their distance from other, less privileged, women rather than the bonds between them. Another writer remarks that the conditions of milliners and dressmakers has left an especially painful impression because their "excess of labour (with all its pernicious and fatal results)," is

> endured in the service, and inflicted in execution of the orders, of a class whose own exemption from toil and privation should make them scrupulously careful not to increase, causelessly or selfishly, the toils and privations of their less favoured fellow-creatures.[73]

Although he characterizes their suffering as class oppression, he too hopes gender will prove transcendent:

> We shall have a heartfelt satisfaction, if, by the wide diffusion which this journal may give these lamentable, these revolting facts, we shall help to awaken some sympathy—some sister feelings—in the breasts of the more kindly and thinking class of our female readers.[74]

He finds it "degrading" to "female feeling, and female character" that "these monstrous pictures of female toil" make the condition of factory workers seem tolerable by comparison.[75]

These appeals to women to forget social and economic differences in the interests of their "sisters" in part replicate the faulty attempts at universalizing made in the needlework books, treating all women as a group at least potentially unified but speaking entirely to a middle-class readership likely to have the time, money, and inclination to enact the elevated ideal of compassionate kinship being advocated. But, by admitting the existence of women outside this privileged category, these writers also expose the partiality—the limits—of the discourse of needlework and the discourse of femininity to which it is so inextricably related. Precisely because all women had some experience of needlework, attention to it draws attention to the differences in these experiences and thus to the dangers of accepting any single definition or narrative of female experience as typical. While its ubiquity as a marker of femininity means needlework is a useful key to the gender markings of the new historiography, needlework's presence across boundaries otherwise ignored or suppressed also reminds us that this feminized historiography itself participated in the construction of gender ideology and myth.

NOTES

1. Rosemary Mitchell's essay "A Stitch in Time? Women, Needlework, and the Making of History in Victorian Britain," *Journal of Victorian Culture* Vol. 1 No. 2 (Autumn 1996), pp. 185-202, researched independently, treats some of the same themes and texts as this chapter, though differing in its particular emphases. I am grateful to Dr. Mitchell for sharing an earlier unpublished version of this essay with me and for discussions of our common interests.

2. Adrienne Rich, "Mathilde in Normandy." *Poems Selected and New 1950-1974* (New York: Norton, 1975), p. 6.

3. John Collingwood Bruce, *The Bayeux Tapestry Elucidated* (London: John Russell Smith, 1856), pp. 2-3.

4. Sandra Gilbert and Susan Gubar, *The Madwoman in the Attic: The Woman Writer and the Nineteenth-Century Literary Imagination* (New Haven: Yale UP, 1979), p. 7.

5. Anne Finch, "The Introduction" (1689), *Norton Anthology of English Literature*, ed. M. H. Abrams et al. 5th edition. 2 Vols. Vol. 1, p. 1960.

6. Mary Cathcart Borer, *Willingly to School: A History of Women's Education* (London: Lutterworth, 1975). My account of needlework's historical associations and significance relies on Rozsika Parker's important study *The Subversive Stitch: Embroidery and the Making of the Feminine* (London: The Women's Press, 1984).

7. Esther Lewis Clark, "A Mirror for Detractors" (1754). See Laurie Yager Lieb, "'The Works of Women are Symbolical': Needlework in the Eighteenth Century," *Eighteenth-Century Life* Vol. X n.s.2 (May 1986), pp. 28-44. For a more literary perspective, see Cecilia Macheski, "Penelope's Daughters: Images of Needlework in Eighteenth-Century Literature," in *Fetter'd or Free? British Women Novelists 1670-1815*, ed. Mary Anne Schofield and Cecilia Macheski (Athens OH: Ohio UP, 1986), pp. 85-100.

8. Deborah Gorham, *The Victorian Girl and the Feminine Ideal* (Bloomington: Indiana UP, 1982), p. 74, quoting *The Mother's Home Book* (1879), p. 220 (original emphasis).

9. Gorham, *The Victorian Girl and the Feminine Ideal*, p. 75.

10. June Purvis, *A History of Women's Education in England* (Philadelphia: Open University P, 1991), p. 14.

11. This figure is cited in T. J. Edelstein, "They Sang 'The Song of the Shirt': The Visual Iconography of the Seamstress," *Victorian Studies* Vol. 23 No. 2 (Winter 1980), pp. 183-210, p. 186.

12. Elizabeth Langland, *Nobody's Angels: Middle-Class Women and Domestic Ideology in Victorian Culture* (Ithaca: Cornell UP, 1995).

13. Joan N. Burstyn, *Victorian Education and the Ideal of Womanhood* (London: Croom Helm, 1980) p. 135.

14. See Santina Levey, *Discovering Embroidery of the Nineteenth Century* (Aylesbury UK: Shire Publications, 1971), p. 4.

15. Mrs. Warren & Mrs. Pullan, *Treasures in Needlework; comprising instructions in Knitting, Netting, Crochet, Point Lace, Tatting, Braiding, and Embroidery; Illustrated with Useful and Ornamental Designs, Patterns, etc.* (London: Ward and Lock, 1855), p. 248.

16. Parker, p. 24.

17. Charles Henry Hartshorne, *English Medieval Embroidery* (London: John Henry Parker, 1848), pp. 1-3.

18. Alice Chandler, *A Dream of Order: The Medieval Ideal in Nineteenth-Century English Literature* (Lincoln: U of Nebraska P, 1970), pp. 12-13. See also Parker, especially Chapter 2, "Eternalising the Feminine: Embroidery and Victorian Mediaevalism 1840-1905," and A. Dwight Culler, *The Victorian Mirror of History* (New Haven: Yale UP, 1985), especially Chapter 7, "Ruskin and Victorian Medievalism."

19. "On Needle-work," *British Lady's Magazine* Vol. 1 No. 4 (April 1815), pp. 257-260; p. 257. Review of *The Art of Needlework*, *Athenaeum* No. 670 (August 29 1840), pp. 675-76; p. 675.

20. [G. H. Lewes], "A Gentle Hint to Writing Women," *Leader* 1 (1850), 189, cited in Elizabeth K. Helsinger, Robin Lauterbach Sheets, and William Veeder, *The Woman Question: Society and Literature in Britain and America 1837-1883, Volume 3: Literary Issues* (Chicago: U of Chicago P, 1983), pp. 4-5.

21. Margaret Oliphant, *Autobiography*, arranged and edited by Mrs. Harry Coghill, foreword by Laurie Langbauer (Chicago: U of Chicago P, 1988), pp. 23-24.

22. Jane Margaret Strickland, *Life of Agnes Strickland* (London: William Blackwood and Sons, 1887), p. 40.

23. George Eliot, *Felix Holt, The Radical*, ed. Peter Coveney (Harmondsworth: Penguin, 1972), p. 176.

24. Elizabeth Barrett Browning, *Aurora Leigh* (Chicago: Academy Chicago Publishers, 1979), p. 15. An interesting recent discussion of

needlework in *Aurora Leigh* is Anne D. Wallace, "'Nor in Fading Silks Compose': Sewing, Walking, and Poetic Labour in *Aurora Leigh*," *ELH* Vol 64 No. 1 (Spring 1997), pp. 223-56.

25. George Eliot, *Middlemarch*, ed. W. J. Harvey (Harmondsworth: Penguin, 1965), p. 307.

26. *Athenaeum* No. 670, p. 675.

27. This problem exemplifies a recurrent conflict between liberal feminist and cultural feminist approaches. Some contemporary critics replicate the liberal rejection of the needle; Catharine Stimpson notes that "[a] pervasive trope [of modernity] is the woman's ultimate decision to substitute the pen that symbolizes writing for the needle that symbolizes her more traditional labor" ["Feminist Criticism," in *Redrawing the Boundaries*, ed. Stephen Greenblatt and Giles Gunn (New York: MLA, 1992), pp. 251-70; p. 255]. But many feminist critics and theorists have returned to images of sewing, weaving, or other traditional female art forms in an effort to reconcile the two.

28. In "A Stitch in Time? Women, Needlework, and the Making of History in Victorian Britain," Rosemary Mitchell similarly emphasizes needlework's multiple potentialities.

29. Warren & Pullan, *Treasures in Needlework*, p. v.

30. [Elizabeth Stone], *The Art of Needlework from the Earliest Ages* (London: Henry Colburn, 1840), p. v.

31. Miss Lambert, *Hand-Book of Needlework* (Philadelphia: Willis P. Hazard, 1851; first published London, 1843), p. 1.

32. [Christian Johnstone], Review of Stone, *Tait's Edinburgh Magazine* Vol. VII (November 1840), pp. 715-723; p. 715.

33. *Treasures in Needlework*, p. vi.

34. Amy Boyce Osaki, writing in an American context, notes that sewing "bound a woman to a larger group of friends and community members." "A 'Truly Feminine Employment': Sewing and the Early Nineteenth-Century Woman," *Winterthur Portfolio* Vol. 23 No. 4 (Winter 1988), pp. 225-41; p. 225.

35. *Art of Needlework*, p. 405; *Hand-Book of Needlework*, n.p.

36. *English Medieval Embroidery*, p. 111.

37. [Johnstone], p. 723; p. 716.

38. [H. R. Bagshawe], Review of Strickland's *Queens of England* Vol. IV, *Dublin Review* Vol. 12 (May 1842), pp. 518-25; p. 518.

39. [R. H. Patterson], Review of Alison's Histories of England, *Blackwood's Magazine* Vol. 79 (April 1856), pp. 404-21; p. 406.

40. Review of Macaulay's *History*, *North British Review* Vol. 10 (February 1849), pp. 367-424; pp. 388-89.
41. *Blackwood's Magazine* Vol. 101 (March 1867), pp. 317-337; p. 317.
42. [J. W. Croker], Review of Macaulay's *History of England*. *Quarterly Review* Vol. 84 (March 1849), pp. 549-630; p. 551.
43. Review of Macaulay's *History*, p. 578-9.
44. [Johnstone], p. 716.
45. [Johnstone], p. 723.
46. [Croker], Review of Macaulay's *History*, p. 552.
47. See, for instance, Jonathan Culler, *On Deconstruction: Theory and Criticism After Structuralism* (Ithaca: Cornell UP, 1982), p. 103: "The supplement is an inessential extra, added to something complete in itself, but the supplement is added in order to complete, to compensate for a lack in what was supposed to be complete in itself."
48. Agnes Strickland, *Lives of the Queens of England, from the Norman Conquest* (Philadelphia: Lea & Blanchard, 1848). 12 Volumes. I:xvi. All subsequent references are to this edition and are given in the text.
49. A volume is missing from the edition of Strickland's *Queens* otherwise cited. Quotations about Katherine Parr and Mary I are from *Lives of the Queens of England* (Philadelphia: George Barrie & Sons, 1902), Volumes V & VI. V:211; VI:83-4.
50. In an engaging contemporary extension of this chain of associations, the British magazine *New Stitches* recently published patterns for cross-stitched portraits of Henry VIII and all of his six wives (Issues 6-12).
51. *Lives of the Queens of England* (Philadelphia: George Barrie & Sons, 1902), VI:84, VI:89; VI:211.
52. *Lives of the Queens of England*, V:190.
53. E. H. Carr, *What is History*. 2nd edition, ed. R. W. Davies (London: MacMillan, 1961), p. 6.
54. Mitchell focuses on the Bayeux Tapestry as a means of exploring "the ambiguities of women historians' self-definition, expressed within the framework of conventional ideology" (192-3); one of her key texts is a novel by Emma Lienard called *Les Broideries de la Reine Matilde* (1847), translated into English in 1858 as *The Bayeux Tapestry: An Historical Romance of the Eleventh Century*.
55. *English Medieval Embroidery*, p. 1.
56. Review of Strickland's *Queens of England*, *Dublin Review* No. 20 (May 1841), pp. 506-18; p. 507.
57. Parker, *The Subversive Stitch*, p. 27.

58. See especially Thomas Amyot, "A Defence of the Early Antiquity of the Bayeux Tapestry," Vol. XIX (1821), pp. 192-206.

59. [Palgrave], Review of *Memoirs of the Queens of France. Quarterly Review* Vol. 71 (1843), pp. 411-16; p. 416.

60. Bruce, *The Bayeux Tapestry Elucidated*, p. 15.

61. [Margaret Oliphant], "Family History," *Blackwood's* Vol. 80 (October 1856), pp. 456-471; p. 458.

62. [Elizabeth Stone], *The Art of Needlework from the Earliest Ages; including some notices of the Ancient Historical Tapestries.* 3rd edition. (London: Henry Colburn, 1841), p. 10. All subsequent references will be to this edition and will be given in the text.

63. Eliot, *Middlemarch*, p. 896.

64. *What Is History?* p. 6.

65. [Johnstone], Review of Stone, p. 723.

66. See Christina Walkley, *The Ghost in the Looking Glass: The Victorian Seamstress* (London: Peter Owen, 1986), and Wanda F. Neff, *Victorian Working Women: An Historical and Literary Study of Women in British Industries and Professions 1832-1850* (London: Frank Cass & Co., 1966).

67. [Anonymous], "Milliner's Apprentices," *Fraser's Magazine* Vol. 33 (March 1846), pp. 308-16; p. 308.

68. Both Neff (pp. 116ff) and Walkley (pp. 20ff) cite Grainger's findings.

69. Quoted in full in Walkley, pp. 130-31.

70. Walkley includes reproductions of all of these paintings as well as of many cartoons and sketches, including the *Punch* cartoon from which she takes her title.

71. Walkley, pp. 93-4.

72. "Milliner's Apprentices," p. 312.

73. [W. R. Greg], "Juvenile and Female Labour," *Edinburgh Review* Vol. 79 (January 1844), pp. 130-56; p. 145.

74. "Juvenile and Female Labour," p. 148.

75. "Juvenile and Female Labour," p. 148.

CHAPTER FOUR
Gender and Historiography in *Romola*

A correct generalization gives significance to the smallest detail.[1]

Critics have long considered *Romola* the black sheep of Eliot's novels. "The initial and inescapable fact about *Romola*," writes George Levine in a representative comment, "is that of its failure."[2] Recently some feminist critics have offered recuperative interpretations of *Romola*, although often still with an apologetic undertext;[3] despite the insights their readings offer, however, the novel remains on the margins even of most Eliot scholarship. Although critics differ both in their specific readings of the novel and in their diagnoses of its faults, three aspects of the novel have consistently called forth comment since its first publication in 1863: first, the abundant, many think *over*-abundant, historical detail; second, the idealized, essentialized heroine, who seems glaringly out of place in either realist or historical fiction; and, finally, the abrupt departure from realism in the novel's penultimate sequences. In this chapter, I argue that these features of the novel, often considered its fatal flaws, are in fact thematically related. In the first place, the debates I examined in Chapter One about the appropriate selection and presentation of details in historical writing illuminate Eliot's practice, which, in its wide-ranging attention to the minute particularities of everything from clothing to diet, aligns her with the new and controversial field of social history. Social history, as we have seen, was associated with women's history because of its focus on domestic life and the private sphere; insofar as *Romola* recounts the conditions of a woman's life in Renaissance Florence, the novel makes explicit this historiographical connection and contributes to the revisionist project it underwrites.

Second, Romola is clearly no ordinary woman, and here the novel's relationship to both social and women's history becomes more complex. Like the women in, say, Strickland's *Queens of England* or Kavanagh's *Women of Christianity*, Romola embodies qualities that appear universally feminine rather than historically determined. She stands outside her milieu, rather than emerging from it, in a manner that strikingly contradicts the emphasis of the rest of the novel on historical specificity. Many critics have offered interpretations of what Romola "stands for," most of which are convincing as far as they go, but none of which examine the effect of placing such a fabulous, symbolic, or allegorical figure at the center of a novel the mode of which is conspicuously—oppressively, some might think—historical.[4] I argue here that this paradoxical placing highlights the incompatibility between two possible approaches to women's history, one pursuing, as the women historians did, an abstract, idealized notion of woman's nature, the other combining a social historian's scrupulous attention to detail with a conception of character as determined, at least partly, by historical context. *Romola* dramatizes the impossibility of sustaining a realistic narrative of a woman's historical life within the constraints of the first model; the tremendous weight of historical particularity Eliot brings to her story presses on the notion of an essential female identity until the pretense of historicity cracks, exposing ideology and myth. History must be written on different terms, *Romola* demonstrates; the novel's lesson for the would-be women's historian is, to paraphrase Carlyle, "Close thy *Comte*; open thy *Scott!*"[5]

I

Romola's most obvious feature is its wealth of information about Florentine life in the fifteenth century. The portrait of the Mercato Vecchio in the first chapter typifies Eliot's attention to details. We see "the vendors of macaroni, corn, eggs, milk, and dried fruits"; we hear the "ringing of pots and pans, the chinking of the money-changers, the tempting offers of cheapness at the old-clothes stalls, . . . the vaunting of new linens and woollens, of excellent wooden-ware, kettles, and frying pans"; there are "brood-rabbits," "doves and singing-birds," "even kittens for sale"; and, "better than all," there are people, young

Gender and Historiography in Romola 105

ones with "softly-rounded cheeks and bright eyes" and "older faces with the unfading charm of honest goodwill in them."[6] This is no grand, impressive panorama but a bustling hive of commonplace people engaged in their daily activities.

The chapter's first sentences suggest a disjunction between the world of the marketplace and the historical world, offhandedly contrasting "the shout and clash of fierce battle between rival families" with "the unhistorical quarrels and broad jests of wool-carders" (53). But the description of the Old Market begins with the information that the piazza "had been the scene of a provision-market from time immemorial" (57) and ends with the impact of the news of Lorenzo the Magnificent's death, which "had for the moment distracted the attention both of buyers and sellers from their proper business" (58) and which excites a lively political discussion among a motley assortment of Florentines that includes a pedlar, a barber, a notary, and a "fat purchaser of leeks" (62). This framing makes nonsense of the initial distinction between "historical" and "unhistorical" events. The lives of the marketgoers are suffused with history, and their own mundane activities are part of its fabric.

Juxtaposing descriptions such as the one of the public market with accounts of the political and religious conflicts of Savonarola's Florence, however, produces just the mixture of high and low historical matter that caused nineteenth-century reviewers so much annoyance in other contexts. In *Romola's* first few chapters, for instance, we get a virtual catalogue of items of clothing; a rapid survey of some of Florence's architectural treasures as they appeared in 1492; an overview, in several contexts, of the conflict between Christianity and pagan humanism; a look at Renaissance hairdressing and shaving practices; details about antique gems and cameos; insight into the practice of patronage; a glimpse of anti-Semitic attitudes and practices; an array of strange idioms and customs; and, through the gossip at the marketplace and in Nello's shop, a wide-ranging but incoherent introduction to the central political issues of the time. Each particular is presented as part of a complex historical milieu, with no lines dividing foreground from background, the conventionally significant from the minutiae.

Eliot's contemporary critics were quick to criticize this mode of presentation, in terms strikingly like those in which they decried non-fictional history showing a similar lack of discrimination. Just as

Archibald Alison complains that Macaulay's pages display a miscellany of ill-assorted items "crammed together without mercy, and with an equal light thrown on the most insignificant as the most important part of the piece," so an early reviewer of *Romola* protests that Eliot's research had "resulted only in an accumulation of details.... All the minute details of Florentine life with which the canvas is crowded do not produce a lasting and enduring impression." "This historical background," this writer continues,

> somewhat oppresses the human interest of the tale, and in its ultimate impression affects us like a mediaeval painted window, in which the action has to be disentangled from the blaze of colour and overwhelming accessories. [7]

Resorting, as Macaulay's critics often do, to analogies with the visual arts, he admires Eliot's accuracy in "accessories" but complains that this strength is really a weakness, since its chief effect is to obscure her overall design. Similarly, the critic in the *British Quarterly* finds much of the historical detail at best incidental to the novel's plot and themes, and he protests that "the historical alloy has been to the tale of nearly as much hurt as benefit"; "the history, especially the minute points of Florentine policy," he complains, "have [sic] no interest for the general reader, and a very subdued one even for the historical student."[8]

Given the context already explored, in which every aspect of historical writing is contested and every contest is gendered, the form of and response to Eliot's only overtly historical novel seem charged with significance. *Romola* was a historical work of conspicuous weight and seriousness, and thus, in one respect at least, masculine, but it was also a novel and thus feminized; it impressed its readers with its scholarly detail but relied on a controversial aesthetic and historiographical model which threatened masculinist norms; and these contradictions were mirrored in the open secret that this ponderously learned production was written by a woman under a man's name. Eliot's project upset both gender and genre expectations: too historical for fiction, too fanciful for history, too studious for a woman but not orderly enough for a man, at once an encyclopedia and a romance, *Romola* fit neither into the mainstream, whether of history or of the novel, nor into the separate sphere so decorously occupied by the "lady historians." One of *Romola*'s reviewers noted Eliot's status as "a veritable successor of Sir Walter Scott," but if he had reinvigorated historical fiction with his manly presence, what had she done?[9]

Eliot plays on the gender stereotypes her own work transgresses by making a woman's education and scholarly aspirations part of her novel. Although Bardo's misogynist platitudes accurately represent fifteenth-century attitudes about women's capacity for learning, similarly patriarchal assumptions would have been familiar to Eliot's nineteenth-century audience as part of their own world.[10] The irony of someone as ostentatiously educated as Eliot penning these words cannot have been lost on many readers:

> 'the sustained zeal and unconquerable patience demanded from those who would tread the unbeaten paths of knowledge are still less reconcilable with the wandering, vagrant propensity of the feminine mind than with the feeble powers of the feminine body.' (97)

"'I constantly marvel,'" Bardo later says to Tito, confiding in the strength of their common masculine superiority,

> 'at the capriciousness of my daughter's memory, which grasps certain objects with tenacity, and lets fall all those minutiae whereon depends accuracy, the very soul of scholarship.' (110)

Again, this passage is inevitably tinged with irony, as the woman novelist's grasp of "minutiae" has already, by this point in the novel, been overwhelmingly demonstrated. Moreover, the comradely smile Tito directs at Romola denies Bardo's attempt at male bonding, trivializing the old man's complaint and suggesting, to Romola at least, that perhaps hers is not a gender-specific failing: "'Does *he* forget too, I wonder?' thought Romola" (111).

But it is through her own practice more than through such oblique metacommentaries that Eliot enters into the ongoing debates about historiographical possibilities and priorities. Here she proves herself as much a successor of Macaulay as of Scott. In a brief notice in the *Westminster Review* roughly contemporaneous with her first venture into fiction, Eliot had commented on the triumph of social history:

to exhibit the condition of the people has now become the ambition of historians, and every book which helps us to picture to ourselves the life of ordinary men and women in past ages is sure of due appreciation.[11]

Works such as the one under review, George Roberts's *Social History of the People of the Southern Counties of England in Past Centuries*, are, she adds,

useful addenda to those grave ante-Macaulayan histories which took little note of life outside of courts, and senates, and battlefields.[12]

Perhaps unconsciously, she echoes a great historian who decades earlier had predicted that such a shift in historical principles would come, that "the Court, the Senate and the Battlefield, receding more and more into the background, the Temple, the Workshop and Social Hearth will advance more and more into the foreground."[13] Eliot's concern in *Romola* with conjuring up, in highly visual detail, "the life of ordinary men and women," a marketplace and barber shop rather than "courts, and senates, and battlefields," suggests one way in which she, like the other "active mind[s] of [her] generation," had been "modified" by Carlyle's influence.[14]

There is an equally striking congruence between *Romola*'s concerns and Macaulay's claims for his *History* in another passage we have looked at before:

to relate the history of the people as well as the history of the government, to trace the progress of useful and ornamental arts, to describe the rise of religious sects and the changes of literary taste, to portray the manners of successive generations, and not to pass by with neglect even the revolutions which have taken place in dress, furniture, repasts, and public amusements.[15]

It would be impossible to illustrate just how thoroughly *Romola* fulfills this promise without becoming as prolix and expansive as the novel itself. Clearly the novel centers on "the rise of religious sects," while numerous passages and even whole chapters deal with "changes of literary taste" and every page contains references to at least one of "dress, furniture, repasts, and public amusements." The "Learned Squabble" of Chapter 7, the "Peasants' Fair" in Chapter 14, the "Supper in the Rucellai Gardens" in Chapter 39, the procession of the "Unseen Madonna" in Chapter 44, Chapter 45 "At the Barber's Shop"—all contain innumerable details about diet, dress, manners, changing tastes, and popular customs, according to Macaulay's recipe.

And, as in Macaulay's text, implicit in all this abundance of historical particulars is the possibility of women's history. Just as the Pitying Mother is the "nucleus" of the procession the Florentines stage in their attempt to bring divine salvation to their suffering city (455), so women are at the heart of many scenes in the novel. There is Romola herself, of course, and I will look more closely at her presently, but the exclusive masculinity of the novel's political scenes is offset in other, subtler ways as well. In the first scenes, for instance, Bratti's basket is filled with "small woman's-ware, such as thread and pins" (53), and in the marketplace

> it was the great harvest-time of the market-gardeners, the cheesemongers, the vendors of macaroni, corn, eggs, milk, and dried fruits: a change which was apt to make the women's voices predominant in the chorus. (57)

The first specific account given of Savonarola's teaching is Monna Brigida's, in which she rattles on about the way he excoriates women:

> 'How he rated us poor women! . . . He called us cows, and lumps of flesh, and wantons, and mischief-makers . . . . And then he cried, and wrung his hands at us, and I cried too.' (178)

Many of his directives target women specifically; the Pyramid of Vanities contains "all the implements of feminine vanity—rouge-pots, false hair, mirrors, perfumes, powders, and transparent veils intended to provoke inquisitive glances" (498), and the young boys, Savonarola's "beardless inquisitors" (499), zero in on Tessa and later on Monna Brigida, demanding that they yield up their frivolous adornments in obedience to the Frate's creed. Particularly in the crowd scenes, there is always an abundance of female figures, often the contadine, such as the "hardy, scant-feeding peasant-women from the mountains of Pistoia"

(193) whose numbers drive Tito to take refuge from the peasants' fair in the church of the Nunziata, which he finds

> filled with peasant-women, some kneeling, some standing; the coarse bronzed skins, and the dingy clothing of the rougher dwellers on the mountains, contrasting with the softer-lined faces and white or red head-drapery of the well-to-do dwellers in the valley. . . . (200)

Without much fanfare, *Romola* shows us a Florence and a fifteenth century inhabited by both men and women, not, as Macaulay does in his famous third chapter, devoting a few pages to women as a separate historical category (like newspapers, transportation, or taxes), but simply weaving them in as part of the whole historical tapestry.

In Eliot's only ostentatiously historical novel, then, we have gender intersecting with historiography in a number of different ways. First, the novel's form, with its overflow of minutiae and intermingling of high and low concerns, invites the common and heavily gender-inflected criticism that its author has failed to discriminate between trivial and significant historical material. Second, in its attention to everyday life and commonplace people the novel resembles social history, a category potentially and problematically feminized because of its serious treatment of life in the private sphere and of women's concerns—dress, diet, manners. Third, writing social history means bringing women into the picture; political history, as *Romola* demonstrates, inevitably focuses on the men who hold the reins of power, but the rarified atmosphere of male bonding that we find, for instance, in the supper at the Rucellai Gardens, or in Nello's barber shop, quickly dissipates in the bustle of the marketplace or the countryside, in the incense-filled air of the churches, or in the home, where the bond of marriage makes different demands.

Finally, and more directly, this novel's main character herself makes gender and history a central problem. Besides being Eliot's most historical novel, *Romola* is the only one of her novels to bear a woman's name. We might reasonably expect Romola to embody what seem to be the lessons of all these historiographical undercurrents. But in a novel that celebrates ordinary life and people, that lingers lovingly over mundane details and labors to bring even the minutest historical fact to life again, the heroine stands oddly aloof from history, extraordinary, grand, majestic, beautiful. My next sections address this striking incongruity.

II

The wealth of historical information in the early chapters of *Romola* disorients rather than educates the reader; one is plunged into an unfamiliar and unwelcoming environment. Numerous Italian words and phrases, many of which Eliot herself translates in parentheses or in footnotes, enhance the distancing effect—we enter into this world only with considerable effort and some outside assistance. Significantly, readers confront this mass of material at the same time as Tito, who arrives in Florence a stranger to the sights and sounds of the city, oblivious to its most pressing concerns and ignorant of its idiom. He wanders away from the crowd at the market, "hopeless of learning what was the cause of the general agitation, and not much caring to know what was probably of little interest to any but born Florentines" (68). Like Tito, readers are outsiders in Florence. More particularly, readers find themselves strangers in *Renaissance* Florence; the morass of details functions crucially to establish the past as a foreign country— not a place where a nineteenth-century English audience (much less a twentieth-century North American one) can feel at home.

By thus characterizing the historical world as primarily unlike the present, Eliot rejects a venerable theory of history, one which in some respects peaked in popularity during the Enlightenment but which lingered on in a variety of nineteenth-century texts: the view that past and present societies differ chiefly in costume. Historical understanding, according to this model, requires no particular effort beyond the antiquarian reconstruction of superficialities, because human nature—and thus human behavior and priorities—is uniform and unchanging. The classic statement of this belief is Hume's:

> Would you know the sentiments, inclinations, and course of life of the Greeks and Romans? Study well the temper and actions of the French and English: You cannot be much mistaken in transferring to the former *most* of the observations which you have made with regard to the latter. Mankind are so much the same, in all times and places, that history informs us of nothing new or strange in this particular. Its chief use is only to discover the constant and universal

principles of human nature, by showing men in all varieties of circumstances and situations, and furnishing us with materials from which we may form our observations and become acquainted with the regular springs of human action and behaviour.[16]

This belief in the uniformity of human nature underwrites the definition of history as 'philosophy teaching by example': history resembles a series of laboratory experiments which cumulatively enable the careful student to identify patterns and constants, insights about 'man in general.'

Romanticism, with its emphasis on national traditions and its desire "to realize [the historical object] in all its individuality,"[17] posed the first serious challenge to this view. Under its influence, the emphasis on 'man in general' gave way to an interest in 'man in history'; gradually human nature as well as human values came to be seen as "also conditioned by the circumstances of history."[18] In English literature, a pivotal figure in this transformation is, of course, Sir Walter Scott.

Scott's explicit allusions to human nature and history show him on the cusp between Enlightenment and Romantic attitudes. In *Waverley's* introductory chapter, for example, the narrator asserts that he will "[throw] the force of [his] narrative upon the characters and passions of the actors";

—those passions common to men in all stages of society, and which have alike agitated the human heart, whether it throbbed under the steel corslet of the fifteenth century, the brocaded coat of the eighteenth, or the blue frock and white dimity waistcoat of the present day. Upon these passions it is no doubt true that the state of manners and laws casts a necessary colouring; but the bearings, to use the language of heraldry, remain the same. . . .[19]

Here he sounds distinctly like Hume. But as the novel progresses, it becomes clear that many of its characters experience "passions" peculiar to their particular historical situation, and in the "Postscript which should have been a Preface" the narrator dwells on his desire to preserve a society rapidly disappearing, citing "feelings," not as constants disguised by superficial variations in costume and behavior, but along with "habits" and "manners" as part of the "evanescent" past.[20] *Waverley* presents so intricate and detailed a picture of social and historical relationships that it becomes impossible to imagine its characters—Evan Dhu, for instance—existing at any other time; the form and substance of the whole novel move the reader away from simple assumptions about the uniformity of human nature. "Scott's novels," as Harry E. Shaw says, "embody a clear but not an overwhelming recognition that we are different from the men and women of the past";[21] Scott's work represents a stage in the transition to a more fully historicized concept of character.

Like the "Introductory" chapter to *Waverley*, the "Proem" to *Romola* initially puts forward what sounds like a distinctly eighteenth-century model of history. The "angel of the dawn," travelling across the Mediterranean in 1492, sees "the same outline of firm land and unstable sea," "the same great mountain shadows on the same valleys," "the domes and spires of cities rising . . . in the same spots where they rise today" (43). Not only have the paths of the rivers "hardly changed," but also "the human lot" shows a "broad sameness," its "main headings" still (and always) "hunger and labour, seed-time and harvest, love and death" (43). As the narrator's focus narrows from this expanse of space and time to "a certain historical spot" (48)—the city of Florence in the nineteenth century—the Renaissance Florentine whose perspective we share sees mostly signs of similarity, recognizing the hills and the river, the villas and the towers. "[T]he sense of familiarity is so much stronger than the perception of change" that he believes "there must still be fellowship and understanding for him among the inheritors of his birthplace" (44).

Immediately, however, an even stronger emphasis on discontinuity and change undercuts this view and controverts the spirit's sanguine expectation of comfort and welcome in the transformed Florence of the nineteenth century. "Is not the anxious voting with black and white beans still going on down there?" he wonders. "Are not the significant banners still hung from the windows—still distributed with decent pomp under Orcagna's Loggia every two months?" (46). "How has it all turned out?"

> Which party is likely to be banished and have its houses sacked just now? Is there any successor of the incomparable Lorenzo. . . . And

what famous scholar is dictating the Latin letters of the Republic—what fiery philosopher is lecturing on Dante in the Duomo . . . ? (49)

The ancient Florentine assumes that there is "'knowledge of these things to be had in the streets below . . . . For are not the well-remembered buildings all there?'" (50). But were he to descend into the streets he would find that only the buildings are the same and his many questions are meaningless, so altered are the ways and habits of Florence. "Go not down, good Spirit!" exclaims the narrator, "for the changes are great and the speech of Florentines would sound as a riddle in your ears" (50).

Moreover, the "Proem" emphasizes the historically specific character of the Florentine himself. Nothing about him suggests any "broad sameness" with other "human lots"; rather, he is

> a man of the fifteenth century, inheriting its strange web of belief and unbelief; of Epicurean levity and fetichistic dread; of pedantic impossible ethics uttered by rote, and crude passions acted out with childish impulsiveness; of inclination towards a self-indulgent paganism, and inevitable subjection to that human conscience which, in the unrest of a new growth, was filling the air with strange prophecies and presentiments. (48)

His yearnings are peculiar to his moment:

> He loved his honours and his gains, the business of his counting-house, of his guild, of the public council-chamber; he loved his enmities too, and fingered the white bean which was to keep a hated name out of the *borsa* with more complacency than if it had been a gold florin. (46)

If universal qualities underlie these particulars, they are so enmeshed in the web of social, economic, political, and religious motives that make up this man's historical life that they cannot be separately identified.

Like the Florentine of the Proem, most of the novel's characters are painstakingly historicized. When we meet Bardo, for instance, we learn that he is a descendant of an old Florentine family. He has

Gender and Historiography in Romola   115

inherited some of "the family passions," but because they live on "under altered conditions" they manifest themselves in strikingly different ways:

> [T]his descendant of the Bardi was not a man swift in street warfare, or one who loved to play the signor, fortifying strongholds and asserting the right to hang vassals, or a merchant and usurer of keen daring, who delighted in the generalship of wide commercial schemes: he was a man with a deep-veined hand cramped by much copying of manuscripts, who ate sparing dinners, and wore threadbare clothes, at first from choice and at last from necessity; who sat among his books and his marble fragments of the past, and saw them only by the light of those far-off younger days which still shone in his memory: he was a moneyless, blind old scholar. ... (92)

Bardo himself yearns to have a "'share in the triumphs of this [fifteenth] century'" (98); the strongest impulses of his heart and spirit are inseparable from his historical moment. The main currents of his life are determined by his full participation in the values of his time, particularly his dedication to the Renaissance humanist ideal of immortality through scholarship.

Tito, too, is a child of his times; even his descent into dishonesty and dishonor, though stemming from his many defects of character, is fully enabled by his humanistic education, which has stripped him of respect for the moral standards he abandons:

> [H]e had been nurtured in contempt for the tales of priests whose impudent lives were a proverb, and in erudite familiarity with disputes concerning the Chief Good, which had after all, he considered, left it a matter of taste. (169)

Confronting Romola about the sale of her father's library, he rejects her scruples as irrelevant and outdated:

> 'If we believed in purgatory, I should be as anxious as you to have masses said; and if I believed it could now pain your father to see his library preserved and used in a rather different way from what he had set his mind on, I should share the strictness of your views. But a little philosophy should teach us to rid ourselves of those air-woven

fetters that mortals hang round themselves, spending their lives in misery under the mere imagination of weight.' (353)

Such an attitude would have been inconceivable in a well-educated European in most other periods.[22]

Probably the most fully developed instance of this melding of character and context is Eliot's intense and microscopic portrait of Savonarola. Here, as the reviewer in the *Athenaeum* writes, she shows

> the influence of his surroundings, the peculiar nature of the human and political elements among which he worked, their influence upon him, and the aspect they bore to him.[23]

Savonarola's inner strivings, his spiritualism, his ego, interact endlessly with his circumstances, which give them shape and direction and determine their external manifestations. The complex web of motivations and actions that make up Savonarola's life cannot be detached from fifteenth-century Florence without completely losing its shape. During the turbulent days while Florence struggles towards a new form of government, for example, Savonarola's preaching plays an important part:

> Impelled partly by the spiritual necessity that was laid upon him to guide the people, and partly by the prompting of public men who could get no measures carried without his aid, he was rapidly passing in his daily sermons from the general to the special—from telling his hearers that they must postpone their private passions and interests to the public good, to telling them precisely what sort of government they must have in order to promote that good—from 'Choose whatever is best for all' to 'Choose the Great Council,' and 'the Great Council is the will of God.' (385)

Inner and outer needs and demands merge for him; he cannot draw a line between himself, his God, and his politics. "[H]alf the tragedy of [Savonarola's] life," the narrator tells us, is

> the struggle of a mind possessed by a never-silent hunger after purity and simplicity, yet caught in a tangle of egoistic demands, false ideas,

Gender and Historiography in Romola   *117*

and difficult outward conditions, that made simplicity impossible. (576)

No intelligible account of Savonarola's life could be made by extracting his mind and character from his "outward conditions."

III

This model of character, as some critics have pointed out, typifies Eliot's practice as a realist novelist; moreover, as they go on to argue, it provides some justification for the novel's abundant historical detail. "The frequent charge that *Romola* is too researched, too decorated with cultural data," Avrom Fleishman says, "... misses Eliot's point: the social medium of the characters is the substance of their lives, out of which they draw their ideas, values, and options."[24] "[Eliot's] 'encyclopedic' efforts in the composition of *Romola*," Sally Shuttleworth asserts in her turn, "stem from her adherence to Comte's organicist conception that the individual is the product of the medium in which he dwells."[25] This reading gets some support from Eliot herself. She defended *Romola* by pointing out its resemblance to her English novels, in which details establish the milieu that in turn generates both character and action:

> It is the habit of my imagination to strive after as full a vision of the medium in which a character moves as of the character itself. The psychological causes which prompted me to give such details of Florentine life and history as I have given, are precisely the same as those which determined me in giving the details of English village life in 'Silas Marner,' or the 'Dodson' life, out of which were developed the destinies of poor Tom and Maggie.[26]

But these explanations, including Eliot's own, leave the title character anomalous, neither acknowledging nor offering any rationale for her very different relationship to her circumstances. Although the immediate context of Romola's life is historically specific—her dress, education, and options carefully reconstruct the life of a fifteenth-century Florentine woman—she is repeatedly described as separate from or exceptional in that context. We first see her providing the "only spot of bright colour" in her father's library, her youthful radiance unsubdued by her somber surroundings (93). Romola shines out with similar grandeur whenever she is present; indeed, the metaphors most frequently associated with her identify her with royalty. She moves about Bardo's library with her "queenly step" (95) and stands by his chair awaiting their visitors with "quiet majestic self-possession" (104). On his way to Bardo's, Tito pleasurably anticipates Romola's reaction to his presence, "the transient pink flush on Romola's face and neck, which subtracted nothing from her majesty, but only gave it the exquisite charm of womanly sensitiveness" (144). When Romola and Tito declare their love for one another, she looks at him "with the same simple majesty as ever" (173), and on the day of their betrothal Tito greets her with "'Regina mia!'" (259). Through Tito's influence, visitors come increasingly to Bardo's home, where

> it was pleasant to look at Romola's beauty; to see her, like old Firenzuola's type of womanly majesty, 'sitting with a certain grandeur, speaking with gravity, smiling with modesty, and casting around, as it were, an odour of queenliness;' and she seemed to unfold like a strong white lily under this genial breath of admiration and homage. (249)

Unlike the narrator in *Middlemarch*, who consistently if gently undermines Dorothea's magnificence by pointing out her childlike naiveté, this narrator comments that Romola "loved homage" (190) but gives no indication that she deserves anything else.

Romola's rarity defines her. "[T]here [is] no woman in all Florence like Romola," Tito thinks (170). "'[T]hou art not like the herd of thy sex,'" Bardo tells his daughter;

> 'thou art such a woman as the immortal poets had a vision of when they sang the lives of the heroes—tender but strong, like thy voice, which has been to me instead of the light in the years of my blindness.' (181)

In the early days of their love, Tito calls her "'a Pleiad that may grow dim by marrying any mortal'" (186), a "'goddess'" (235), a "'golden-tressed Aurora'" (237). "'My goddess! is there any woman like you?'" Tito exclaims, "with a mixture of fondness and wondering admiration at the blended majesty and simplicity in her" (239). The "subjection" and "awe" Tito feels in Romola's presence resemble

> the worship paid of old to a great nature-goddess, who was not all-knowing, but whose life and power were something deeper and more primordial than knowledge. (145)

And much as he adores her, he occasionally wishes she were "something lower" (234).

Later in the novel, Romola's sovereignty takes on more definite shape as she is identified repeatedly with the Madonna, as the title of Chapter 44, "The Visible Madonna," makes explicit; in that chapter, the poor women and children she tends bless her "in much the same tone as that in which they had a few minutes before praised and thanked the unseen Madonna" of the procession (462). When Savonarola's "beardless inquisitors" accost Tessa,

> [s]uddenly a gentle hand was laid on [Tessa's] arm, and a soft, wonderful voice, as if the Holy Madonna were speaking, said, 'Do not be afraid; no one shall harm you.' . . . [Tessa] had never seen any one like this lady before. (511)

Tessa never quite disentangles Romola from the Madonna:

> in the dream-like combination of small experience which made up Tessa's thought, Romola had remained confusedly associated with the pictures in the churches, and when she reappeared, the grateful remembrance of her protection was slightly tinctured with religious awe. (546)

When she arrives in the plague-stricken village,

> Romola certainly presented a sight which, at that moment and in that place, could hardly have been seen without some pausing and palpitation. With her gaze fixed intently on the distant slope, the long lines of her thick grey garment giving a gliding character to her rapid walk, her hair rolling backward and illuminated on the left side by the sun-rays, the little olive baby on her right arm now looking out with jet-black eyes, she might well startle that youth of fifteen,

accustomed to swing the censer in the presence of a Madonna less fair and marvellous than this. (644)

The "[m]any legends . . . afterwards told in that valley" perpetuate this vision of a "blessed Lady who came over the sea" (649).

Romola's distance from the historical world of the novel is not on this metaphorical or symbolic level alone. Her sequestered upbringing has kept her ignorant of and detached from everyday life. She approaches Dino's deathbed with apprehension because "[t]he Church, in her mind, belonged to that actual life of the mixed multitude from which they had always lived apart" (209-210). "She had been brought up in learned seclusion from the interests of actual life," and comes to take an interest in the "grave political changes" transforming Florence only because she fears they will impede her efforts to preserve Bardo's library:

> the expulsion of the Medici meant little more for her than the extinction of her best hope about her father's library. . . . [H]er new keen interest in public events, in the outbreak of war, in the issue of the French king's visit, in the changes that were likely to happen in the State, was kindled solely by the sense of love and duty to her father's memory. (311)

When the Great Council is established, Romola recoils from the celebratory bells:

> [T]he general joy seemed cruel to her: she stood aloof from that common life—that Florence which was flinging out its loud exultation to stun the ears of sorrow and loneliness. (387)

Although, at Savonarola's command, she eventually devotes herself to tending the poor and sick in Florence, she remains detached and remote from her surroundings, moving through the crowds which part to make way for her, watching from a window as the procession goes by, acting always out of a sense of moral obligation rather than fellowship.

Since the novel's first publication, critics have commented on the poor fit between Romola and her novel. R. H. Hutton, writing in the *Spectator*, thought her "the least perfect figure in the book," "a shade

Gender and Historiography in Romola

more modernized than the others, several shades less individual."[27] His word "modernized" anticipates a recurrent strain in commentaries on *Romola*: that she is anachronistic, a child of the nineteenth century, not the fifteenth. The critic in the *Westminster Review*, for instance, protests that

> it would be very difficult to produce any evidence of claims to the kind of union to which Romola aspired as existing in the minds of the women of the fifteenth century . . . and here again we find another reason for wishing that Romola had been a modern Englishwoman, she having so much more the character of one than that of an Italian lady of four centuries since.[28]

No other character in the book could conceivably be transplanted, but Romola does seem easily uprooted. As George Levine says, "in Romola's story, the details of Florentine life are largely irrelevant"; her "problems are universal and ultimately not dependent on the contingent and the conditional."[29] Alison Booth, who wants to interpret *Romola* as a feminist reclamation of historiography, "[s]eizing the world for women," nevertheless has to admit that Romola "seems one of the least historical of Eliot's heroines," while Deirdre David argues that, like Eliot's characterizations of intellectual women in her essays "Woman in France" and "Silly Novels by Lady Novelists," Romola is located in a "realm of inherency," outside the "contingency of history."[30]

A satisfactory reading of *Romola* surely must not skip over the oddity of making such an ahistorical woman the heroine of a heavily historical text. And we know that this seemingly paradoxical move was not accidental; when Sara Hennell wrote to Eliot that in Romola she had "painted a goddess, and not a woman," Eliot replied,

> You are right in saying that Romola is ideal—I feel it acutely in the reproof my own soul is constantly getting from the image it has made. . . . The various *strands* of thought I had to work out forced me into a more ideal treatment of Romola than I had foreseen at the outset.[31]

What "strands of thought" could have led so self-conscious a novelist into what most critics perceive as a tangle? A plausible answer is that one strand of *Romola* is Eliot's intervention in a particular tradition of women's history, one which, as we have already seen, characterized women much as Romola is characterized, and, moreover, one with which Eliot was almost certainly familiar.

IV

Eliot need not have even known of the women historians whose volumes were so popular throughout the century for *Romola* to bear interestingly on their work and the issues it raises, but in fact, although no direct evidence, such as quotations in her published work or references in her notebooks, proves that Eliot read any of this material herself, numerous oblique connections, combined with her well-known voracity as a reader and general familiarity with the literary context of her times, justify the inference that she would have known something of or about it. To begin with, from 1852 to 1854 she was the intellectual force behind the scenes at the *Westminster Review*. Although none of the articles in the journal from that period can be definitively attributed to her, as chief editor she would have been fully acquainted with their contents.[32] Many of the ten numbers of the *Review* produced under her supervision contain at least some mention of women historians.

In the very first volume of the new series, for example, is a long review article by J. A. Froude called "Mary Stuart"; one of the three texts he discusses is Agnes Strickland's two-volume edition of Mary Queen of Scots's letters, published in 1848. The April 1852 number mentions Julia Kavanagh's *Women of Christianity* in the "Contemporary Literature" section, and there is a notice of Julia Pardoe's biography of Marie de Medicis in the July 1852 number, the same number that contains George Henry Lewes's essay "The Lady Novelists." In the October 1852 number, in a review of a newly-issued catalog of the Library of the London Institution, the critic remarks disdainfully on finding Agnes Strickland added to the collection's History section. The January 1853 number contains a review of Tytler's *England Under Edward VI and Mary* that cites Agnes Strickland's life of Queen Mary, and the same issue reviews Volume III of Strickland's *Queens of Scotland*, the volume treating the life of Mary Queen of Scots. Finally, the Contemporary Literature section of the July 1854 number mentions both Mrs. Newton Crosland's *Memorable Women* and Clara Lucas Balfour's *Working Women of the Last Century*.[33]

Clearly, women historians and their works were part of the body of material with which Marian Evans and her colleagues were concerned. Moreover, these reviews, though brief, evaluate these texts and writers in familiar terms. The volume of Strickland's *Queens of Scotland* is, for example,

> not the best book that ever was written, nor can its author take the first rank as an historian; but she has the art of collecting what is most picturesque in the old chroniclers, and of working up her 'notes and extracts' in a very graceful manner into a fresh and lively narrative, in a style plain and unaffected.[34]

Typically, the critic damns Strickland with faint praise, demoting her without explanation from "the first rank" of scholars but conceding the ease and grace of her writing, qualities which, as we have seen, were associated with the feminized genre of the novel and thus considered only dubiously appropriate in historical prose. Similarly, Julia Pardoe's biography of Marie de Medicis is "a work of considerable research, written in a style of vivacious, but somewhat inflated eloquence," its sprightliness of tone undercutting whatever status its scholarship might have earned it.[35] Julia Kavanagh's *Women of Christianity* is pronounced

> [i]llustrative in character, and written with an amount of capacity and good taste no less remarkable than the research it embodies ... [an] excellent book [that] may be recommended to all classes for the purity of its tone and its freedom from religious prejudices.[36]

The book is evaluated, not for its historical content, but for its ideological and aesthetic virtues. And, consistent with the demand that women's histories be didactic, Crosland's *Memorable Women* and Balfour's *Working Women of the Last Century* are both praised because they "hold up the lives of eminent persons as patterns to be admired and imitated."[37]

Further and more direct evidence of Eliot's interest in questions of historiography and gender emerges from her own writing. From July 1855 to January 1857, she was responsible for the *Belles Lettres* section of the *Westminster Review*, a job for which she reviewed, by Gordon Haight's count, an astounding 166 books.[38] Some of these short notices are now well-known, such as her reviews of Kingsley's *Westward Ho!*, Geraldine Jewsbury's *Constance Herbert*, or Tennyson's "Maud." Particularly interesting for my purposes is a brief commentary in the July 1855 number on C. W. Fullom's *History of Woman*.

Eliot's comments on Fullom are concise but devastating. "[H]is scraps of knowledge," she says, "here and there give him stepping-stones through the immeasurable morass of his ignorance," and she attacks him for having "the audacity to call a book stuffed with vulgar anecdotes and vulgar errors, the mere froth and scum of historical reading, a 'History of Woman.'"[39] These cutting remarks were published soon after Eliot's long article "Woman in France" appeared in the October 1854 *Westminster*, and also soon after Eliot proposed an article on "Ideals of Womanhood" or, as an alternative, "Woman in Germany."[40] "I still think the 'Ideals of Womanhood' a good subject and one I should like to treat," she wrote to John Chapman in January 1855;

> The subject I now propose is 'Woman in Germany'—not simply the modern German woman ... but woman as she presents herself to us in all the phases of development through which the German race has run from the earliest historic twilight, when it was still blended with the Scandinavian race and its women were prophetesses, through the periods of the Volkswanderung and the romantic and *bürgerlich* life of the Middle Ages up to our own day.[41]

Eliot evidently took considerable interest in the condition and history of women during the years just before her first venture into fiction.

Almost every study of Eliot's fiction traces to some extent her probing of both historical and gender questions. Commentators frequently note her attention to the kinds of questions addressed earlier in this chapter and elsewhere in this study: social history, the impact of insignificant people and unrecorded actions on the larger unfolding of history, the historical interest and significance of the quotidian. In her novelistic representations and analyses of these historiographical issues, she shows herself fully involved with the discourse of history discussed, for example, in Chapter One. Both of the full-length novels that preceded *Romola—Adam Bede* (1858) and *The Mill on the Floss* (1861)—contain repeated meditations on these questions. They also

Gender and Historiography in Romola

focus on women; their heroines' experiences provide most of the dramatic interest and thematic depth. *The Mill on the Floss* in particular deals with problems of history and gender, but in a very different way than *Romola*. Unlike Romola, Maggie is embedded in her historical circumstances; her crises result from conflicts between her desires and her historical possibilities. Contingency, to return to the vocabulary of *Romola*'s critics, is crucial to her.

Romola is thus not a completely new departure for Eliot, as she had been interested in and experimenting with this constellation of problems throughout her writing career. The novelty lies in the resolution of her most direct intervention into the debates and discourses of history and gender. In *Romola* Eliot imports a familiar figure from contemporary historical literature into the complex historical world of a realist novel. The resulting incongruity thoroughly undermines the notion that women's history can be written using such an idealized, essentialized model of women's character.

V

Two sequences in *Romola* bring the problems of idealized gender and historical narrative particularly into focus: the two scenes in which Romola runs away. In the first such episode, Romola seeks to free herself of the constricting narrative in which she finds herself trapped; like Maggie's flight to the gypsies in *The Mill on the Floss*, Romola's flight to Venice and Cassandra Fedele represents her attempt to bring her life in line with her desires. Disillusioned with her marriage, alienated from her husband, Romola resolves "to solve the problem in a way that seemed to her very simple" (392): she will leave Tito and Florence behind and remake her life. She has no model for her actions—"[s]he was not acting after any precedent, or obeying any adopted maxims" (392). Given strength partly by desperation and partly by ignorance,

> she [has] invented a lot for herself—to go to the most learned woman in the world, Cassandra Fedele, at Venice, and ask her how an instructed woman could support herself in a lonely life there. (393)

Romola's ambition defies what Carolyn Heilbrun has argued is a fundamental restriction on women's life stories: she seeks a quest plot for herself.[42] Moreover, the careful historical placing of her story makes this particular quest one she might plausibly fulfill. After all, Cassandra Fedele *did* achieve fame and independence through scholarship, though only temporarily, and thus she is, as Deirdre David has noted, "an intimation for the reader of how Romola might have lived," and female learning was regarded more highly during the Italian Renaissance than perhaps at any other time before the nineteenth century.[43] Although some critics have argued that Savonarola's intervention sends Romola back to the world of history or realism, it seems more accurate to say that he cuts her off from a particular historical possibility, one that potentially means her self-fulfillment, in favor of another that entails self-sacrifice and actions based on a specific definition of appropriate womanly behavior.[44]

Romola's return to Florence restores her to the thematic or symbolic pattern from which her desperate flight promised (or threatened) to free her. Indeed, not until she is back "in her usual place" (439) do we see clearly just what that pattern is. Romola is not just any queenly romantic heroine; she is a Comtean heroine, and the qualities she embodies correspond with Comte's idealized vision of womanhood. Like the women historians, Comte placed the burden of moral and civilizing influence on women, believing that they embodied, naturally and essentially, the qualities his Religion of Humanity sought to promote in mankind, "forms of social feeling—veneration, attachment, and benevolence."[45] Women were, Comte thought, inferior intellectually and so unfit for work outside the domestic sphere, but their stronger emotional ties gave them a special role:

> It is indisputable that women are, in general, as superior to men in a spontaneous expansion of sympathy and sociality, as they are inferior to men in understanding and reason. Their function ... must therefore be to modify by the excitement of the social instinct the general direction necessarily originated by the cold and rough reason which is distinctive of Man.[46]

In his *System of Positive Polity*, Comte wrote still more explicitly about the importance of women's "modifying influence"; Positivism, he emphasized, "marks out for [women] a noble field of social usefulness,

Gender and Historiography in Romola

embracing a public as well as private life, and yet in a way thoroughly in harmony with their nature."[47] Frederic Harrison, Positivist and friend and consultant of George Eliot, wrote in his essay on "The Future of Woman,"

> The true function of woman is to educate, not children only, but men, to train to a higher civilisation, not the rising generation, but the actual society, by diffusing the spirit of affection, of self-restraint, self-sacrifice, fidelity, and purity . . . not by writing books . . . but by manifesting [these qualities] hour by hour in each home by the magic of the voice, look, word, and all the incommunicable graces of woman's tenderness.[48]

"Our true ideal of the emancipation of Woman," he wrote in another essay, "is to enlarge in all things the spiritual, moral, affective influence of Woman."[49] The key word and governing theory here, as in the women historians' texts, is "influence"; women's contribution to the new social order will be crucial but indirect.[50]

Many critics have commented on Romola's obvious likeness to Comte's idealized woman.[51] Moreover, Romola's story traces Comte's three stages of society, in which selfishness is superseded by familial love and then by dedication to humanity in general. Romola embarks on her journey to Venice when the ties of family, her love for her father and then for her husband, seem irrevocably lost; Savonarola's intervention restores her to the Comtean progression:

> All that ardour of her nature which could no longer spend itself in the woman's tenderness for father and husband, had transformed itself into an enthusiasm of sympathy with the general life. (463)

Romola's Catholicism manifests itself through good works rather than spiritualism; in this too she reflects a Comtean ideal, as he admitted the benefits that had accrued to mankind through the church but believed the religion itself false.[52]

Steeped as *Romola* is in Positivist ideas and imagery, however, J. B. Bullen's reading of the novel as "an allegorical account of the development of man's moral consciousness from the earliest times," "an attempt to realize Positivist ideas in narrative form,"[53] has been critiqued or complicated by several subsequent critics who argue that

Romola endorses neither Comte nor Positivism. As T. R. Wright suggests, "Eliot's fiction ... can be considered as a critique of Comte ... in which Positivist concepts are examined and sometimes found wanting."[54] "The repetitive pattern of doubt, flight, and affirmation in *Romola*," Sally Shuttleworth argues, "reflects George Eliot's uncertain relationship to Comtean philosophy."[55] Critics have pointed out, for instance, that *Romola* does not present anything like the Comtean ideal of marriage. Nancy Paxton argues that

> [b]y repeatedly defining Tito's and Romola's reactions [in their quarrels] as those of husband and wife [generically], Eliot deflates the idealism of Comte's theory of domestic relations by showing the dominance exercised by the husband and the submission required by the wife.[56]

For Paxton, it is, somewhat ironically, the very qualities Comte wished women to epitomize—altruism, submission, love—that allow Tito to master Romola and destroy their marriage.[57] Felicia Bonaparte similarly sees *Romola*'s portrayal of marriage as the novel's key departure from Comte, although her argument is that Romola and Tito's marriage, which according to Comtean theory should have led to an expansion of love, teaches rather that it is pain which leads us to compassion.[58] This array of objections and complications prevents any simplistic alignment of the novel with Comtean theory or values.

In the novel itself, too, there are signs of doubt about the inevitability or naturalness of both the historical progression Comte predicted and his version of woman's nature. Romola, superficially the perfect Comtean heroine, must be forcibly sent back to take up her role in society; an early critic protested that Savonarola's arguments don't seem "cogent enough to turn aside a purpose as determined as Romola's,"[59] and today's readers surely respond to Romola's return to Florence with disappointment at the opportunity lost, even if they concede its thematic interest and importance. Romola herself is persuaded more by the force of Savonarola's personality than by any real conviction that the path he chooses for her is the right one, and once back in Florence she turns out not to have any "innate taste for tending the sick and clothing the ragged" (463). "Her early training had kept her aloof from such womanly labours," the narrator explains

(463), but no education should be able to completely suppress an instinct supposedly so strong. Romola may live out a Comtean plot, but not without external prodding.

Comte's essentialized, sympathetic, benevolently influential woman is close kin to the woman who appears, in a multitude of costumes, in the volumes by the women historians, the queens who, as Strickland says, have been "instruments in the hands of God, for the advancement of civilization and the exercise of a moral and religious influence."[60] Eliot's critique of Comte, then, provides a parallel critique of this approach to women's history, and the novel's final, heavily symbolic, chapters demonstrate the fatal flaw in both theories: because they deal in abstract, ahistorical idealizations, ultimately they defeat efforts at historical representation. In *Romola*, the heroine comes into her own through an apotheosis that literalizes her physical and symbolic identification with the Madonna. In the "drifting" and "awakening" sequence, Romola finally finds a narrative that suits her, but in the process the novel abandons its realist, historicist mode for an overtly mythical one. "The experience [is] like a new baptism to Romola";

> In Florence the simpler relations of the human being to his fellow-men had been complicated for her with all the special ties of marriage, the State, and religious discipleship. (650)

While thus "sever[ed] from [her] wonted life" (651), she commits the "beautiful loving deeds" that become the stuff of legend in the valley (649) and attains the inner peace as well as the outward glory that eluded her when she was enmeshed in the infinitely complex milieu that is history.

Does *Romola* then "defy the exclusion of women and 'others' from contemporary historiography," as Alison Booth has suggested?[61] The answer, I think, is 'not exactly.' *Romola* dramatizes the consequences of attempting to compensate for women's absence from conventional history by substituting the kind of model the women historians adopt. Romola is a misfit in the world of historical realism; her first flight from Florence almost propels her into a new and promising historical possibility, but her second flight ends, as Deirdre David says, in "a realm of inherent sexual characteristics."[62] Although it may be true that these chapters provide a founding legend which will become the model for new narratives of female experience, as Susan Winnett has recently argued,[63] the resulting legend, like the plot of the women's histories, is severely limited and limiting. After all, her "new baptism" sends Romola back to the home, not out into the world. Dorothy Mermin puts it bluntly:

> All the men with whom she had any connection are dead and she is her own mistress, free to do what she wants; and what she does is devote herself to making a home for her aunt and her dead husband's mistress and children.[64]

Here is surely no feminist triumph over patriarchy, useful as such a reading might be as ammunition in the long controversy over Eliot's gender politics. The mythical baggage Romola carries throughout the novel contains nothing but more of the same: domesticity, passivity, and service to men. Indeed, even though Romola *does* have the last word, she uses it to tell, not her story, but Bardo's, Savonarola's and Tito's, and not to a daughter who may carry Romola's legacy forward, perhaps into a new kind of freedom for women, but to Lillo, over whom she can only hope to exert some degree of beneficent influence. She has lived her possibilities to the full, possibilities defined by a specific vision of woman's nature and relationship to historical process, and she has ended up, as before, "in her place."

The novel does call for a revisionist historiography, then, but in opposition, not to patriarchal practice, but to a development in women's writing that, for all its appearance of radicalism, ultimately continued to deny women access to history. *Romola* pushes to the imaginative limit the ideal of womanhood and woman's influence promoted by Comtean Positivism and by the women historians, and finds a dead end. The novel itself implicitly offers an alternative. With the wealth of historical knowledge available, a far different approach to historical narrative was possible, one that in turn underwrote a different approach to character. Social history, painstaking attention to detail and to relationships between context and character, exemplified in much of Scott and in aspects of *Romola*, was the way to historical understanding as well as the way to women's history. But as long as ideological preconceptions excluded women from this methodology, as long as essentializing myths constructed women as ahistorical beings detached

Gender and Historiography in Romola

from their context, women would continue to be misfits, out of place in historical representation as Romola is out of place in her novel. And until such a transformation wrote women into history, historiography would continue to be partial, inadequate, and, in its own way, mythical.

NOTES

1. George Eliot, "R. W. Mackay's *The Progress of the Intellect*," *Selected Critical Writings*, ed. Rosemary Ashton (Oxford: Oxford UP, 1992), pp. 18-36; p. 21.

2. "'Romola' as Fable," *Critical Essays on George Eliot*, ed. Barbara Hardy (London: Routledge & Kegan Paul, 1979), pp. 78-98; p. 78.

3. Alison Booth, *Greatness Engendered: George Eliot and Virginia Woolf* (Ithaca: Cornell UP, 1992); Nancy Paxton, "Feminism and Positivism in George Eliot's *Romola*," in *Nineteenth-Century Women Writers of the English-Speaking World*, ed. Rhoda B. Nathan (New York: Greenwood, 1986), pp. 143-150; and Susan Winnett, "Coming Unstrung: Women, Men, Narrative, and Principles of Pleasure," *PMLA* Vol. 105 No. 3 (May 1990), pp. 505-518.

4. See particularly J. B. Bullen's persuasive "George Eliot's *Romola* as a Positivist Allegory," *Review of English Studies* Vol. 26 No. 104 (November 1975), pp. 425-435, or George Levine's "'Romola' as Fable." I agree with Avrom Fleishman that Levine's reading, insightful though it is, dodges "most of the questions about [*Romola*'s] historical realism." *The English Historical Novel: Walter Scott to Virginia Woolf* (Baltimore: Johns Hopkins UP, 1971), p. 162 n. 11.

5. "'Close thy *Byron*; open thy *Goethe!*'" *Sartor Resartus*, ed. Kerry McSweeney and Peter Sabor (London: Oxford UP, 1987), p. 146.

6. George Eliot, *Romola*. Ed. Andrew Sanders (Harmondsworth: Penguin, 1980), pp. 57-58. All subsequent references are to this edition and are given parenthetically in the text.

7. [Archibald Alison], Review of Macaulay's *History*, *Blackwood's* Vol. 65 (April 1849), p. 390; Review of *Romola*, *Westminster Review*, p. 346; p. 347.

8. Review of *Romola*, *British Quarterly Review* Vol. 38 (October 1863), pp. 448-65; pp. 461-2.

9. Review of *Romola*, *British Quarterly Review*, p. 453. See Ina Ferris, *The Achievement of Literary Authority* (Ithaca: Cornell UP, 1991), for Scott's masculinization of the novel.

10. For more about women scholars in the Renaissance, see Margaret L. King's "Book-Lined Cells: Women and Humanism in the Early Italian Renaissance," in Patricia Labalme, ed., *Beyond Their Sex: Learned Women of the European Past* (New York: NYU P, 1980), pp. 66-90.
11. *Westminster Review* Vol. XI (January 1857), pp. 292-3; p. 292. Attributed to GE by Gordon S. Haight, in *George Eliot: A Biography* (Oxford: Clarendon, 1968), p. 185, and Thomas Pinney, in *Essays of George Eliot* (London: Routledge & Kegan Paul, 1963), p. 455.
12. *Westminster Review* Vol. XI, p. 293.
13. Thomas Carlyle, "Boswell's *Life of Johnson,*" *Selected Essays* (N.p.: T. Nelson & Sons, n.d.), pp. 165-227; p. 183.
14. George Eliot, "Thomas Carlyle," *Selected Critical Writings* pp. 187-92; p. 188.
15. *History of England from the Accession of James II.* 3 Volumes. (London: J. M. Dent & Sons Ltd., 1913.) Vol. I, p. 10.
16. David Hume, *An Enquiry Concerning Human Understanding*, ed. Antony Flew (La Salle IL: Open Court, 1988), p. 121.
17. Rosemary Jann, *The Art and Science of Victorian History* (Columbus: Ohio UP, 1985), p. xxiii.
18. Joseph Levine, *Humanism and History: Origins of Modern English Historiography* (Ithaca: Cornell UP, 1987), p. 192.
19. Sir Walter Scott, *Waverley*, ed. Andrew Hook (Harmondsworth: Penguin, 1972), pp. 35-6.
20. *Waverley*, pp. 493-494.
21. Harry E. Shaw, *The Forms of Historical Fiction: Sir Walter Scott and His Successors* (Ithaca: Cornell UP, 1983), p. 148.
22. Felicia Bonaparte cites Tito as the clearest example of a character shaped by context. *The Triptych and the Cross: The Central Myths of George Eliot's Poetic Imagination* (New York: NYU P, 1979), pp. 118-120.
23. Review of *Romola*, *Athenaeum* No. 1863 (July 11 1863), p. 46.
24. Fleishman, *The English Historical Novel*, p. 158.
25. Sally Shuttleworth, *George Eliot and Nineteenth-Century Science: The Make-Believe of a Beginning* (Cambridge: Cambridge UP, 1984), p. 99.
26. *The George Eliot Letters*, ed. Gordon S. Haight. 7 Volumes. (New Haven: Yale UP, 1954-1978), Vol. IV, p. 97.
27. Review of *Romola*, *Spectator* No. 1829 (July 18, 1863), pp. 2265-67; p. 2266.
28. Review of *Romola*, p. 348.

29. "*Romola* as Fable," p. 92; p. 90.
30. Alison Booth, *Greatness Engendered*, p. 178; p. 190; Deirdre David, *Intellectual Women and Victorian Patriarchy: Harriet Martineau, Elizabeth Barrett Browning, George Eliot* (Ithaca: Cornell UP, 1987), p. 188; p. 196.
31. *Letters*, Vol. IV, p. 104 n.8; p. 103-4, emphasis in original.
32. Gordon Haight says that "in the absence of strong evidence to confirm her authorship, attributions are hazardous." *George Eliot: A Biography*, p. 98. See also Pinney, ed., *Essays of George Eliot*, p. 452.
33. [J. A. Froude], "Mary Stuart." *Westminster Review* Vol. 1 (January 1852), pp. 96-142; [Ebenezer Syme], *Westminster Review* Vol. 1 (April 1852), pp. 660-61; [Ebenezer Syme], Vol. 2 (July 1852), p. 258; [Ebenezer Syme], *Westminster Review* Vol. 2 (October 1852), p. 583; [J. A. Froude], *Westminster Review* Vol. 3 (January 1853), p. 19; [Ebenezer Syme?], Vol. 3 (January 1853), p. 279; [J. A. Froude], *Westminster Review* Vol. 6 (July 1854), p. 268.
34. [Ebenezer Syme], *Westminster Review* Vol. 3 (January 1853), p. 279.
35. [Ebenezer Syme], *Westminster Review* Vol. 2 (July 1852), p. 258.
36. [Ebenezer Syme], *Westminster Review* Vol. 1 (April 1852), p. 661.
37. [J. A. Froude], *Westminster Review* Vol. 6 (July 1854), p. 268.
38. Haight, *George Eliot: A Biography*, p. 186.
39. *Westminster Review* Vol. 8 (July 1855), pp. 301-2.
40. Haight, p. 173.
41. *Letters*, Vol. I, p. 190.
42. Carolyn Heilbrun, *Writing a Woman's Life* (New York: Ballantine, 1988).
43. Deirdre David, *Intellectual Women and Victorian* Patriarchy, p. 190. Fedele gave up her studies after her marriage. See King, "Book-Lined Cells."
44. For the former argument, see, for instance, Levine, "*Romola* as Fable."
45. Arline Reilein Standley, *Auguste Comte* (Boston: Twayne, 1981), p. 103.
46. August Comte, *Positive Philosophy*. Translated and abridged by Harriet Martineau. 3 Volumes. (London: George Bell, 1896). Vol. 2, p. 285.
47. August Comte, *System of Positve Polity*. Translated by Richard Congreve, Frederic Harrison, et al. 4 Volumes. (London: Longmans, Green, and Co., 1875-77). Vol. I, p. 170; p. 183.
48. Frederic Harrison, "The Future of Woman," in *Realities and Ideals, Social, Political, Literary, and Artistic* (New York: Macmillan, 1908), pp. 63-81; p. 70.
49. "The Realm of Woman," *Realities and Ideals*, pp. 82-101; p. 100.

50. Nancy Paxton points out that Comte's support for women's education as well as the religious significance he gave to the family and the role of mothers led many Victorian feminists to support him. See her "Feminism and Positivism in George Eliot's *Romola*" or *George Eliot and Herbert Spencer: Feminism, Evolutionism, and the Reconstruction of Gender* (Princeton: Princeton UP, 1991).

51. See, for example, T. R. Wright, *The Religion of Humanity: The Impact of Comtean Positivism on Victorian Britain* (Cambridge: Cambridge UP, 1986), pp. 189-90; Bullen, "George Eliot's *Romola* as Positivist Allegory," especially pp. 433-34; Paxton, "Feminism and Positivism in George Eliot's *Romola*" or *George Eliot and Herbert Spencer*; and U. C. Knoepflmacher, *Religious Humanism and the Victorian Novel* (Princeton: Princeton UP, 1965), p. 40.

52. T. R. Wright notes that Savonarola's achievements as well as his faults, as GE portrays them, correspond to Comte's analysis of Catholicism. *The Religion of Humanity*, p. 190. See also Bullen, pp. 431-32.

53. Bullen, "George Eliot's *Romola* as Positivist Allegory," p. 428; p. 433.

54. *Religion of Humanity*, pp. 180-81.

55. *George Eliot and Nineteenth-Century Science*, p. 100.

56. "Feminism and Positivism in George Eliot's *Romola*," p. 147.

57. "Feminism and Positivism in George Eliot's *Romola*," p. 148.

58. *The Triptych and the Cross*, p. 106.

59. *British Quarterly Review* Vol. 38 (October 1863), p. 461.

60. *Lives of the Queens of England*. 12 Volumes. (Philadelphia: Lea & Blanchard, 1848). Vol. 12, p. viii.

61. *Greatness Engendered*, p. 180.

62. *Intellectual Women and Victorian Patriarchy*, p. 194.

63. Susan Winnett, "Coming Unstrung: Women, Men, Narrative, and Principles of Pleasure," *PMLA* Vol. 105 No. 3 (May 1990), pp. 505-18.

64. Dorothy Mermin, *Godiva's Ride: Women of Letters in England, 1830-1880* (Bloomington: Indiana UP, 1993), p. 122.

CHAPTER FIVE
"'Not At All Like Being A Queen'"?
Historicizing Female Sovereignty in *Middlemarch*

> *'It is a pity she was not a queen,'* said the devout Sir James. *'But what should we have been then? We must have been something else,'* said Celia, objecting to so laborious a flight of imagination. *'I like her better as she is.'*[1]

> *'There isn't any power. But there can be influence.'*
> —Prince Charles[2]

The Prelude and Finale to *Middlemarch* frame the novel in terms of two major issues. First and most obviously, the opening passages about Saint Theresa and "the social lot of women" indicate that what follows will be a contribution to the 'woman question.' Most of Eliot's contemporary reviewers read and sought to understand the novel in this way, and modern critics continue, with good reason, to interpret it as crucially concerned with questions of gender, woman's nature, and feminism.[3] The Prelude and Finale also link the novel to a second set of problems, one which they (and the novel as a whole) insistently pair with the first. Phrases and passages in both of these framing sections speak directly to the discourse of history which the rest of this study has explicated. The Prelude concludes with a vision of a life "unmarked by any signal event," the kind of "noiseless" existence hailed by Carlyle and Macaulay as genuinely historical:

> Here and there is born a Saint Theresa, foundress of nothing, whose loving heart-beats and sobs after an unattained goodness tremble off and are dispersed among hindrances, instead of centering in some long-recognizable deed. (26)

As I discussed in Chapter Two, both Carlyle and Macaulay hint at but do not overtly point to women when they look into "the dark untenanted places of the past," to the transformations effected "in every school, in every church, behind ten thousand counters, at ten thousand firesides."[4] In contrast, Eliot explicitly genders this historiographical theme. Saint Theresa's life is the model for a life historicized through some "long-recognizable deed," but it is also the touchstone for the lives of later women who share her "ardour" but find no such fulfilling project, whose ideals and opportunities never coalesce into direct, meaningful action. Those who care to "know the history of man," the Prelude insists, must look to the history of woman.

The Finale closes the novel in terms still more clearly emerging from the discourse of history, and just as directly linking it to gender. The famous concluding passage conspicuously echoes Carlyle's essay "On History" (itself, written in 1832, exactly contemporaneous with the action of the novel):

> Her finely-touched spirit had still its fine issues, though they were not finely visible. Her full nature . . . spent itself in channels which had no great name on the earth. But the effect of her being on those around her was incalculably diffusive: for the growing good of the world is partly dependent on unhistoric acts; and that things are not so ill with you and me as they might have been, is half owing to the number who lived faithfully a hidden life, and rest in unvisited tombs. (896)

Her aquatic metaphor also evokes Strickland's image of those "undercurrents" of the "broad stream of history" that influence "the tide of events."[5] Like Strickland, Eliot emphasizes the historical significance of "unhistoric acts" which are inconspicuous but consequential; although consigning Dorothea to a life of obscurity, with her closing words Eliot reminds her audience that her heroine shares her fate with the majority of the world and that this silent majority in fact constitutes history's most important population. To a certain extent, then, the relationship of *Middlemarch* to the Victorian discourse of history is obvious. Rather than further explicating Eliot's consistent endorsement of a model of incremental change and the historical significance of minute events, for the rest of this chapter I want once again to read her fiction as intervening in a specific aspect of the discourse of history: the intersection of models of ideal womanhood with historiography which I have already argued illuminates otherwise puzzling aspects of *Romola*. Here I focus on Dorothea Brooke, who, like Romola de' Bardi in her novel, is the vehicle for Eliot's social and historiographical critique. She carries the novel's thematic burden on her shoulders: she is the modern-day Saint Theresa of the Prelude and the "unhistoric" agent of the Finale. But what kind of historical heroine is she? In Chapter Four I argued that Romola is *not* really a historical heroine but rather a figure of universalized, essentialized womanhood, drawn to the same pattern as the idealized women in the volumes by the "lady historians." I argue here that these women provide a crucial touchstone for Dorothea as well, but that *Middlemarch* brings them—or what they represent—back into the historical narrative from which they were expelled in *Romola*. Dorothea redefines female sovereignty, replacing the ahistorical ideal Romola personifies with a queenly identity suitable for realist and historical representation. In *Middlemarch*, Eliot continues, if more obliquely than in *Romola*, to endorse what I will call for shorthand the "queenly ideal." The crucial difference is that in *Middlemarch* the queenly ideal is a potential rather than a standard, and one more perfectly realized within the private, rather than the public, sphere.

I

Although not only her novels but also her letters, essays, and reviews reveal a persistent interest in the social, psychological, and historical development of women, Eliot disliked making direct statements on the 'woman question'; in 1857 she wrote to Charles Bray of her reluctance to give any "specific enunciation of doctrine on a question so entangled," and in 1868 she told Barbara Bodichon, "I never like to be quoted in any way on this subject."[6] While many of her closest women friends were activists for feminist causes, Eliot herself generally stayed aloof, perhaps because of anxiety that her own unusual personal situation might compromise their efforts, but more clearly because of her uncertainty that any but educational reforms were in fact for the best. Although she deplored the inadequate education generally offered to women and the debased state into which she considered social prohibitions and constraints reduced them, she opposed arguments for equality as equivalence, insisting rather that the ideal relation between the sexes was one of complementarity. "Let the whole field of reality be laid open to woman as well as to man," she wrote in 1854,

> and then that which is peculiar in her mental modification, instead of being, as it is now, a source of discord and repulsion between the sexes, will be found to be a necessary complement to the truth and beauty of life. Then we shall have that marriage of minds which alone can blend all the hues of thought and feeling in one lovely rainbow of promise for the harvest of human happiness.[7]

In "Silly Novels by Lady Novelists," she argued that women could produce novels with "a precious speciality, lying quite apart from masculine aptitudes and experience."[8] Women novelists can "fully equal men"—but "after their kind," taking advantage of the particular "aptitudes and experience" they have by virtue of their sex.[9]

Eliot believed that women's special character developed out of the uniquely female experience of motherhood. "Under every imaginable social condition," she writes in her 1854 essay "Woman in France,"

> [woman] will necessarily have a class of sensations and emotions—the maternal ones—which must remain unknown to man; and the fact of her comparative physical weakness, which, however it may have been exaggerated by a vicious civilization, can never be cancelled, introduces a distinctively feminine condition into the wondrous chemistry of the affections and sentiments, which inevitably gives rise to distinctive forms and combinations.[10]

When she makes explicit what she considers "distinctively" feminine characteristics, her specifications accord easily with general Victorian presuppositions and prejudices about woman's nature—maternity (or the capacity for it) breeds into women capabilities for other-directedness, for sympathy, empathy, and selflessness. In 1868, she wrote to Emily Davies that the "physical and physiological differences between women and men," while in a certain sense superficial, nonetheless are the "deep roots of psychological development"; one's experience of one's physical self is "the deepest and subtlest sort of education that life gives." The differences thus nurtured lead men and women to different functions, women's "peculiar constitution" preparing them for a "special moral influence":

> In the face of all wrongs, mistakes, and failures, history has demonstrated that gain. And there lies just that kernel of truth in the vulgar alarm of men lest women should be 'unsexed.' We can no more afford to part with that exquisite type of gentleness, tenderness, possible maternity suffusing a woman's being with affectionateness, which makes what we mean by the feminine character, than we can afford to part with the human love, the mutual subjection of soul between a man and a woman—which is also a growth and revelation beginning before all history.[11]

At the heart of this view of women is an essentialist notion: women's unique capacity to bear children, an inescapable physiological fact, results in an ahistorical "feminine character" marked by the qualities necessary for nurturing children.

The gentle, affectionate woman with a "special moral influence" is a familiar figure by now, one we have seen here in the writings by women historians as well as in Positivist theory, and one who also appears frequently in Eliot's fiction. Dorothea is only one in a line of Eliot's women held up for her readers' admiration for realizing an ideal of womanliness as an extension of maternal instincts. Milly Barton and Dinah Morris are the two clearest examples. They embody loving selflessness and affect those around them as much by their mere presence as by any direct action. Like Romola, these women are never criticized or ironized by their narrators; they enjoy unambiguously and unproblematically the status of exemplars. "Soothing, unspeakable charm of gentle womanhood!" pronounces the narrator of "The Sad Fortunes of the Rev. Amos Barton,"

> which supersedes all acquisitions, all accomplishments. You would never have asked, at any period of Mrs Amos Barton's life, if she sketched or played the piano. You would even perhaps have been

rather scandalized if she had descended from the serene dignity of *being* to the assiduous unrest of *doing*.[12]

"*Being*" versus "*doing*": thus the narrator reminds us that ideal femininity excludes agency in favor of essence or influence. Milly Barton is "a large, fair, gentle Madonna," a "tall, graceful, substantial presence" that is "imposing in its mildness"; her chief characteristic is a "sublime capacity of loving."[13] The tone of reverential admiration with which the narrator describes her is especially striking given the satirical, if kindly, tone he adopts toward her pathetic and commonplace husband. But this story aims to awaken in its readers a sense of "the poetry and the pathos" of ordinary experience, an effect that relies on their yielding to the unassuming beauty of Milly's life and death.[14] The narrator cannot afford to ironize Milly, for she and her perfect, devout, unselfish, womanly love carry the story's moral and affective burden.

Dinah Morris plays a more active role than Milly, but she, too, acts with unerring and peculiarly feminine grace, tact, and beneficence. More conspicuously than Milly, she brings good to the lives of those around her in the true queenly manner, from her first visit to the Bedes after Thias's death, when she has a "subduing influence" on poor Lisbeth's grief, to her visit to Hetty in prison when she brings the frightened sinner to confess and repent.[15] Her preaching strains the convention of female piety by placing her in the public gaze, but it remains an unusual extension of woman's spiritual influence rather than an attempt to redefine woman's sphere. And in the novel's conclusion Dinah, too, conforms to the principle laid down in *Scenes of Clerical Life*:

> A loving woman's world lies within the four walls of her own home; and it is only through her husband that she is in any electric communication with the world beyond.[16]

When Adam and Dinah marry, Mr. Irwine rejoices that Adam will now be the beneficiary of Dinah's "strong, gentle love," and indeed all the energies she had expended on others are ultimately devoted to her family.[17] Throughout the novel, the narrator's tone towards Dinah never varies from the solemn admiration he evinces when describing her preaching on the green: "She was not preaching as she heard others preach, but speaking directly from her own emotions, and under the inspiration of her own simple faith."[18] Like Milly's, Dinah's virtues carry too much thematic weight for the narrator to subject them to belittling commentary.

As the presence in both novels of a wide variety of female characters clarifies, neither Milly nor Dinah is offered as an example of a typical woman. Rather, Eliot presents them as touchstones, ideals of perfect womanly love, virtue, and generosity—examples of what women can be, if "that exquisite type of gentleness, tenderness, possible maternity suffusing a woman's being with affectionateness, which makes what we mean by the feminine character" ripens into reality. This model of what the very best women are like—or would be like, given the opportunity, or could have been like, had things been different—is consistent throughout Eliot's fiction, although her later heroines are more complex and often manifest intellectual passion and yearning not easily reconciled with it. The only thoroughly unwomanly woman in all of Eliot is, I think, Daniel Deronda's mother, the singer Alcharisi, and she, like Elizabeth I in Strickland's biography, has succeeded by renouncing her sex: when Daniel talks with her, for instance, it seems that "all the woman lacking in her was present in him."[19] Her impassioned eloquence about the "slavery of being a girl" resonates with twentieth-century readers more than Dinah's pious sincerity, no doubt, but she is a disturbing and tragic rather than heroic or exemplary figure.[20] Real women, to adapt a familiar saying, do not abandon their children.

II

These examples serve to remind us that it is at once tempting, easy, and inaccurate to overestimate Eliot's unconventionality about women's roles.[21] Eliot's own life is paradigmatic in this respect: although she defied the strictures of Victorian morality in order to live, unmarried, with George Henry Lewes, this superficially radical gesture is offset by her own conception of their relationship as a marriage and her insistence on being addressed as "Mrs. Lewes." Like Eliot's, Dorothea's unconventionality appears greater than it is. The people in Dorothea's world certainly perceive her as unusual, and their responses range from unease to appreciation. The confusion and suspicion aroused in her neighbors by her spiritual and intellectual intensity tempers the admiration they feel for her physical beauty:

> The rural opinion about the new young ladies, even among the cottagers, was generally in favour of Celia, as being so amiable and innocent-looking, while Miss Brooke's large eyes seemed, like her religion, too unusual and striking. (31)

After his encounter with her at Mr. Brooke's party, Lydgate thinks that her "youthful bloom, with her approaching marriage to that faded scholar, and her interest in matters socially useful, gave her the piquancy of an unusual combination" (119), and Will, even before his feelings for her shape themselves into love, feels she is "not a woman to be spoken of as other women were" (249). When Will visits Dorothea at Lowick, he thinks she looks, "in her plain dress . . . without a single ornament on her besides her wedding-ring, as if she were under a vow to be different from all other women" (398); later he rebuffs Rosamond's jealous, coquettish inquiries about Dorothea with the dampening remark that "'Mrs Casaubon is too unlike other women for them to be compared with her'" (474).

Dorothea's difference, however, lies not in any wish to be "unlike" all other women but in her aspiration to fulfill her culture's highest ideal of womanly strength and goodness, to apply herself energetically to the goals of exemplary action and beneficent influence widely touted as women's social mission. Dorothea cannot be satisfied with "the perusal of *Female Scriptural Characters* . . . and the care of her soul over her embroidery in her own boudoir" (50-51). She takes Mrs. King's scriptural characters as genuinely exemplary, seeking to realize in her own life the excellences they manifest. "From the pity, gentleness, and forbearance of women," writes Mrs. King,

> spring most of the Christian virtues that adorn society; and from the tenderness and compassion stamped on their hearts, arise the greatest number of those benevolent deeds, that form the chief blessings of life.[22]

Like the queens in the volumes by the women historians, Mrs. King's scriptural women distinguish themselves by their charity, their benevolence, and their piety; they do good in the world by public applications of these private feminine virtues. Dorothea accepts this pattern of female behavior as an ideal and cannot "live in a pretended admission of rules which were never acted on" (51)—"shut out" from passive contentment, she yearns to "'lead a grand life'" herself (51). In short, Dorothea aspires to be queenly, where "queenly" refers to the model of behavior and values developed and extolled in the many popular biographies of royal and other notable women, a genre already prevalent during the decade of her education.

In the volumes by women historians, as Chapter Two showed, queens fulfill a special social, spiritual, and historical role characterized by indirect agency serving benevolent ends. They ameliorate harsh conditions, often intervening with their husbands on behalf of the poor and weak. They found churches, or schools, or orphanages; they patronize literature and the arts. In Mary Hays's *Memoirs of Queens, Illustrious and Celebrated*, for example, which Dorothea might have read, George II's consort Caroline receives high praise for her domesticity, her patronage of the arts and letters, and her role as "protectress and benefactress" to the poor and unhappy.[23] Or in her *Celebrated Female Sovereigns*, first published at just the time when the action of *Middlemarch* is set, Anna Jameson emphasizes Berengaria's exercise of her beneficent influence over Richard I to help the poor.[24] These women exercise their sovereignty in womanly ways, extending their capacity for maternal tenderness to their subjects. They sympathize with suffering and appreciate beauty, and, driven by feminine feeling rather than masculine ambition, they find their vocation in relieving the one and cultivating the other.

Dorothea's queenliness is a constant theme in the novel. Not only comments by the narrator but remarks by many other characters mark her, as Romola is marked, as a regal figure. She savors her authority in her uncle's household, for instance, "with the homage that belonged to it" (33); the narrator calls her "majestic" (592), and to the Lydgates's maid she appears a "queenly young widow" when she arrives for her fateful visit to Rosamond (831). Her admirers, particularly Sir James and Will Ladislaw, tend to think of her as royalty. "'She is a noble creature,'" Sir James exclaims after watching Dorothea's ardent and repentant display of affection for the ailing Casaubon (319); later, and again to Celia, who fortunately is too placid to resent the admiration he continues to lavish on her sister, he says devoutly, "'It is a pity she was not a queen'" (580). Will is less literal but just as ready to subject himself to Dorothea's rule: he longs for "some queenly recognition, some approving sign" from "his soul's sovereign" (250), and he thinks of her as

> for ever enthroned in his soul: no other woman could sit higher than her footstool; and if he could have written out in immortal syllables the effect she wrought within him, he might have boasted after the example of old Drayton, that—
> Queens hereafter might be glad to live
> Upon the alms of her superfluous praise. (510)

Unlike Romola's, Dorothea's queenliness is frequently undercut or ironized, either explicitly, through narratorial comment, or implicitly because of the source or context of these remarks. Despite this undermining, however, the implications of which I discuss further below, queenliness is a metaphor with which our thoughts of Dorothea get repeatedly entangled.

Beyond such direct references, some characters obliquely reinforce her association with the queenly ideal, either by their faith in her power to do good through influence or by their vision of her enlightening the world in the manner so frequently attributed to the queens in the women historians' volumes. Sir James, for instance, has a "constant belief in Dorothea's capacity for influence" (422); he wishes she had stayed with her uncle, because her influence might have persuaded him to carry out reforms on his land:

> 'She might have got some power over him in time, and she was always uneasy about the estate. She had wonderfully good notions about such things. But now Casaubon takes her up entirely.' (416)

And Casaubon imagines her brightening his life with her gentle radiance, bringing "that cheerful companionship with which the presence of youth can lighten or vary the serious toils of maturity" (48-9), "adorn[ing] his life with the grace of female companionship" and "irradiat[ing] the gloom which fatigue was apt to hang over the intervals of studious labour with the play of female fancy" (87). Both men prove more comfortable with female influence in theory than in practice; their frequent resistance to Dorothea's plans and desires despite their ostensible support and admiration typifies the way "rules of conduct" contradict "loudly-asserted beliefs" in their society, something Eliot sharply criticized in the first edition of the novel:

> Among the many remarks passed on her mistakes, it was never said in the neighbourhood of Middlemarch that such mistakes could not have happened if the society into which she was born had not smiled on propositions of marriage from a sickly man to a girl less than half his own age—on modes of education which make a woman's knowledge another name for motley ignorance—on rules of conduct which are in flat contradiction with its own loudly asserted beliefs.[25]

Dorothea herself, with her longing for "work which would be directly beneficent like the sunshine and the rain" (516), shows the influence on her of queenly models, from her impulse to do good to her image of herself as a natural force bringing health and happiness by her presence rather than by any specific actions. She wishes from the start "to make her life greatly effective" (50), a desire which means, for her, turning her sympathies into concrete activity. She seeks a means "by which her life might be filled with action at once rational and ardent" (112); she is "alive to anything that [gives] her an opportunity for active sympathy" (236). She starts a school in the village and devotes herself to designing better cottages for her uncle's tenants, both good examples of queenly projects. She hopes that her marriage will expand her sphere of beneficent influence, but she finds Lowick prosperous and comfortable:

> She felt some disappointment, of which she was yet ashamed, that there was nothing for her to do in Lowick; and in the next few minutes her mind had glanced over the possibility, which she would have preferred, of finding that her home would be in a parish which had a larger share of the world's misery, so that she might have had more active duties in it. (103)

And her husband, whose life she expected would absorb and exalt her own, proves at first reluctant about and finally averse to including her in his work—which, in any case, she soon ceases to see as a repository of greatness. Her "ardent woman's need to rule beneficently by making the joy of another soul" (396) is constantly frustrated.

Neither her extended nor her immediate home, then, provides "room for the energies which stirred uneasily under the dimness and pressure of her own ignorance and the petty peremptoriness of the world's habits" (67). "The duties of her married life," she finds,

> contemplated as so great beforehand, seemed to be shrinking with the furniture and the white vapour-walled landscape. . . . When would the days begin of that active wifely devotion which was to strengthen her husband's life and exalt her own? (307)

The womanly arenas of philanthropy and marriage both fail her:

> the sense of connection with a manifold pregnant existence had to be kept up painfully as an inward vision, instead of coming from without in claims that would have shaped her energies. (307)

Ironically, having achieved a position of aristocratic grandeur equal to her own regal bearing and aspirations, Dorothea finds herself paralyzed rather than liberated. Every generous impulse, every affectionate urge, is checked by some constraint, some demand of propriety. Even her widowhood does not bring relief, for although freed from Casaubon's inhibiting presence, she finds herself still more closely observed and restrained by her family and neighbors. Her most ambitious plan, to

> 'take a great deal of land, and drain it, and make a little colony, where everybody should work, and all the work should be done well [and where] I should know every one of the people and be their friend' (594)

falls apart because, although she is wealthy, she is not wealthy enough. She suffers, as she says, from having her feelings checked at every turn (792); she seems likely never to have any opportunity to translate her powerful emotions into some tangible project.

Not until she lowers her sights from sweeping social problems to discrete domestic ones does she in fact have any success as an agent of beneficent change. Thwarted in her grander aims, she finds in Lydgate's crises a new direction for her energies:

In her luxurious home, wandering under the boughs of her own great trees, her thought was going out over the lot of others, and her emotions were imprisoned. The idea of some active good within her reach, 'haunted her like a passion', and another's need having once come to her as a distinct image, preoccupied her desire with the yearning to give relief. (817-18)

Although her intervention on Lydgate's behalf does not save his career from its descent into the slough of mediocrity, it fortifies him; "'you have made a great difference in my courage by believing in me,'" he tells her (825). And her visits to Rosamond avert a potential catastrophe by disrupting her attempts to entangle Will Ladislaw in an affair. "[W]hat sort of crisis might not this be in three lives" closely entwined with hers, she wonders (846). This is not the kind of work she had meant to do, but she realizes that the "objects of her rescue were not to be sought out by her fancy: they were chosen for her" (846). In both instances her ardor more than her actual words brings results—she succeeds, as a queen should, through influence. "The presence of a noble nature, generous in its wishes, ardent in its charity," comments the narrator, "changes the lights for us .... That influence was beginning to act on Lydgate" (819). Rosamond "felt something like bashful timidity before a superior, in the presence of this self-forgetful ardour" (853), while Dorothea "felt the relation between them to be peculiar enough to give her a peculiar influence" (854). Rosamond's explanation of Will's conduct is begun "under the subduing influence of Dorothea's emotion" (856), an influence of the highest womanly kind, as we see when Dorothea clasps Rosamond's hand "with gentle motherliness" (851). Finally Dorothea's feminine sympathy becomes an active force in the world, not for her own glorification—these deeds do not exalt her, as she had once hoped her actions would—but·for the ease and improvement of those around her.

III

Dorothea, then, participates in the tradition of queenliness we have already looked at in several contexts. But in Chapter Four I argued that this model of female identity defies historicization, that Romola's essentialized, idealized status makes her fit for a mythic rather than a historical narrative. Eliot's achievement in *Middlemarch* is sustaining a vision of women's capacity for queenliness without sacrificing her realism—or, conversely, sustaining her realist, historical narrative without sacrificing her long-held belief in woman's special powers. Such a result is possible because she presents Dorothea as admirable but not, in fact, exemplary, approaching but not embodying an ideal, and because she shows her as embedded in historical particularity and necessity, as Romola so conspicuously is not. In the first place, the novel abounds with explicit warnings against preconceptions and formulas about women, whether flattering or belittling. In her review essay "Margaret Fuller and Mary Wollstonecraft," Eliot had expressed her approval of Fuller's comments on "the folly of absolute definitions of woman's nature and absolute demarcations of woman's mission."[26] The Prelude to *Middlemarch* concludes with cautionary remarks about just such absolutism, noting that the "limits of variation are really much wider than any one would imagine"; this "inconvenient indefiniteness" makes "scientific certitude" impossible (26). Characters in the novel who believe they have achieved a state of formulaic "certitude" about women inevitably have their "folly" exposed. Dorothea's disdain for Sir James confounds Mr Brooke, for instance:

> Mr Brooke wondered, and felt that women were an inexhaustible subject of study, since even he at his age was not in a perfect state of scientific prediction about them! (63)

Mr. Brooke concludes that woman is "a problem ... hardly less complicated than the revolutions of an irregular solid" (65); his scientific analogy alerts us to his continuing error—he treats women as a category amenable to "prediction," to "certitude," rather than as complex individuals.

Mr. Brooke's wish to solve the woman problem causes him no particular harm. Lydgate, however, who thinks he *has* settled the matter, suffers for his error. After his painful experience with Laure, Lydgate resolves to "take a strictly scientific view of woman" (183), expecting only what he has already sufficient evidence for. He thus subscribes to the scientific fallacy the Prelude warns against—and, ironically, given his profession, proves a faulty scientist, theorizing well ahead of his data. He brings

> a much more testing vision of details and relations into [his] pathological study than he had ever thought it necessary to apply to the complexities of love and marriage, these being subjects on which he felt himself amply informed by literature, and that traditional wisdom which is handed down in the genial conversation of men. (193)

From literature and tradition, Lydgate has distilled a pattern of "perfect womanhood" to which he clings in spite of his professions of objectivity and to which, he concludes, Rosamond perfectly conforms (387). She has, he confidently reflects,

> just the kind of intelligence one would desire in a woman—polished, refined, docile, lending itself to finish in all the delicacies of life, and enshrined in a body which expressed this with a force of demonstrations that excluded the need for other evidence. Lydgate felt sure that if ever he married, his wife would have that feminine radiance, that distinctive womanhood which must be classed with flowers and music, that sort of beauty which by its very nature was virtuous, being moulded only for pure and delicate joys. (193)

"But Lydgate," the narrator has already warned us, "might possibly have experience before him which would modify his opinion as to the most excellent things in woman" (120). Lydgate's new home will be the laboratory for experiments in love and marriage which may challenge his theories, perhaps even inducing a paradigm shift.

Sure enough, Lydgate finds that Rosamond's "combination of correct sentiments, music, dancing, drawing, elegant note-writing, private album for extracted verse, and perfect blond loveliness," conceals obstinacy, ignorance, and narrow-minded egotism (301). In part, Lydgate suffers because he, like Dorothea, reads superficial signs as indicating deeper virtues; Rosamond makes him miserable because she does not really correspond to his ideal. But he also resists the "inconvenient indefiniteness" of woman's nature, preferring reductive categorization to complexity and variation. Disillusioned with Rosamond and remembering Laure, he immediately universalizes their failings: "'It is the way with all women,'" he thinks (638). Just as Dorothea troubles her uncle's efforts at "scientific prediction," however, she thwarts Lydgate's "power of generalizing" (638). In his early encounters with her, he is too distracted by thoughts of Rosamond to find Dorothea appealing. She is "'a little too earnest,'" he thinks (119), "not," the narrator expands, "Mr Lydgate's style of woman" (120). "Women just like Dorothea had not entered into [Lydgate's] traditions" (323); if they had, he might have revised or, better yet, discarded his formula for feminine perfection before making his fateful (and fatal) choice. Once entangled in Rosamond's web, Lydgate recalls Dorothea's impassioned selflessness, her "voice of deep-souled womanhood," with a mixture of admiration and bemusement (638). Apparently unable to find a happy medium, to see and treat women as real people rather than as embodied abstractions and ideals, he eventually reveres Dorothea instead of Rosamond as the epitome of feminine perfection; even Rosamond's egotism cannot blind her to his change of allegiance, and she lives out the final years of their marriage in the shadow of "Mrs. Ladislaw, whom he was always praising and placing above her" (893).

Despite the contrast she provides to Rosamond, however, Dorothea is not held up as a true example of "perfect womanhood"; to idealize her in this way would be to repeat Brooke's and Lydgate's errors of overconfident generalization, their desire for "scientific certitude" about women. A constant flow of ironic commentary forestalls this misreading by undercutting Dorothea's seeming grandeur. Dorothea does impress many of her friends and neighbors as an image of perfection. "'What is it that you gentlemen are thinking of when you are with Mrs Casaubon?',," Rosamond pettishly asks Will. "'Herself,'" Will responds; "'When one sees a perfect woman, one never thinks of her attributes—one is conscious of her presence'"(473). Lydgate remembers her speaking with the "voice of deep-souled womanhood" (638), and after she offers him her belief and loyalty he compares her to the Virgin Mary (826). The narrator sometimes joins in the chorus of admiration: the epigraph to Chapter 43, for instance, which speaks of the "pure and noble lines / Of generous womanhood that fits all times," clearly refers to Dorothea (469), and during her night of agony what the narrator calls her "grand woman's frame" is shaken by sobs (844). But skeptical, even occasionally derisive, remarks run in conspicuous counterpoint to this theme of reverential admiration in a manner rare indeed in Eliot's treatment of her heroines. No opportunity is missed to remind readers that Dorothea is naive, unworldly, impetuous, and even foolhardy. "Poor Dorothea!" we hear early on; "compared with her, the innocent-looking Celia was knowing and worldly-wise" (31), and a little later, "Miss Brooke was certainly very naive with all her alleged cleverness" (88). Surrounded as she initially is with people notable for intellectual shallowness or coarse materialism, Dorothea's simplicity seems at first a guarantee of her strength and virtue: she lives in so faulty and inadequate a world that her distance from its mundane concerns and realities appears essential to her hopes of achieving something grand. But, of course, her first decisive action in the novel is a terrible mistake which Celia's worldly wisdom, had Dorothea shared it or at least attended to it, would have forestalled. Dorothea's first marriage eloquently testifies to the inadequacy of her beliefs.

Frequently, moreover, Dorothea's generous impulses are shown to be flawed, the means she settles on deficient to the noble ends she desires. When she wishes to give money to the hospital, for example, the narrator sides with Casaubon in finding her plan inappropriate:

> Mr Casaubon made no objection beyond a passing remark that the sum might be disproportionate in relation to other good objects, but when Dorothea in her ignorance resisted that suggestion, he acquiesced. (479)

Her irritating shortsightedness and obstinacy offset the appeal of her ardent altruism. This effect is most strikingly evident in her climactic encounter with Lydgate, who of all Dorothea's acquaintance knows best the complexity and difficulty of real-world problems. Throughout this scene, the narrator balances appreciation of Dorothea's lofty motivations against cutting criticism of her "childlike" perspective. Her voice, with its "searching tenderness," "might have been almost taken as a proof" that her efforts will succeed, the narrator comments, the excess of qualifiers underlining the insubstantiality of Dorothea's promises (820). "Lydgate did not stay to think that she was Quixotic," but this observation ensures that readers will think so (820). And just when the narrator seems, like Lydgate, to be softening under Dorothea's influence, finding her "childlike grave-eyed earnestness" "irresistible," there comes a caustic reminder of her limitations:

> The childlike grave-eyed earnestness with which Dorothea said all this was irresistible—blent into an adorable whole with her ready

understanding of high experience. (Of lower experience such as plays a great part in the world, poor Mrs Casaubon had a very blurred shortsighted knowledge, little helped by her imagination.) (822)

Even the word "adorable" diminishes her, reducing her to the status of a cute toy or an affectionate puppy. As Dorothea Barrett comments about the scenes of Dorothea's restlessness prior to her climactic interview with Will, we are given in such instances "painfully diminished descriptions of the heroine whose 'grand woman's frame' moved us to both pity and respect" earlier in the novel.[27] Without pretension or arrogance, Dorothea reaches out to offer help and sustenance to a man eminently worthy of her assistance; although her gesture is surely queenly in its munificence and selflessness, rather than elevating her the narrator emphasizes the contrast between the nobility of her aspirations and the paucity of her understanding. The effect is to lower her from ideal to real: she has tremendous potential for greatness, but her highest qualities make up only part of her character.

Finally, Dorothea is no more a universal figure than she is an unproblematically heroic or ideal one. As the insistence on her imperfections humanizes her, so the emphasis on the ways in which Dorothea's circumstances affect her historicizes her; the development of even her highest individual characteristics is constrained by the conditions of possibility. Like *Romola*, *Middlemarch* abounds with historical details.[28] Unlike Romola, though, who seems detached from her surroundings and who ultimately escapes the constraints of both society and history, Dorothea is entangled in her moment,

> struggling in the bands of a narrow teaching, hemmed in by a social life which seemed nothing but a labyrinth of petty courses, a walled-in maze of small paths that led no whither[.] (51)

Dorothea is who she is, does what she does, because of when she is. Her shallow, restricted education ill-equips her for the noble life she hopes to lead even as it dictates the terms in which she imagines that life. Her ardor and tenderness do not have free play but rather shape themselves according to the available scripts, for, as the Finale reiterates, there is no creature whose inward being is so strong that it is not greatly determined by what lies outside it. A new Theresa will hardly have the opportunity of reforming a conventual life, any more than a new Antigone will spend her heroic piety in daring all for the sake of a brother's burial: the medium in which their ardent deeds took shape is for ever gone. (896)

Romola escapes from her medium and while thus liberated shapes her "ardent deeds" to her own nature. Dorothea enjoys no such transcendence from "the unfriendly mediums of Tipton and Freshitt" (62) but struggles throughout the novel to accommodate her yearnings to her options. She finds her idealism chastened by her experience: "'I used to despise women a little for not shaping their lives more, and doing better things,'" she tells Will sadly (589). She comes to see that there are limits to life's plasticity as well as to her own abilities, that she could have done "better things" "if she had only been better and known better" (893). Even those who regret her fate cannot state "exactly what else that was in her power she ought rather to have done" (894). Symbolic apotheosis is not an option in the real (or realist) world, or in history.

IV

Dorothea thus seems to be peculiarly positioned. Although she manifests qualities which Eliot elsewhere characterized as quintessentially and ideally feminine, and although she appears to participate in a tradition of queenly magnificence and beneficence, her noble aspirations are frustrated, her grandeur undermined, and her universality denied. What remains, then? What kind of figure is Dorothea? Near the end of the novel, Celia, attempting to prevent Dorothea from marrying Will, tells her,

> 'James always said you ought to be a queen; but this is not at all like being a queen. You know what mistakes you have always been making, Dodo, and this is another.' (879)

As usual, Celia's sharp but shallow perception leads her to the truth, but, also as usual, not to the whole truth. Dorothea's self-effacing but influential role after her marriage to Will is indeed "like being a queen," but a queen of a different kind, a queen suited for a "home epic" rather than a heroic one. Dorothea lives

> a life filled also with a beneficent activity which she had not the doubtful pains of discovering and marking out for herself. Will became an ardent public man . . . . Dorothea could have liked nothing better, since wrongs existed, than that her husband should be in the thick of a struggle against them, and that she should give him wifely help. (894)

Her special qualities are not lost or rejected; rather, they resolve themselves into domestic and individual virtues with historically localized manifestations.

The novel's resolution, then, transplants rather than transforms the queenly ideal. In doing so, it literalizes the impulse in the volumes by the women historians to represent queenliness in middle-class terms. While the queens in these volumes exercise their sovereign power in ways and towards ends consistent with bourgeois Victorian gender ideology, they remain public, aristocratic figures, literally queens and only by analogy good Victorian women. Dorothea really is a good Victorian woman, and so she epitomizes rather than contradicts the tradition. Queenliness, which in the volumes by the women historians means beneficent influence, piety, compassion, munificence, and wifely devotion, becomes a metaphor invoking exactly the same qualities; the circle of identification is complete.

Other texts or developments from the period make a similar transition between literal and symbolic queenship. I suggested in Chapters Two and Three that middle-class Victorian women looking into the mirror of history saw royal and aristocratic women as elevated, idealized versions of themselves, a vision of similarity enabled in general by abundant representations of historical women exemplifying Victorian virtues and in particular by their shared interest in needlework. This ennobling analogy is the central conceit of Ruskin's 1865 lecture "Of Queens' Gardens," a treatise on women's potential for "royal authority."[29] Ruskin's description of woman's "royal or gracious influence" coincides with the queenly ideal.[30] It is "a *guiding*, not a determining function," first of all, passive rather than active.[31] Secondly, it is primarily a moral influence, one governed by concern for others and infused with womanly tenderness, "self-renunciation" and "the passionate gentleness of an infinitely variable, because infinitely applicable, modesty of service."[32] Ruskin eloquently expounds the by now familiar doctrine of beneficent feminine power:

> Power to heal, to redeem, to guide, and to guard. Power of the sceptre and shield; the power of the royal hand that heals in touching,—that binds the fiend, and looses the captive; the throne that is founded on the rock of Justice, and descended from only by steps of Mercy.

"Will you not covet such power as this," he demands of his female audience, "and seek such thrones as this, and be no more housewives, but queens?"[33] But the identification is not really optional:

> whether consciously or not, you must be, in many a heart, enthroned: there is no putting by that crown; queens you must always be: queens to your lovers; queens to your husbands and your sons; queens of higher mystery to the world beyond, which bows itself, and will for ever bow, before the myrtle crown and the stainless sceptre of womanhood.[34]

The mirror has been permanently affixed to the drawing-room wall; queenliness has become synonymous with true womanhood.

By the time *Sesame and Lilies* and *Middlemarch* were published, of course, queenliness had acquired a different connotation because of one particular real woman: Queen Victoria, who in three decades of rule had epitomized the transformation of sovereign power into domestic influence. Dorothy Thompson nicely articulates one of the central paradoxes of nineteenth-century Britain:

> It is an odd contradiction that in the period in which the doctrine of separate spheres of activity for men and women was most actively developed and propounded, the highest public office in the land was held by a woman.[35]

Although the English throne *is* patrilineal, as Margaret Homans emphasizes, it is important to remember that England has no law equivalent to France's Salic Law, which prohibits women from inheriting the throne, and thus the phenomenon of a Queen Regnant was in fact neither strange nor unknown in the nineteenth century.[36] Indeed, as Thompson points out, England had

> a strong folk memory—perhaps more a mythology—of good times for England under previous women rulers, from Boadicea through Good Queen Bess to Queen Anne.[37]

But Victorian gender ideology did not easily accommodate women as warriors or autocrats, while contemporary politics was increasingly at odds with overt exercises of any form of sovereign control. During the period of *Middlemarch*'s composition and publication, there was a rise in republican and anti-monarchist sentiment, checked in December 1871 by an outpouring of public sympathy and support for the royal family as the Prince of Wales struggled to survive a severe case of typhoid.[38] Not only, then, is the novel set during a period of agitation for democratic reform, but its immediate context was one of political questioning and sensitivity to the implications of sovereignty, complicated by restrictive assumptions about woman's sphere.

Queen Victoria, herself outspokenly opposed to women's rights, recognized the tension between her views ("Let woman be what God intended; a helpmate for a man—but with totally different duties & vocations") and her own situation; in an 1870 letter to Gladstone protesting plans to permit women to study medicine alongside men, she admitted,

> The Queen is a woman herself—& knows what an anomaly her *own* position is:—but that can be reconciled with reason & propriety tho' it is a terribly difficult & trying one.[39]

She achieved the reconciliation between femininity and power, royalty and democracy, by domesticating and privatizing the monarchy.[40] Playing to the hilt the role of devoted wife and mother, and downplaying her participation in state affairs, Victoria invented the version of the British monarchy that survives to the present day, making the queenly ideal of indirect influence rather than active intervention the standard for rulers of either sex. As Walter Bagehot observed in 1867, the power of the monarchy had become obscure, secret, hidden—based on persuasion and suggestion rather than command or direct control.[41] Bagehot also noted the Queen's other chief strategy: "A *family* on the throne is an interesting idea also. It brings down the pride of sovereignty to the level of petty life."[42] As Margaret Homans says, adapting Nancy Armstrong's well-known formulation, "the modern British monarch was first and foremost a woman —to be specific, a wife, and a middle-class one."[43] Modern commentators on the monarchy agree that these changes to the monarchy's image and function have determined the role of the sovereign and her family today. Ilse Hayden, for instance, notes that "the Queen's formal jural power may be limited but . . . her informal influence is enormous"; Hayden credits Victoria and Albert with redefining the monarchy as a moral institution and associating royalty and domesticity. "In a sense," she comments, echoing Bagehot, "they put the Royal Family on the throne."[44] The shift from power to influence, from master or mistress to model, largely explains the current fascination with the personal lives of the royal children; a dysfunctional family on the throne will be unable to fulfill what is now its chief, perhaps only, role, and unless the monarchy can once again adapt, its evolutionary gains will be negated and the species may not survive.

By literalizing this redefinition of queenliness as a middle-class, domestic, private, influential role in the person of Dorothea, Eliot resolves an incoherence that lurks in the volumes by the women historians. While they developed and advocated a theory of history emphasizing undercurrents and "noiseless revolutions" which legitimized their interest in women and feminine concerns, they nonetheless wrote about unmistakably public figures. The image of the privatized queen preserves their vision of woman's potential for moral influence and beneficent activity but accommodates it to their valorization of invisibility and to Eliot's own commitment to representing everyday life.

This shift in focus, from the conspicuous to the hidden, from Saint Theresa to Dorothea, returns us to the question of genre with which I began this study. Consistent application of the feminized historiographical theories which I have argued dominated the Victorian discourse of history requires minute and serious treatment of "unhistoric" lives, lives which thus *become* "historic" in all but one important sense. Though now considered suitable objects of study and representation, and thus "historic" in the sense of possessing historical significance, they remain "unhistoric" in the sense that they have not been documented, made part of the historical record. How, then, to reconstruct the past world made up of these lives? The historical discourse in which Agnes Strickland or Hannah Lawrance sought to participate increasingly defined itself by its commitment to scholarly forms, apparatus, and standards; though they stretched and challenged the boundaries of this discourse in ways that to many severe critics threatened to taint history with the inaccuracy, triviality, and sentimental indulgence of fiction, the women historians remained faithful to its formal requirements. These constraints, however, made it impossible for them to depict any but the widely visible. The harder but also, by their own standards, more important task of representing those who live a hidden life they had to leave to the novelists.

NOTES

1. George Eliot, *Middlemarch: A Study of Provincial Life*, ed. W. J. Harvey (Harmondsworth: Penguin, 1965), p. 580. All further references are given in the text and are to this edition.

2. Prince Charles, *In His Own Words*, p. 99, quoted in Tom Nairn, *The Enchanted Glass: Britain and its Monarchy* (London: Radius, 1988), p. 197.

3. Contemporary reviews emphasizing this aspect of the novel include the *Fortnightly Review* Vol. 19 (January-June 1873), pp. 142-47 and the *British Quarterly Review* Vol. 57 (April 1873), pp. 407-29. Twentieth-century examples include Gillian Beer, *George Eliot* (Bloomington: Indiana UP, 1986) and Alison Booth, *Greatness Engendered: George Eliot and Virginia Woolf* (Ithaca: Cornell UP, 1992).

4. Carlyle, "On History," *A Carlyle Reader*, ed. G. B. Tennyson (Cambridge: Cambridge UP, 1984), pp. 55-66, p. 58; Macaulay, "History," *Lays of Ancient Rome and Miscellaneous Essays and Poems* (London: J. M. Dent & Sons, 1910, rpt. 1963), pp. 1-39, p. 34.

5. *Lives of the Queens of England, from the Norman Conquest*. 12 Volumes. (Philadelphia: Lea & Blanchard, 1848; orig. pub. London: Henry Colburn, 1840-1848.) Vol. 1, p. 25.

6. *The George Eliot Letters*, ed. Gordon S. Haight. 7 Volumes. (New Haven: Yale UP, 1954-78). Vol. 2, p. 396; Vol. IV, p. 425.

7. "Woman in France: Madame de Sablé," in *Selected Critical Writings*, ed. Rosemary Ashton (Oxford: Oxford UP, 1992), pp. 37-68; p. 68.

8. "Silly Novels By Lady Novelists," in *Selected Critical Writings*, pp. 296-321; p. 320.
9. "Silly Novels," p. 320.
10. "Woman in France," pp. 37-8.
11. *Letters*. Vol. IV, pp. 467-8.
12. George Eliot, *Scenes of Clerical Life*, ed. David Lodge (Harmondsworth: Penguin, 1973), p. 54.
13. *Scenes*, pp. 54-55.
14. *Scenes*, p. 81
15. George Eliot, *Adam Bede*, ed. Stephen Gill (Harmondsworth: Penguin, 1980), p. 159.
16. *Scenes*, pp. 99-100.
17. *Adam Bede*, p. 578.
18. *Adam Bede*, p. 72.
19. *Daniel Deronda*, ed. Barbara Hardy (Harmondsworth: Penguin, 1967), p. 723.
20. "'You are not a woman. You may try—but you can never imagine what it is to have a man's force of genius in you, and yet to suffer the slavery of being a girl.'" *Daniel Deronda*, p. 694.
21. The debate about Eliot's "feminism" is ongoing. Dorothea Barrett, in *Vocation and Desire: George Eliot's Heroines* (London: Routledge, 1989), includes an interesting overview and analysis of recent contributions in Chapter 9, "George Eliot and Twentieth-Century Feminist Perspectives" (pp. 175-88).
22. Mrs. F. E. King, *Female Scriptural Characters, exemplifying Female Virtues* (Boston: Wells & Lilly, 1816), pp. 59-60.
23. Mary Hays, *Memoirs of Queens, Illustrious and Celebrated* (London: T. & J. Allman, 1821), p. 93.
24. Anna Jameson, *Lives of Celebrated Female Sovereigns and Illustrious Women*, ed. Mary E. Hewitt (Philadelphia: Porter and Coates, 1870; first published London, Henry Colburn, 1831). Mary Roberts's *Select Female Biography* was also published around the novel's time frame (London: Harvey & Darton, 1829).
25. *Middlemarch*, ed. Gordon S. Haight (Boston: Houghton Mifflin, 1956), p. 612. Eliot removed this passage from subsequent editions, mostly because of objections from critics that it misrepresented the response of Dorothea's family and friends to her first marriage.
26. "Margaret Fuller and Mary Wollstonecraft," *Selected Critical Writings*, pp. 180-86; p. 183.
27. Dorothea Barrett, *Vocation and Desire*, p. 139.

28. See Jerome Beaty, "History By Indirection: The Era of Reform in *Middlemarch*." *Victorian Studies* Vol. 1 (December 1957), pp. 173-79.

29. John Ruskin, "Of Queens' Gardens," in *Sesame and Lilies, The Two Paths, and the King of the Golden River* (London: J. M. Dent & Sons, 1907), pp. 48-79; p. 49.

30. "Of Queens' Gardens," p. 49.

31. "Of Queens' Gardens," p. 58.

32. "Of Queens' Gardens," p. 60.

33. "Of Queens' Gardens," pp. 72-3.

34. "Of Queens' Gardens," p. 74.

35. Dorothy Thompson, *Queen Victoria: Gender and Power*. (London: Virago, 1990), pp. xiv-xv.

36. Margaret Homans, "'To the Queen's Private Apartments': Royal Family Portraiture and the Construction of Victoria's Sovereign Obedience." *Victorian Studies* Vol. 37 No. 1 (Autumn 1993), pp. 1-41; p. 1.

37. *Queen Victoria: Gender and Power*, p. xix.

38. See Thompson, p. 105, and Nairns, *The Enchanted Glass*, pp. 331-34.

39. Philip Guedella, *The Queen and Mr. Gladstone*. 2 Volumes (London: Hodder and Stoughton, Ltd., 1933), Vol. I, p. 228; Vol. I, p. 227.

40. "By presenting herself as a wife, Queen Victoria offered the perfect solution to Britain's fears of female rule and of excessive monarchic power." Margaret Homans, "'To the Queen's Private Apartments,'" p. 3.

41. Walter Bagehot, *The English Constitution* (London: C. A. Watts & Co., Ltd., 1964), pp. 99-100.

42. *The English Constitution*, p. 85.

43. "'To the Queen's Private Apartments'," p. 2.

44. Ilse Hayden, *Symbol and Privilege: The Ritual Context of British Royalty* (Tucson: U of Arizona P, 1987), p. 5, p. 66.

CHAPTER SIX
Mary and Elizabeth
Reconfiguring Gender and Power

> *In front of this great glowing gorgeous canvas, the whole foreground is taken up with the figures of two women—representatives, as it were, of the two halves of the world, who tore that world asunder in their day . . . two haughty shades, with a hundred unsolved questions between them, exciting men's passions and disturbing their judgment, though it is nearly three hundred years since once of them died proudly in the height of her life and genius, and the other in the desolation of royalty and old age.*[1]
>
> *The destiny of the world might seem to hang on the conflict, on the opposing characters and fate of these two wonderful women, Elizabeth of England and Mary of Scotland.*[2]

In Chapter Five I argued that Dorothea Casaubon exemplifies a movement from literal to metaphorical queenliness, a shift which, I suggested, was the chief and perhaps the only available strategy for reconciling female power of the particular kind celebrated by Strickland or Ruskin with dominant beliefs about women's proper place in society. For a queen to be compatible with Victorian gender ideology, she had to be dethroned, placed within a private and domestic rather than a public and political context. However, the resolution Eliot's novel achieves between the discourses of history and femininity, and the model *Middlemarch* offers for representations of female rule, do not obviate the difficulty posed by and for historical (or, for that matter, fictional) treatments of real queens. In Chapter Two I noted that most Victorian women historians define their own work in opposition to "general history," the history of the public sphere, but in making this ideologically and thus strategically crucial distinction they rather disingenuously ignore the truth about their subjects: even a queen consort is a public figure as much as a private one, her personal affairs inseparable from the affairs of state. And while at least a queen consort can, as a wife and mother, be seen as strictly analogous to the metaphorical queen who ruled over the Victorian home, a queen regnant, sovereign in her own right, defies such easy containment within conventional parameters. Unlike the novelist, the historian works within a genre still largely defined by its adherence to fact and thus lacks the option of doing away with such difficulties by inventing a heroine to fit her agenda. Her task is not one of simple transcription, of course, but is, as historical writing always is, accounting for and narrating facts so that they cohere, so that they make sense—and what counts as "making sense" depends heavily on the plots and narrative structures available within a given culture.[3] As I have already argued, the plots and narratives most readily available and widely accepted in the nineteenth century did not include stories of female agency, individuality, or self-determination, at least not expressed through public, political, or military action of the kind associated with sovereign rule.

But narrative forms set limits not to our actual or historical possibilities but to our representations, and they change as they are tested against lived experiences that they cannot accommodate. This study has argued from the beginning that the great revolution in nineteenth-century historical discourse was the uneven, controversial, but inexorable expansion of available ways for understanding and representing history in general and women's history in particular. In previous chapters I have focused on ways writers sought to shape the stories they had to tell to suit, if also to stretch, conventions for talking about women's lives. In this chapter I focus on two stories that proved recalcitrant in this respect—those of Mary, Queen of Scots, and Elizabeth I of England. Agnes Strickland's biographies of Elizabeth, from her series *Lives of the Queens of England*, and of Mary, from her *Lives of the Queens of Scotland*, and Froude's *Reign of Elizabeth*, from his *History of England*, nicely illustrate the complex range of problems facing Victorian writers attempting to tell the stories of these famous rivals or, by extension, of any powerful women.[4] These works expose rather than adapt the ideological constraints within which biographers of powerful women had to work because their subjects are what Mary Poovey has called "border cases": they exist along the fault line between the complexities of real life and the certainties of ideology, in this case the ideology of the separate spheres which so many writers thought should determine the structure of historical as well as social discourse.[5] In the end, the facts of these women's lives did not really matter. Although ostensibly the heated debates about the rival queens focused on actual events during their reigns, the real issue, I argue, was the solution each biographer put forward, implicitly or explicitly, to the problem of women and power and to the difficulty of representing women in history.

Intuitively, the twentieth-century expectation would no doubt be that Elizabeth would have proved more attractive to the Victorians than her cousin. In the first place, she was seen as having defended not just England but the whole cause of Protestantism in Europe against the encroachments of the Catholic powers, an accomplishment exemplified in her navy's victory over Spain's mighty Armada in 1588. Mary, in contrast, was not only a devout Catholic herself but also a member of the Catholic League and a constant conspirator with just those papist powers Elizabeth spent her long reign holding at bay. Elizabeth was famous as the "Virgin Queen"; her highly publicized celibacy, we might think, would have elevated her further in the Victorian imagination by turning her into an icon of just the kind of asexual female purity so widely promoted as an ideal. Again in contrast, Mary Stuart married three times, twice in circumstances which might suggest uncontrolled and indiscriminate passions that, if "womanish," are surely not ladylike; even her first marriage, to the young French Dauphin, can be read as an unsuitable willingness to sacrifice female delicacy to political expedience. Finally, Elizabeth reigned over an era perhaps unrivaled in English history for its glory; she inherited a teetering nation, seething with religious discord and barely recovered from the civil wars of the previous century, and left it economically strong, internationally respected, and brimming with the cultural energy embodied, for us as for the Victorians, in the figure of William Shakespeare. Mary, in comparison, fled a Scotland more politically and religiously divided than it had been when she returned from France to begin her reign, and she died a prisoner, if, arguably, a martyr, officially accused of treachery for plotting against Queen Elizabeth and unofficially presumed guilty of adultery and murder.

But, as Leonée Ormond has pointed out, "for the Victorians, the flawed Mary Queen of Scots was more appealing than the efficient Elizabeth."[6] Aside from mentioning the influence of Scott's *Kenilworth* (1824), Ormond offers no explanation for this prejudice, only evidence of it. I would like to suggest that the rather surprising tendency among Victorian writers to prefer Mary to Elizabeth, even when Mary is the villain rather than the heroine of the text, can be explained by Mary's much greater compatibility with both gender and genre conventions, a phenomenon illustrated by the relative ease with which both Strickland and Froude manipulate her story. In the end, however grand Elizabeth's achievements, she poses so many problems to a would-be narrator that she is almost unrepresentable. For a Victorian, writing Elizabeth as a villain was not really an option, but writing her as a heroine would require redefining all the relevant categories: gender, power, history, and heroism. Ultimately even Froude, her greatest nineteenth-century biographer and advocate, writes her instead into insignificance, so that her seeming glory is just that—seeming—and the course of history and historical narrative can go on as before, while Mary, represented alternately as saint and seductress, martyr and charlatan, is, one way or another, comfortably assimilated.

I

Different as their lives were in the details, Mary and Elizabeth as historical subjects posed similar problems for their would-be narrators. One central issue their biographers faced was the conflict between their roles as queens regnant and their natures as women. Both Strickland and Froude comment again and again on the potential split thus created, constantly presenting "woman" and "queen" as alternative, if not necessarily opposing, identities with a rhetorical ease that reveals how fundamental such a distinction was to their patterns of thinking. "[Elizabeth] . . . forgot the dignity of the queen and the delicacy of the woman," Strickland remarks at one point, later noting regretfully that, in meetings with foreign envoys, "[Elizabeth's] deportment towards them . . . occasionally transgressed both the delicacy of a gentlewoman, and the dignity of a queen" (*Elizabeth*, 179, 620). In her account of one of the many phases of the Queen of England's often bizarre marriage negotiations, Strickland describes "the mighty Elizabeth, laying aside the dignified restraints of the sovereign" and behaving "like a perplexed and circumvented woman as she was" (*Elizabeth,* 286). And when Mary flees from her Scottish captors to what she hopes will be safety and succor in England, Strickland indignantly proclaims that

> [w]omanly sympathy, to say nothing of the duties of hospitality and princely courtesy, rendered it incumbent on a sister Sovereign to supply the royal fugitive with everything of which she stood in need, and that in a manner consistent with the honour of the English crown, and the exalted station Mary had occupied both in France and Scotland. Instead, however, of acting with the munificence of a Queen or the delicacy of a gentlewoman on this occasion, Elizabeth was guilty of the meanness of insulting her royal guest.... (*MQS,* II:97)

In contrast, when investigating the allegations that Mary was romantically involved with the poet Chastelard, Strickland finds "nothing in the reports of any of the ambassadors resident at the Court of Scotland, to justify the belief that Mary Stuart would thus have forgotten the dignity of a Queen, or the decorum of a gentlewoman" (*MQS,* I:140). As the repetitive language in these examples suggests, to her the distinction is both simple and consistent. Froude, though his biases clearly run counter to Strickland's, relies on similar categories. Commenting on Elizabeth's public popularity, he is pleased that "the human character [showed] always through the royal robes, yet with the queenly dignity never so impaired that liberties could be ventured in return" (IV:61). Recording Elizabeth's early reaction to Mary's troubles, Froude notes that

> [her] behaviour at this crisis was more creditable to her heart than to her understanding.... [Y]et she forgot her obvious interest; and her affection and her artifices vanished in resentment and pity. Her indignation as a sovereign was even less than her sorrow for a suffering sister. (II:310).

Both Froude and Strickland thus suggest that their subjects are engaged in a delicate balancing or juggling act. The different stories they ultimately tell about Mary and Elizabeth, as I discuss in more detail below, are shaped by their sense of how (or whether) this conflict of identities can be resolved in each case.

That it is a conflict is made clear by both biographers from the beginning, and both tend to characterize the struggle as one between nature and nurture: both Mary and Elizabeth are taught from childhood that they must deny their feminine instincts in order to behave in a manner appropriate to their situation. Strickland, for instance, describes a meeting between Mary and her mother at which "the young Queen was compelled to restrain the warm gush of filial affection," she tells us, "and, instead of rushing to the maternal embrace, to act the part of the Sovereign" (*MQS*, I:11). "Even in infancy," Strickland explains, "[Mary] had been tutored to enact the character of a Queen whenever she was carried abroad, and to restrain her natural emotions" (*MQS*, I:19). The chief obligation of both women, once anointed queens, is to serve their countries; as Froude points out, "[q]ueens do not reign for their own pleasure," and while "[i]ndividuals may trifle at their foolish will with character or fortune[,] sovereigns, on whom depends the weal of empires, contract duties from their high places, which their private humours cannot excuse them for neglecting" (IV:178). "The weal of empires" versus "private humours": thus succinctly can the crucial conflict be summed up, and the key word "private" reminds us that the two roles, regal and personal, were widely understood to be both distinct and indelibly gender-marked, the border between them the same as that between the separate spheres. Elizabeth might have helped Mary, Froude supposes, "had she been a private person; but as a sovereign she was responsible for the welfare of her country; and the very existence of England and Scotland also was at stake" (II:499), and so her personal wishes, those "sisterly" feelings to which he had attributed her earlier inclination to help Mary out, had to be laid aside if she was successfully to fulfill her obligations as ruler of the nation. "The frequent absences of the reckless partner whom she had in evil hour associated with herself in her regal office," Strickland says of Mary's marriage to Darnley,

> placed Mary in a painful dilemma between her duty to her realm and her respect for him; for either the whole business of the State must come to a dead stop while awaiting the leisure and convenience of the truant boy, or she must treat him as a nullity, by exercising the functions of government without his personal co-operation. With

feminine adroitness, she endeavoured to evade these distressing alternatives. . . . (*MQS*, I:250)

By Strickland's lights, the alternatives are "distressing" because if Mary chooses to tend to the State she must betray the wifely loyalty she owes even a bad husband, but if she neglects her official duties she betrays her realm. "[H]ard indeed must have been [Mary's] task to suppress her tears, and act and speak with the calm composure that beseemed the monarch, while the woman's heart was smarting so sorely," Strickland says sympathetically (*MQS*, I:273). Just as orthodox Victorian beliefs would dictate, success as a ruling sovereign relies on the suppression or abandonment of women's natural instincts and feelings, not to mention duties and responsibilities.

This tidy model, in which "queen" is a public identity while "woman" is a private one, is clearly the easiest way to make sense of these prominent women for a Victorian audience widely accustomed to such distinctions. Applied consistently, it supplies a standard by which their success as sovereigns can be measured in terms of their sacrifice of womanly virtues, or by which their exemplarity as women is a measure of their unfitness to rule. Both Strickland and Froude do, in fact, invoke this double standard as a way of evaluating their subjects, as we will see. However, their efforts to make the equation as simple as standard Victorian gender ideology dictated are constantly frustrated, not least by the facts of history—the facts of these women's lives. Experience does not always fall into neat categories, and clearly as Froude and Strickland want, or imagine, the dividing line to be between public and private, personal and political, their own narratives reveal again and again that, for royal women at least, the personal really *is* political. Nowhere is this uncomfortable truth revealed more clearly than in the endless discussion, in all the texts under consideration here, of courtship and marriage. In Victorian bourgeois society, marriage was not, as it had been in earlier times including the sixteenth century, considered analogous to public institutions, but was rather the central, even the defining, institution of the private sphere. Marriage and domesticity were the alternatives to public life, the comforting zone to which men, weary from their labors in the markets, courts, and halls of power, returned to be soothed and calmed. On marrying, women were expected to withdraw from any business they might have had outside their home and to become "angels in the house," influence their only form of power and that influence severely restricted in its appropriate applications. As feminist theorists have argued for decades, this separation of public and private is in many ways mythical, since there is no action, however intimate, that cannot be seen as entangled to some degree in political questions or power relationships. Such an interpretation of private life was antithetical to standard Victorian views, grounded as they were in the ideology of the separate spheres, and much Victorian literature is structured around this division of the world into complementary halves, including those works that ultimately question or criticize this model. But both Froude's and Strickland's biographies end up, almost certainly against their own intentions or expectations, emphasizing the flimsiness of this distinction and, in the process, if only by indirection and implication, making nonsense of the separation of the world into the gendered arenas which formed the basis of so much Victorian social and political thought.

In the first place, from the moment Mary and Elizabeth acceded to their thrones, their marriages became a, sometimes *the*, central political question for them and, even more strikingly, for their councilors. Never at any point in her life could either woman forget that her matrimonial decisions were anything but personal ones. When both were still infants, they were already seen as pawns on a complex international chessboard:

> King Henry [VIII] offered [Elizabeth's] hand to the Earl of Arran for his son, in order to win his co-operation in his darling project of uniting the crowns of England and Scotland by a marriage between the infant queen, Mary Stuart, and his son Prince Edward. (Strickland, *Elizabeth*, 14)

Early in Elizabeth's reign, her parliament's first step,

> after the choice of a speaker, was to petition the queen to marry; this, indeed, appeared the only means of averting the long and bloody successive wars, with which, according to human probability, the rival claims of the female descendants of Henry VII threatened the

nation, in the event of Elizabeth dying without lawful issue of her own. (Strickland, *Elizabeth*, 191)

At one point, Froude recounts, Elizabeth received a direct petition from her council:

> After grateful acknowledgments of the general government of the queen the two Houses desired, first, to express their wish that her highness would be pleased to marry 'where it should please her, with whom it should please her, and as soon as it should please her.' (II:101-102)

Queen Mary "met her nobles in her Parliament Hall in Stirling Castle, on the 15th of May, and signified her intention of contracting matrimony with her cousin Henry, Lord Darnley" (Strickland, *MQS*, I:205). Such intermingling of affairs of the heart with affairs of state was necessary, of course, because royal marriages affected not only domestic stability by promising dynastic continuity but also the international balance of power by creating new political alliances based on family ties. The possibility of Elizabeth's marriage with the Duke of Anjou, for instance, preoccupied her, her ministers, and most European powers for months. "Could the marriage have been arranged," Froude explains,

> an aggressive league with this object [the division of the Low Countries between France and England] would have unquestionably followed between England, France, and the German Protestant states; and a European revolution would have been the inevitable consequence. Without the marriage, it was doubtful whether either of the contracting powers would have sufficient confidence in the other to risk a breach with Spain. (III:295-6)

Strickland reports that Eric of Sweden's wooing of Mary

> was jealously regarded by Elizabeth, on account of his previous pretensions to herself, and also because the naval power of Sweden, united with Scotland, might have rendered Mary too formidable a neighbour. (*MQS*, I:119)

Similarly,

> On the subject of Mary's marriage with Bothwell, Elizabeth expressed herself with great severity, not only on account of its appearing an outrage against every proper feeling, but because she anticipated that an immediate league between the new consort of the Scottish queen and France would be the result. (*Elizabeth*, 235)

And by "entertaining the matrimonial overtures" directed her way from France, Elizabeth was later able to "[disarm] every direct hostile attempt that might otherwise have been made in favour of her royal prisoner, Mary Stuart" (Strickland, *Elizabeth*, 291-2). Parliaments and politics are supposedly the stuff of which "general history" is made, but the inseparability of the putatively "private" question of marriage from such large public questions in these accounts undermines the theory according to which, as we saw in Chapter Two, the women historians distinguished their modest, personal, biographical projects from that more grandiose and masculine enterprise. If the "well-being of [her] people ... hung on the thread of [Elizabeth's] single life" (Froude I:344), to which province of history do Elizabeth's marriage plans belong?

Maternity as much as matrimony was charged with public, political significance in these women's lives. Most of the interest in Elizabeth's possible marriage came from her subjects' wish that she give them an heir to secure the country's future against the civil strife attendant on a disputed succession, as she herself, according to Strickland, well knew:

> The twelfth year of Elizabeth's reign being now completed, the anniversary of her accession was celebrated as a general festival throughout her dominions. The aspect of public affairs was, however, still gloomy, the unsettled state of the succession was more alarming to the nation than ever, and Elizabeth herself began to consider, that the only chance of putting an end to the plots and intrigues of the partisans of Mary Stuart, would be the birth of heirs of her own. (*Elizabeth*, 272)

Whatever her other problems or failings, Mary Stuart gave *her* realm an heir, an event described in both Strickland's and Froude's account as pivotal, not in the context of her personal life, but in the context of national and international affairs. "On the 19th of June, in Edinburgh Castle," Froude relates,

> between nine and ten in the morning was born James Stuart, heir presumptive to the united crowns of England and Scotland. Better worth to Mary Stuart's ambition was this child than all the legions of Spain and all the money of the Vatican; the cradle in which he lay, to the fevered and anxious glance of English politicians, was as a Pharos behind which lay the calm waters of an undisturbed succession and the perpetual union of the too long divided realms. Here if the occasion was rightly used lay the cure for a thousand evils; where all differences might be forgotten, all feuds be laid at rest, and the political fortunes of Great Britain be started afresh on a newer and brighter career. (II:81)

Less flamboyantly, but with her eye turning just as rapidly from the baby's cradle to his regal future, Strickland comments that "Mary Stuart, on the 19th of June, had given birth to a son, who was one day to unite the Britannic Isles in one peaceful and glorious empire" (*Elizabeth*, 221). In neither case is there any hint of conflict between little James's gender identity and his destiny—because neither Strickland nor Froude imagines any discrepancy between masculinity and sovereignty. The solution to the confusion and turmoil created by Mary and Elizabeth—politically in the sixteenth century, ideologically and rhetorically in the nineteenth—is, apparently, a male heir who can restore order and comprehensibility.

Of course, royal marriages had always been and would continue to be political, rather than personal, transactions, for male monarchs as well as female, and marriage for any sovereign is desirable because it produces legitimate heirs to stabilize the nation's power structure; the blurring of boundaries I have been describing occurs in any attempt to treat the life of a public personality, not just in biographies of royal women. But in the most common scenario, wives are the requisite accessory to this politicization of matrimony, not the determining agents; they are sought after, rather than seeking, their soft touch and benevolent influence complementary, as we saw in Chapter Two, to the king's royal, masculine authority. The situation is very different when the wife herself brings agency and power to the relationship from the outset; it differs even more from the conventional Victorian model of courtship when every detail of each prospective match is part of extensive, and highly publicized, negotiations at the highest level of government. Such cases, because they reverse the expected roles and patterns and so defy containment by analogy to bourgeois practice, expose otherwise unquestioned norms as constructions affected by history—and so subject to challenges and change. The continuing emphasis on the queens' matrimonial prospects and the overt concern that they not only wed but bed their husbands in order to provide their countries with heirs meant, both in the sixteenth century, through parliamentary and other debates, and in the nineteenth, through these biographical volumes, a very public focus on the aspects of their life that ought, by Victorian standards, to have been most private. Froude says, with remarkable frankness, about the extended negotiations for Elizabeth's marriage with the Duc d'Alençon, that "nothing but the candle being out and the happy pair established together behind the bed-curtains would be really conclusive" (IV:351); clearly another set of standards is operating here than that which governed ordinary polite conversation about men and women in the mid-1800s. This continuing violation of female modesty coupled with the absence of any apology for it by either Strickland or Froude highlights the arbitrariness of the standards usually applied and suggests that in the genre within which they were working, one bound by fact, if shaped by interpretation, the spheres were not easily or accurately separated, at least not along gendered lines.

II

As biographical subjects, then, Mary and Elizabeth both posed significant problems for the Victorians, because their identities and experiences as women and sovereigns highlighted the inadequacy of standard Victorian categories for discussing the complexities of historical experience. While their stories have in common the basic conflict between their supposedly natural womanly roles and their obligations as sovereigns, as well as the awkward politicization of their private lives, however, Froude and Strickland tell very different narratives about them in attempting to make sense of or resolve these difficulties. Looking first at their accounts of Mary's life, we can see immediately that for both authors she is always at least as much woman as queen. As Froude sums it up, in a telling comparison,

> Elizabeth forgot the woman in the queen, and after her first mortification about Leicester preserved little of her sex but its caprices. Mary Stuart when under the spell of an absorbing inclination could fling her crown into the dust and be woman all. (II:73)

This notion of Mary as "woman all" is an assessment of Mary's character shared by Froude and Strickland but one which has different implications for each of them. Both would agree with the majority of their nineteenth-century readers that to be "woman all" means to be ruled by one's heart, rather than one's head; to be loving, emotional, perhaps even irrational, rather than calculating and dispassionate; to be loyal first to one's family and friends and only second to an abstraction such as a nation or an abstract ideal such as justice. But are such feminine qualities virtues or vices in a ruling monarch? In Strickland's account, they are clearly virtues. Strickland's Mary is benevolent and compassionate, exercising her benign influence in the cause of civilization, religious tolerance, and political harmony just as the queenly ideal dictated she should. Even her first marriage, political alliance though it is, becomes a love match, as is her marriage to Darnley, so in contrast to Elizabeth Mary is never really in the position of trading intimacy for foreign policy; further, as Strickland tells it, she is raped by Bothwell and then forced to marry him, and so not only is her feminine vulnerability confirmed but also she is saved, despite her three marriages, from charges of promiscuity. Mary's imprisonment and execution result from her betrayal by those, including Elizabeth, who follow only political imperatives: her womanly instincts—to trust, to share, to conciliate—make her vulnerable to their schemes and so, ultimately, a martyr not just to Catholicism but to femininity. "Many of her troubles," as Strickland puts it,

> resulted from the unguarded frankness of her character.... True woman, proud and quick to take offence, but quickly mollified, her great weakness was the excess of charity which inclined her not only to forgive, but to believe and trust those who had injured her, and those whose interest it was to deceive and circumvent her. (*MQS*, II:130)

"[T]rue to the sweet and holy instincts of her nature and her sex," Strickland tells us elsewhere, "[Mary] had ever been more ready to pardon than [Darnley] to sin against her—had been only too happy to play the sweet office of a conjugal nurse once more, when she found him languishing for her presence, and willing to resign himself to her care and gentle guidance" (*MQS*, I:390). Strickland's Mary, then, exemplifies the queenly tradition I have outlined in previous chapters, and within this tradition her thoroughgoing femininity is not a problem for her sovereignty but rather the surest guarantee of her fitness to wear a crown.

Mary's exemplarity is explicit in the vocabulary Strickland uses to describe her. On the day of her marriage to the French Dauphin, she appears to everyone as "well fitted to realize the *beau ideal* of a regal bride" (*MQS*, I:29), and during her young husband's fatal illness she is recognized as "the angel of his life" (*MQS*, I:51). When she returns to her native land, "the Scotch were proud of possessing a Queen who was the most beautiful and perfect among ladies of that age" (*MQS*, I:85), and when she appears publicly before her subjects she exhibits "the full perfection of womanly grace and stature" (*MQS*, I:143). Even after the crises of her marriage to Darnley and the murder of her Italian secretary, David Rizzio, Mary is "the idol of her subjects,"

> to whom the fears of losing her, during her late dangerous illness, had shown her value; while her popular and generous demeanour, when she came among them again in her beauty and regal splendour, with the blooming heir she had given to Scotland in her arms, endeared her more than ever to their hearts. (*MQS*, I:363)

By Strickland's account, she is "the loveliest, the most intellectual and liberal-minded Princess in the world, as well as the most clement" (*MQS*, II:220); the string of superlatives comes as no surprise late in the second of two volumes in which Mary's excellence is the constant refrain.

Her perfection manifests itself in ways familiar by now as the ideals of queenly behavior. Her leading characteristics are "benevolence and feminine compassion" (*MQS*, I:244), and her priorities as sovereign of Scotland are peacemaking and civilizing projects, like those cited over and over as the greatest accomplishments of other royal women, which she, like them, will bring about by her benign influence rather than by direct intervention. "Her great desire," Strickland says, "was to render her realm, which had suffered so many miseries during her long minority and absence from the seat of government, peaceful and prosperous under her gentle sway" (*MQS*, I:95-96); she was a "peace-maker by nature, and a peace sovereign by principle" (*MQS*, I:334). During the years of her widowhood, before her marriage to Darnley, "she had won the esteem and love of her people":

> her gentle sway and refining influence had been blessed to Scotland. She had loosed the bonds of the prisoners, and considered the low estate of the poor, in providing officers to distribute her alms to the needy, and advocates to plead the cause of those who had wrong. She had established peace in her borders, and commercial relations with all the nations in the world. (*MQS*, I:201-2)

Her regime of gentle suasion and guidance is so effective that it discourages her subjects from plotting against her:

> The great body of her people were too sensible of the reality of these blessings to desire to exchange the gentle sway of their liege lady for the yoke of the selfish oligarchy then striving to obtain the mastery over their rightful Sovereign by means of English gold. (*MQS*, I:239)

According to Strickland, by the time Mary loses her hold on Scotland she has nearly achieved a revolution, bringing a formerly backward country into a more enlightened state, and all without once overstepping the bounds of her gender:

> [Mary] had healed the wounds and remedied the miseries which nineteen years of war, foreign and internal, had inflicted on that unhappy country. She had employed her gentle influence, as woman should, in reconciling feuds, and teaching vindictive and hereditary foes to learn from her own example the duty of forgiveness. Law reforms of an important nature, and beneficial to all classes, especially to the poor, had been effected under her jurisdiction. She had laboured to mollify the persecuting spirit of the times. . . . She had studied to promote those arts and manufactures, which not only

gave refinement and grace to a hitherto barbarous state of society, but enabled the people to provide for the wants of life. (*MQS*, II:26)

"As woman should": again, although Mary's work as a monarch is Strickland's ostensible focus here, her identity as exemplary woman directs and defines Strickland's interpretation of her actions.

To bolster her claims for Mary's exemplary status, and to secure her within the ranks of the womanly despite her crown, Strickland persistently emphasizes Mary's skill at "the feminine accomplishment of tapestry and embroidery" (*MQS*, I:7), which, as I discussed in Chapter Three, was seen by the Victorians as the quintessential womanly art. Needlework, by Strickland's account, served two important functions for Mary. In the first place, it worked as a means of asserting her gender even as she stepped outside her proper sphere—while sitting in Council with her ministers, she brought her needlework with her:

> Mary sat daily in Council several hours, in deliberation with her ministers and advisers; but, while thus occupied, she employed her hands with her needle—a little table of sandal-wood, with her work-basket and implements of industry, being always placed by her chair of state. Every rightly constituted mind must appreciate this characteristic trait of feminine propriety in a young female Sovereign, whom duty compelled to take the presiding place in a male assembly.... [S]he took refuge from encountering the gaze of so many gentlemen by bending her eyes on her embroidery, or whatever work she was engaged in. She entered the Council chamber in her regal capacity, but she never forgot the delicacy of her sex while there. (*MQS*, I:96)

Needlework enables Mary to walk the fine line between her competing identities by giving her tangible proof of her femininity to carry with her into the public arena, a self-effacing gesture that protects her from, though it does not entirely eliminate, the risks of this movement across gendered boundaries. In this respect, needlework serves much the same purpose for her as the women biographers' rhetorical gestures towards feminine propriety (such as their conspicuous deference to "historians") do for them: while seeming to endorse conventional hierarchies, including those of both gender and genre, they, like Mary, proceed quite openly into the very territory they seem to be ceding.

One reason Mary proves so amenable to Strickland's interpretation of her as the "*beau ideal*" of queenliness, however, is that the time she spent actually in this delicate position was relatively short; less than a decade after her return to Scotland as queen regnant, she was imprisoned, her potential power and agency subject to physical rather than ideological limits. Like the Lady of Shalott's tower in Tennyson's poem, the walls of Mary's many prisons literalize the constraints of Victorian gender ideology; like the Lady herself, Mary finds consolation for her confinement by applying herself to the one creative and emotional outlet left to her, appropriately, in both cases, a form of "woman's work." Needlework proved a great "solace to her in her house of bondage," Strickland tells us (*MQS*, I:12), and again, "the favourite occupation with which the royal captive beguiled the tedium of her prison hours, was the composition of devices for pictorial needle-work, in which she greatly excelled" (*MQS*, II:48). Discussing Mary's stoicism during her nineteen-year captivity, Strickland poses a rhetorical question: "How is it that women support calamities with greater fortitude than men?" "Men," she concludes,

> give themselves up to morbid melancholy, brooding incessantly over their troubles: women divert their thoughts from dwelling exclusively on subjects of a painful nature, by employing their fingers in the sedative occupation of needlework. The salutary effect of sewing, knitting, and embroidering in calming the nerves of female patients is constantly proved in lunatic asylums. Mary Stuart probably preserved her overcharged heart from breaking, and her brain from frenzied excitement, by occupying those hands which had been accustomed to wield the sceptre and grasp the orb of empire, in composing and tracing with the needle allegorical illustrations of her misfortunes. (*MQS*, II:214)

It is not precisely that women's greater patience and natural serenity enable them to labor over such painstaking and tedious work without tiring, as was commonly supposed, but that feminine instincts and women's work are reciprocally supportive, the latter requiring and thus reinforcing the former. Mary's excellence at needlework, then, which Strickland emphasizes from the first pages of her biography, not only indicates but also protects her exemplarity. Further, once this logic is accepted, it becomes further evidence for Strickland's belief in Mary's utter innocence of any moral or political wrongdoing, as it is here when Strickland discusses the Babington plot:

> [W]e find [Mary], on the 18th of July, the very day after the letter to Babington was despatched, calmly employing herself in looking over her numerous pieces of embroidery and pictorial needlework, finished and unfinished, in the charge of Mademoiselle Beauregard, and superintending the classing and drawing up a curious descriptive inventory of these specimens of feminine taste and industry, which was made in her presence.... A woman whose pastimes and propensities took so elegant and innocent a turn, was unlikely to have embarked in projects of a bloody and barbarous nature, which emanate from restless minds, unaccustomed to the peaceful and sedative labours of the needle. (*MQS*, II:408)

It is simply unthinkable, Strickland would have us conclude, that a woman could be involved in both tapestries and conspiracies. Of course, to make this point she has to skim quickly over the work Mary in fact did with her needle, which occasionally included, as she admits in passing, using it to substitute for a pen, depicting "with skilful needle... the story of her wrongs, and the relentless malice of her powerful foe," "composing and tracing with the needle allegorical illustrations of her misfortunes" (*MQS*, II:49, II:214). Such substitutions of needle for pen, as we saw in Chapter Three with Matilda of Flanders, were, like so many other aspects of these women's lives (and these women's texts), double-edged: Mary is appropriating the authority of a chronicler by telling her own story, as Matilda, in Stone's and Strickland's accounts, took on herself the responsibility and the privilege of telling William the Conqueror's, but both women decline the masculine implement in favor of their own "pliant instrument."[7] Perhaps because this ambiguous relationship to writing and authority raises too many of the ideological problems solved, for Strickland, by Mary's imprisonment, Strickland does not dwell on the details of Mary's needlework, though she seems never to miss an opportunity to document its making.

Strickland also establishes Mary's true identity as

unproblematically feminine—and unquestionably exemplary—by emphasizing her membership in a community of virtuous women. Mary herself always, we learn, treated other women with respect. "[N]o instance of ill-nature, envy, or tyranny towards her own sex, has ever been recorded of [her]" (*MQS*, I:150), and again,

> Not one instance of unkindness, or even discourtesy, to the ladies of her Court or household, has ever been cited against her. Dearly did they love her in her prosperity, fondly and faithfully did they cleave to her in the dark days when she was a throneless captive. The earnest applications from members of the female aristocracy of Scotland for leave to pass into England and wait upon her in prison, are sufficient evidence of the estimation in which she was held by those who had had the best opportunities of personal knowledge of her manners and characteristics. (*MQS*, II:181)

The unswerving loyalty of Mary's female attendants through even her darkest days indeed becomes, like references to her embroidery, a leitmotif of Strickland's text, and one serving a very similar purpose. "Mary was attended by noble Scotch gentlewomen in the days of her royal splendour," Strickland notes on the very first page of her biography;

> they clave to her in adversity, through good report and evil report; they shared her prisons, they waited upon her on the scaffold, and forsook not her tangled remains till they had seen them consigned to a long denied tomb. Are such friendships usual among the wicked? Is the companionship of virtuous women acceptable to the dissolute?— or that of the dissolute to the virtuous? (*MQS*, I:1)

These rhetorical questions prompt us to follow the same logical path as Strickland's accounts of Mary's needlework: this fact of Mary's life is incompatible with the allegations against her, and so the allegations must be false. And what further proof could be called for? After all, Strickland argues,

> If Mary's conduct, either as the wife or widow of Darnley, had been in the slightest degree culpable, female testimony to that effect would not have been lacking; it never is on such occasions. But to the

honour of womanhood be it repeated, that not one person of her own
sex, from the wives of the Regents Moray and Mar down to the
humblest serving-maid in any of her palaces, could be induced to
corroborate the slanders of her successful foes, by deposing a word to
her disadvantage. (*MQS*, I:439)

Strickland's defense relies on the safe assumption that most of her
readers will, like her, be committed to a theory of womanhood by
which such affectionate loyalty would, indeed, be unthinkable if Mary
were guilty as charged. Other women might in that case have given her
their sympathy, their help, or their charity, but not their love, and they
certainly would not have lied to protect her. The fact that "we never
find her deserted by her own sex under any circumstances" (*MQS* II:79-
80), not, "even in [the] most direful climax of her misery, . . . deserted
by the high and excellent of her own sex" (*MQS*, II:13), that "[w]ith the
exceptions of Queen Elizabeth, Catherine de Medicis, and the Countess
of Shrewsbury [all harsh, powerful, and unwomanly women], Mary had
no female enemies" (*MQS* I:1), testifies to her acceptance within a
sisterhood governed by strict moral codes, those dictated, as Victorian
gender ideology would have it, by nature. By implication, the faith of
nineteenth-century women readers in Mary's innocence is a test of their
own allegiance to this ideology and their own adherence to these codes,
for to persist in doubting her becomes equivalent to doubting women's
ability to discern and repudiate depravity among their own kind, from
which it is only a few small steps to rejecting the whole doctrine of the
separate spheres.

In the end, Strickland's picture of Mary is one in which her two
identities, sovereign and woman, become a single harmonious one
corresponding to what I have been calling the "queenly ideal."
Absolute power is, indeed, not compatible with true femininity, but in
every aspect of her life and reign Strickland's Mary converts her regal
authority into womanly influence, her public role into one consistent
with her private inclinations. The world would be a better place, we are
left to conclude, if such beneficent rule really were feasible, as under
such "gentle sway" we would soon be led to a kinder, more civilized
future—as Scotland was during the first years following Mary's return
from France. But the world's progress lags behind this enlightened
ideal, and so the game is won by those who play by different, harsher,

more masculine rules. For all that Strickland idealizes Mary, then, her account of her ultimately, and not surprisingly, confirms the basic premise of the other biographies of royal women I have examined in this study: women—*real* women—make better queens consort than queens regnant, for survival in the man's world of politics and the public sphere means suppressing one's true nature and becoming more the queen than the woman, something Strickland's Mary never even considers. Strickland leaves us with the image of Mary's effigy in Westminster Abbey:

> Nothing can be more graceful and majestic than the form, or more lovely and intellectual than the face, which indicates every noble and benevolent quality that could adorn the character of queen or woman—such, indeed, as a careful investigation of her personal history from authentic and documentary sources of information, proves that she possessed. (*MQS*, II:466)

"Of queen or woman": the opposition is gone, the identities reconciled, the qualities indicating perfection in one the same as those indicating it in the other. Strickland has found, in the facts which, she prided herself, were the sole basis of her conclusions, confirmation of this possibility reflected in the mirror of history, a genuine embodiment of the queenly women she and her female contemporaries were supposed to see when they looked into the mirrors on their own drawing room walls.

To Froude, being "woman all" meant something rather different. Froude's Mary comes not out of the pages of a conduct book but out of a sensation novel: while Froude admits and even admires her daring, her cleverness, her courage, and her beauty, ultimately he wants his readers to recognize these manifold attractions as snares for the unwary, a pretty cloak over a scheming woman driven by lust, passion, jealousy, and ambition. Like the title character in Mary Elizabeth Braddon's *Lady Audley's Secret* (1861), Froude's Mary is a brilliant actress; like Braddon's protagonist Robert Audley, Froude plays historical detective and, with the data he accumulates, destroys his prey's credibility and constructs a narrative of the "true" story of the woman behind the mask. During the skirmishes that followed Mary's marriage to Bothwell, Mary appears "in a short jacket with a red petticoat which scarcely reached below her knees, the royal dignity laid aside with the royal costume—but once more herself in her own free fierce nature, full of fire and fury" (II:279-80); in this brief but typical description, in which he emphasizes the discontinuity between her theatrical posing and her true self, the excess of alliteration reveals both his appreciation of her almost satanic stature and his pleasure in containing her powers with his own masterful rhetoric. Froude's Mary is "woman all" because she is emotional, passionate, self-centered, and unable to suppress these qualities in service of her public duties:

> Here lay the vital difference of character between the Queen of Scots and her great rival, and here was the secret of the difference of their fortunes. In intellectual gifts Mary Stuart was at least Elizabeth's equal; and Anne Boleyn's daughter, as she said herself, was 'no angel.' But Elizabeth could feel like a man an unselfish interest in a great cause; Mary Stuart was ever her own centre of hope, fear, or interest; she thought of nothing, cared for nothing, except as linked with the gratification of some ambition, some desire, some humour of her own; and thus Elizabeth was able to overcome temptations before which Mary fell. (I:251-2)

Strickland ultimately praises Mary for never sacrificing her true nature to a role thrust upon her by circumstance. Froude too sees her always more "woman" than "queen," but to him this triumph of femininity over sovereignty has no redeeming features; rather, the combination of regal power with womanly vices threatens with potential catastrophe not just two nations but the whole course of the Reformation in Europe.

Perhaps out of deference to the legions of Mary Stuart's nineteenth-century admirers, Froude does not simply paint her as a villainess. "Whatever credit is due to iron fortitude and intellectual address," he says at one point, "must be given without stint to this extraordinary woman" (II:67), and such admiring remarks appear in regular counterpoint to his more damning indictments. Mary combines in herself "many noticeable qualities":

> Though luxurious in her ordinary habits, she could share in the hard field life of the huntsman or the soldier with graceful cheerfulness; she had vigour, energy, tenacity of purpose, with perfect and never-failing self-possession; and as the one indispensable foundation for

the effective use of all other qualities, she had indomitable courage.... (I:251)

She was "never false to her friends, and stood through good and evil by those who risked their lives to serve her" (V:247). But these strengths of character, impressive as they are even to Froude, are only the tip of what Froude portrays as a deep and dangerous iceberg. His Mary has no share in "the deeper and nobler emotions" (I:252); she uses her substantial gifts only in service of her own selfish interests:

> Philip cared sincerely for Romanism, Elizabeth cared for English liberty, the Earl of Murray cared for the doctrines of the Reformation; Mary Stuart was chiefly interested in herself and she was without the strength of self-command which is taught only by devotion to a cause. (II:15)

His concessions to her beauty and accomplishments, then, are only a means for him to introduce his real estimation of her as a consummate performer. At intervals she reveals her true self, as when, "weary of the mask which she had so long worn," she determines "to marry Darnley and dare the worst which Elizabeth could do" (I:478), but the very moments at which, in Strickland's account, Mary appears at her most heroic show her, in Froude's account, at her most deceitful. The enlightened attitudes for which Strickland heaps praise upon Mary are entirely discounted by Froude as moves in Mary's political game: "[a] Catholic sovereign sincerely pleading to a Protestant assembly for liberty of conscience," he says, for instance, "might have been a lesson to the bigotry of mankind; but Mary Stuart was not sincere" (II:7). As the imminence of her death becomes more and more a certainty, she is

> determined that, if die she must, she would give her death the character of a martyrdom.... From this moment all her efforts were directed to making her Romanism as conspicuous as possible, and to enforcing upon every one that she was to die in the cause of the faith. (V:301)

Somewhat callously, Froude finds even in this scenario an opportunity for a double-edged compliment: "it would be affectation to credit her with a genuine feeling of religion," he says, "but the imperfection of her motive exalts the greatness of her fortitude. To an impassioned believer death is comparatively easy" (V:315). In a strategically similar and even more rhetorically impressive passage about her involvement in Darnley's death, he exclaims,

> [W]e are called upon to believe that the queen, the arch-plotter of Europe, the match in intellect for the shrewdest of European statesmen, was the one person in Scotland who had no suspicion of his guilt, and was the victim of her own guileless innocence. Victim she was, fooled by the thick-limbed scoundrel whom she had chosen for her paramour, duped by her own passions, which had dragged her down to the level of a brute. But the men were never born who could have so deceived Mary Stuart, and it was she herself who had sacrificed her own noble nature on the foul altar of sensuality and lust. (II:251)

In both examples he gives with one hand even as he takes away with the other, admitting her impressive courage and intelligence only to find in them the proof of her villainy—paradoxically, to be innocent she would, he argues, have had to be lesser.

Froude's Mary conceals beneath her dazzling surface the guile and ruthlessness of a wild animal:

> sleeping behind that grace of form and charm of manner lay a spirit which no misfortune could tame—a nature like a panther's, merciless and beautiful—and along with it every dexterous art by which women can outwit the coarser intellects of men. (II:63)

His recurrent animal metaphors invoke the familiar flip side of the Victorian idealization of womanhood, the conviction that the alternative to the angel in the house is a demonic figure of ungovernable urges, unfathomable designs, and limitless cunning. Mary's contemporaries, Froude asserts, easily saw through her façade: "In their eyes, the gentle sufferer of modern sentimentalism was a trapped wild cat, who if the cage was opened would fix claw and fang into their throats" (II:309). After her flight to England, the beautiful and interesting sufferer was manifestly a dangerous animal which had run into a trap, difficult to keep, yet not to be allowed to go abroad until her teeth were drawn and her claws pared to the quick. (II:385)

And during her years of captivity in England she continues the charade of artless innocence, but without deceiving either her captors or her historian:

> She was the old Mary Stuart still, the same bold, restless, unscrupulous, ambitious woman, and burning with the same passions, among which revenge stood out predominant. Hers was the panther's nature—graceful, beautiful, malignant, and untamable. (V:258)

The association of her with wild cats summons up a long chain of familiar negative connotations for such feline femininity, including predatoriness of a specifically sexual kind. By such sideways devices Froude turns Mary's very strengths against her so that her intelligence and courage become craftiness and audacity, her beauty camouflage. He sustains the common link between womanliness and nature, but his nature is "red in tooth and claw," and his Mary exemplifies its dark, rather than its pure, possibilities.

For all his conspicuous hostility toward her, Froude is clearly comfortable with Mary, able as easily as Strickland to fit her into a preconceived narrative pattern. Strickland's account of Mary's life is essentially tragic, but Froude explicitly rejects that familiar model for another more consistent with his emphasis on her artifice and theatricality: melodrama. Her history is frequently marked, he comments early on, by "strange adventures" which give it "the interest—not perhaps of tragedy, for she was selfish in her politics and sensual in her passions—but of some high-wrought melodrama" (I:345). Summarizing Mary's career, he casts her as "the heroine of an adulterous melodrame [sic]": "[h]er husband was murdered, and she married the murderer. Her subjects took arms, dethroned, imprisoned, and intended to send her to the scaffold" (V:256). These last remarks occur under the running head "Mary's Character Unchanged"; in her continuity as such a figure is his strength as a narrator, for he has no tricky maneuvers to perform, no rhetorical sleight-of-hand to do in order to sustain his characterization. Unlike Elizabeth, who, as we'll see below, causes all sorts of confusion for both him and Strickland, Mary conforms to, or is easily contained by, modes of framing and discussing a woman's life readily available to him and comprehensible to his audience.

Froude clearly expected that this audience would recoil from his rather lurid portrait of the unfortunate queen, however carefully he adapted it to their generic expectations. His remarks about how Mary's story was passed down to and received by posterity suggest that he, like Strickland, hoped to direct his readers' responses by alerting them to how different reactions to it reflect on the readers themselves. In particular, he is impatient with the romantic views of her popular in the nineteenth century, presumably exemplified by works such as Strickland's, although, oddly, he never once refers directly to her biography. "The evidence [about Mary's complicity in Darnley's death]," he says bluntly, "is neither conflicting nor insufficient . . . but the later sufferings of Mary Stuart have surrounded her name with an atmosphere of tenderness, and half the world has preferred to believe that she was the innocent victim of a hideous conspiracy" (II:129). Casting such beliefs as irresponsible concessions to emotion, rather than rational responses to the evidence, marks them as at once foolish and typically feminine, an implication reinforced by his attributing such errors of judgment to only "half the world." While Strickland encouraged women's loyalty to Mary as a gesture of community and shared values, Froude roundly condemns such partiality and, significantly, implies that it is profoundly anti-historical, as it means neglecting facts, "evidence," for feelings—a gendered division of territory that, rhetorically, once more expels women from the historian's turf. Of course, it was not *just* women who believed in Mary's innocence, and Froude does not let her masculine admirers off without admonition. "The hardihood of Mary Stuart's advocates has grown with time," he comments;

> The Catholics made her innocence an article of faith. Under the Stuarts it became an article of loyalty. Through religious and political tradition it has been passed on to the spurious chivalry of modern times, which assumes that she could not have been wicked because she was beautiful and a queen. (II:496)

Like the women who sentimentalize her plight, the men who flock to her standard out of chivalrous impulses are responding, not objectively to the facts, but emotionally to an idealized image and a model of queenly behavior to which, as Froude is at pains in all of his comments to point out, Mary conformed only superficially. All of these modern supporters are fighting a rearguard action against not just common sense but historical progress, for, as Froude points out about Mary's sixteenth-century champions, they manifest "a blind, passionate, devoted loyalty, appealing to the impetuous instincts of generosity and heroism," while their opponents show "the unromantic intelligence of a people whose history was beginning, and in whose veins instead of noble blood was running the fierce fever of Calvinism" (II:368). Her contemporaries had, in his view, few excuses for their misguided behavior, however instinctive or generous, but how much more to blame are those who after the passage of three centuries persist in upholding such a reactionary cause! Mary herself had trusted, Froude says, to her own eloquent defenses of herself, believing "that her pathetic and passionate words would pass at all times for current coin" (III:340). Her advocates among his Victorian audience have only, like so many before them, fallen victim to her seductive charm.

III

While they are clearly at odds with each other, Strickland's and Froude's narratives of Mary Stuart's life are each internally consistent, with Strickland casting her unequivocally as a queenly ideal and Froude characterizing her throughout as a scheming deceiver. Both versions are also, I have suggested, consistent with Froude's statement that at heart Mary was "woman all," with the differences in their interpretations turning on their basic understanding of what such a gendered identity might be. In contrast to these conflicting pictures of Mary, their portraits of Elizabeth are strikingly similar, although Froude tends to be more forgiving of her faults and to offer more excuses for her behavior than Strickland does. More than Mary's, Elizabeth's life story defies conventions, particularly gender-specific ones, and in their efforts to make its various events comprehensible, both writers try out different ways of emplotting them and characterizing her. Elizabeth herself famously tried to have her sex and renounce it too, as indicated by her oft-quoted speech to her troops at

Tilbury before the defeat of the Armada: "'I know I have the body of a weak, feeble woman,'" she told them, "'but I have the heart and stomach of a king—and of a King of England too'" (Strickland, *Elizabeth*, 531). Froude and Strickland sometimes emulate this strategy, rejecting her feminine identity in favor of a masculine one more compatible with her sovereign power and her historical status. At other times, they insist that, despite everything, Elizabeth really was just another woman—a conclusion which has different implications for their assessments of her just as it did for their assessments of Mary.

Strickland is specific about Elizabeth's masculine traits, asserting her divergence from the "feminine propensity of leaning on others for succour in the time of danger": "she partook not of the nature of the ivy, but the oak, being formed and fitted to stand alone," Strickland says (*Elizabeth*, 146). At other points Strickland gives her credit for possessing "masculine intellect" and "masculine energy" (*Elizabeth*, 620, 712). But with what comes to seem typical perversity, Elizabeth resists being thus rewritten as more man than woman. Part of the problem is that her sex was always an important part of her public identity, not to mention her foreign policy. For one thing, although in the end she died single, she was almost always on the brink of matrimony; as we have seen, the possibility that she would marry and bear an heir was never far from anyone's mind. She was also famous for her coquetry, her vanity, and her love of fine clothes and jewels, all stereotypically feminine traits. Unable, then, to treat Elizabeth's actual sex as irrelevant, and no doubt reluctant to expel from her pantheon of "woman worthies" one of the most conspicuously successful historical women of all time, Strickland expends substantial textual energy trying to reclaim her *as* a woman. She plays up Elizabeth's associations with unproblematically exemplary female figures, as when she reminds us that "[t]his great female sovereign . . . was born on the day celebrated as the nativity of the Virgin Mary, and she died, March 24th, on the eve of the festival of the annunciation, called Lady Day" (*Elizabeth*, 704). Despite her own childless state, Strickland assures us, "Elizabeth was all her life remarkable for her love of children" (*Elizabeth*, 87), and, like her distant cousin the Queen of Scots, Elizabeth "greatly excelled" at "the feminine accomplishment of needlework" (*Elizabeth*, 11), which was "one of the resources with which she wiled away the weary hours of her imprisonment at Woodstock" (*Elizabeth*, 95). References to needlework disappear once Elizabeth actually sits on the throne and, in this case unlike Mary, gives up the needle for the sceptre, but Strickland works to minimize the unladylike implications of this choice by stressing Elizabeth's benevolent impulses as a ruler. "The royal eye, like sunshine," she reports, "fostered the seeds of useful enterprise, and it was the glory of the last of the Tudors, that she manifested a truly maternal interest in beholding [crafts and industries] spring up and flourish" (*Elizabeth*, 361); "[her] greatness was as a peace sovereign," she continues, "[and] she was formed and fitted for domestic government" (*Elizabeth*, 363).

The road to Elizabeth's reclamation is a rocky one, though. Both of the comments quoted above, with their strategic inclusion of key terms such as "maternal" and "domestic," are juxtaposed against descriptions of Elizabeth that cast her in a much less flattering light. Elizabeth enjoyed "sports unmeet for any Christian lady to witness, much less to provide for the amusement of herself and court," Strickland admits before softening this criticism with her remarks about Elizabeth's motherly care for her people's industries (*Elizabeth*, 360). And her admiration for Elizabeth's greatness as a "peace sovereign" is followed by a regretful but severe commentary on the queen's less benign aspect:

> Alas! that the biographer of Elizabeth should be compelled to turn from the lovely picture of an enlightened female sovereign, smiling on the labours of the children of her own subjects, . . . to depict her presiding like Atropos, over racks and gibbets, and all the horrible panoply of religious and political tyranny. (*Elizabeth*, 363)

Alas indeed, as such a picture is entirely incompatible with the queenly ideal; Strickland's obligation, as a historian, to give her readers the facts makes her ideological project almost impossible to sustain.

Strickland's best efforts at damage control are her claims that many of Elizabeth's most questionable (that is, least womanly) actions and policies originated not with her but with her ministers, who, according to Strickland, frequently overpowered Elizabeth's personal preferences and pressured her into acting as they wished. "Well did the pitiless men by whom Elizabeth's better feelings were smothered, understand the arts of bending her stormy temper to their determined purposes," she declares (*Elizabeth*, 327); similarly, the implacable junta by whom Elizabeth's resolves were at times influenced, and her better feelings smothered, had sinned too deeply against Mary Stuart, to risk the possibility of her surviving their royal mistress. (*Elizabeth*, 455)

It is hard not to take Strickland's hint that the conflicts here are gendered and the "better feelings" against which these "pitiless men" conspire are those womanly instincts that shine through on other occasions. These implications become perfectly explicit when Strickland reaches the difficult chapter of Mary Stuart's condemnation and execution, for Strickland clearly the darkest stain on Elizabeth's record and thus the episode requiring the most careful explication if Elizabeth is to retain any of her biographer's (or *her* readers') sympathy:

> Elizabeth's relentings were overruled, and her female heart steeled against the natural impulses of mercy by the ruthless men whose counsels influenced her resolves[.] Had Elizabeth exercised her own unbiassed judgment, and yielded to the angel whisperings of woman's gentler nature, which disposed her to draw back from affixing her signature to the fatal warrant, her annals would have remained unsullied by a crime, which can neither be justified on moral nor political grounds. (*Elizabeth*, 477)

Here Elizabeth, for all her faults, is part of the tradition of gentle, virtuous, benevolent queens Strickland wishes to document and glorify, but she is a fallen angel who strays from the path of true femininity—or, more accurately and still more forgivingly, is driven from it by the harassment of men themselves motivated by purely public, political concerns. But Strickland's account maintains neither this view nor its opposite—that Elizabeth's greatness is enabled by her abandonment of womanly values—with any consistency, and the resulting portrait of "this great queen and extraordinary woman" is as uneven and divided as this phrase, which concludes Strickland's biography, suggests (*Elizabeth*, 712). No wonder Strickland opens her volume with an apology:

> It is not, perhaps, the most gracious office in the world to perform, with strict impartiality, the duty of a faithful biographer to a princess so endeared to national pride as Elizabeth, and to examine, by the cold calm light of truth, the flaws which mar the bright ideal of Spenser's 'Gloriana,' and Shakespeare's.... The web of her life was a glittering tissue, in which good and evil were strangely mingled, and as the evidences of friend and foe are woven together, without reference to the prejudice of either, or any other object than to shew her as she was, the lights and shades must sometimes appear in strong and even painful opposition to each other, for such are the inconsistencies of human nature, such the littlenesses of human greatness. (*Elizabeth*, 1-2)

The same unevenness which Strickland finds plagues Elizabeth's history infects her own biography, reflecting not just the foibles and anomalies of human nature but also the resistance of real life, of fact, to the pressures of plot and ideology.

Froude shares Strickland's problems with Elizabeth, unable to deny the accomplishments of her reign but unable also to ascribe them to either her masculine greatness or her feminine perfection. Unlike Strickland, however, he does have a consistent strategy for dealing with his elusive subject: over and over he reduces her historical stature and significance, with the result that the question of her gender diminishes in importance because she ceases to be exemplary in any case. The less credit she gets for political successes or personal nobility the more she fades into the background of Froude's canvas, and thus he manages to contain entirely the potential threat posed by this outstanding example of female participation and agency in history. To a large extent, Elizabeth's own behavior helps him in this project, particularly her notorious indecisiveness, her tendency to be passive in the face of even the most pressing diplomatic problems, and, most crucially given Froude's explicit intention to document the triumph of the Reformation over the dark powers of Rome and the Catholic League, her consistent refusal to stand forth as the outright defender of the Protestant cause. "If, as is sometimes said, Elizabeth was the greatest of English sovereigns, one is tempted to suppose that the average stature cannot have been excessive," is Froude's rather belittling conclusion (IV:174); if such is the case, there remains little need to redeem or reclaim

Elizabeth for any particular ideological agenda.

Froude is quite willing to praise Elizabeth when he thinks she deserves it, or when he thinks the general judgment of history has unfairly gone against her. He feels particularly strongly that her conduct towards her cousin Mary has been misinterpreted: "the fairest feature in her history," he argues,

> the one relation in which from first to last she showed sustained and generous feeling, is that which the perversity of history has selected as the blot on her escutcheon. Beyond and beside the political causes which influenced Elizabeth's attitude towards the Queen of Scots, true human pity, true kindness, a true desire to save her [Mary] from herself, had a real place. . . . From the beginning to the end no trace can be found of personal animosity on the part of Elizabeth; on the part of Mary no trace of anything save the fiercest hatred. (V:477)

Such unqualified approbation is, however, the exception rather than the rule in his account. Most of the time his support invites the old cliché that with such friends, Elizabeth needs no enemies. "How [Elizabeth] worked in detail," he says, for example,

> how uncertain, how vacillating, how false and unscrupulous she could be, when occasion tempted, has appeared already and will appear more and more; but her object in itself was excellent, and those who pursue high purposes through crooked ways deserve better of mankind, on the whole, than those who pick their way in blameless inanity, and if innocent of ill, are equally innocent of good. (IV:68)

The "excellence" of Elizabeth's general goals is nearly obscured by the string of epithets with which he opens his sentence, and the qualifier "on the whole" makes his defense seem tepid and half-hearted at best. The following passage similarly fluctuates between admiration and criticism:

> Opinion which has credited Elizabeth with a statesmanship which she did not possess has condemned her no less unreasonably for qualities which in a private person are blameless and interesting. She was a woman of clear intellectual perception, but without intellectual

passion; singularly careless of herself and therefore of undecided temperament. On great questions, where arguments are equally balanced, the loves and hates of men, their beliefs and sympathetic convictions, rather than conclusions of reasoning, give them resolution to plant their steps firmly. Elizabeth had none of these, and was in consequence uncertain, unstable, and vacillating. (V:287)

Though ostensibly offered in the interests of balanced reporting, such alternations between endorsement and censure have a deadening effect on one's interests and sympathies, cumulatively undermining more than they establish. "Great in her general attitude, great in her own heart and bearing at special moments of danger," Froude begins with a flourish at one point, "Elizabeth could yet stoop to these poor tricks, which, after all, were not to serve her" (III:445), a masterful deployment of the art of sinking. "If Elizabeth's conduct in its details [towards the Queen of Scots] had been alike unprincipled and unwise," he argues, "the broader bearings of her policy were intelligible and commendable; her caprice and vacillation arose from her consciousness of the difficulties by which she was on every side surrounded" (II:72). Elizabeth lacked "any larger or deeper conviction of her own," he says near the end of his five volumes, as he attempts to sum up her character; "[s]he was without the intellectual emotions which give human character its consistency and power." In the same breath, however, he admits that she possessed "[o]ne moral quality ... in an eminent degree; she was supremely brave." Moreover, he goes on, "[s]he lived simply, worked hard, and ruled her household with rigid economy. But her vanity was as insatiable as it was commonplace," he continues, and "[e]xcept when speaking some round untruth Elizabeth never could be simple" (V:475). The twists and turns of this small passage typify the convolutions of Froude's approach to Elizabeth overall.

This pattern of reversals and retractions is also evident in Froude's discussions of religion and of Elizabeth's role in the great struggle between Popery and Protestantism, with the slight difference that here his tone becomes more overtly censorious. "[Elizabeth's] own [religious] creed was a perplexity to herself and to the world," he observes (I:467), and this lack of religious commitment combined with her failure of leadership offends him. He cannot deny that his cause prospered during her reign, but as far as he is concerned no thanks are due to Elizabeth. "She appears in history the champion of the Reformation, the first Protestant sovereign in Europe," he says, but the word "appears" is critical: "it was a position into which she was driven forward in spite of herself, and when she found herself there, it brought her neither pride nor pleasure" (IV:65). She saw "no reason to risk her throne" for the Reformation, "a cause for which at best she had but a cold concern. She preferred," he goes on damningly,

> to lie, and twist, and perjure herself, and betray her friends, with a purpose at the bottom moderately upright; and nature in fitting her for her work had left her without that nice sense of honour which would have made her part too difficult. (V:2)

No saving "but" comes in here to counteract the effect of this stern assessment. Still, most of the time he continues to offset his complaints with, if not compliments, then at least excuses, as here:

> [T]hat Elizabeth remained in essentials true to the great cause of the Reformation to which she owed her birth and crown, must never be forgotten when we are provoked to condemn her inconsistencies. That she was without distinct doctrinal conviction was rather her merit than her fault. That she was irresolute—that she listened to all sides—that she was unwilling to risk a throne in defence of opinions with which she had but a moderate sympathy—that she was irritable and impatient—that she quarrelled with her truest friends—all this is plain enough, but it is also reasonable enough. If she had other faults, she was young—and she was a woman. It is sufficient praise that she perilled crown and life in a bold and noble policy. (I:183)

Interestingly, in this example her sex is Froude's trump card: such inadequacies are "reasonable" and "sufficient," all that we ought to expect from a woman in her position. His final comment about Elizabeth's role in the religious struggle is extremely grudging:

> The greatest achievement in English history, the 'breaking the bonds of Rome,' and the establishment of spiritual independence, was completed without bloodshed under Elizabeth's auspices, and Elizabeth may have the glory of the work. (V:478)

Thus easily does he at once yield to the obvious—that credit for this great "achievement" does in some sense belong to Elizabeth—*and* make this concession seem chivalrous on his part, a small triumph, he would have his readers believe, of the gentleman over the historian, of pleasant fancy over strict fact.

A final measure of Froude's unwillingness to leave Elizabeth comfortably on her throne is his treatment of the victory over the Armada. In Strickland's account this episode is the highlight of Elizabeth's career, with the famous Armada speech its crowning moment:

> The day on which Elizabeth went, in royal and martial pomp, to visit her loyal camp at Tilbury, has generally been considered the most interesting of her whole life. Never, certainly, did she perform her part, as the female leader of an heroic nation, with more imposing effect than on that occasion. (Strickland, *Elizabeth*, 529)

Not only does Froude, perhaps uniquely among Elizabeth's historians and biographers, not mention, much less quote, the famous speech, but he moves promptly to strip away this heroic image, dismissing it as the result of skillful public relations:

> The nation knew Elizabeth only by her public acts. The harassed hours of her ministers, the struggles by which the measures were forced out of her by which England had been barely saved, these of course were unrevealed to the world, and altogether undreamt of. . . . To her people she was always plausible; always to appearance frank and free-spoken. She was now the heroine of the hour. The wreath of victory which her subjects had won for her they laid at the feet of their sovereign . . . . (V:432)

Victorian readers who persist in seeing Elizabeth as a great leader are, as her subjects were before them, simply dupes. Here, as in his account of Mary Stuart, Froude claims the right, through his privileged position as historian, as possessor of the facts, to correct his audience's misguided beliefs about his subject. In the end, his goal seems to be to overturn the common notion that, for all her faults, for all her failings as a woman, or perhaps because of them, Elizabeth was entitled to the adulation and gratitude of her nation. Gloriana, the Virgin Queen, the

Fairy Queen: in Froude's hands, she is a strangely shrunken figure indebted for the prominent place she had held for so long to circumstances, to her subjects, and, above all, to the great men who looked after the real business of the realm while she dilly-dallied:

> Effects must have had causes equal to them, and that she left England at her death the first of European powers is accepted as proof that she was herself the first of princes. It was not however the ability of Elizabeth, it was the temper of the English nation which raised her in her own despite to the high place which she ultimately filled. The genius and daring of her Protestant subjects, of whom Walsingham was no more than a brilliant representative, formed the splendid pedestal on which her own small figure was lifted into dignity. (IV:364)

Thus he clears away from the masculine turf of English history the one woman who seems most entitled to a place on it, obviating the need to rethink the rules and distinctions—such as that between the public and private spheres—which had guaranteed women's exclusion for so long.

NOTES

1. [Margaret Oliphant], "Mr. Froude and Queen Mary." *Blackwood's* Vol. 107 No. 651 (January 1870), pp. 105-23; p. 105.

2. [H. H. Milman], Review of Froude's *Reign of Elizabeth*. *Quarterly Review* Vol. 114 No. 228 (October 1863), pp. 510-37; p. 516.

3. See, for instance, Louis O. Mink, "Narrative Form as Cognitive Instrument," in *Historical Understanding*, ed. Brian Fay, Eugene Golub, and Richard Vann (Ithaca: Cornell UP, 1987), pp. 182-203.

4. Agnes Strickland, *The Life of Queen Elizabeth* (London: J.M. Dent, 1906), henceforth cited in the text as *"Elizabeth"*; Agnes Strickland, *The Life of Mary Queen of Scots* (London: George Bell and Sons, 1888), 2 volumes, henceforth cited in the text as *"MQS"*; and James Anthony Froude, *The Reign of Elizabeth* (London: J. M. Dent, 1911), 5 volumes, henceforth cited in the text as "Froude."

5. Mary Poovey, *Uneven Developments: The Ideological Work of Gender in Mid-Victorian England* (Chicago: U of Chicago P, 1988), p. 12.

6. Leonée Ormond, "'The Spacious Times of Great Elizabeth': The Victorian Vision of the Elizabethans." *Victorian Poetry* Vol. 25 Nos. 3-4 (Autumn-Winter 1987), pp. 29-46; p. 31.

7. Charles Henry Hartshorne, *English Medieval Embroidery* (London: John Henry Parker, 1848), p. 3.

Conclusion

The burden of this study has been to show the ways in which gender complicated the Victorian discourse of history, disrupting tidy distinctions between genres, styles, and subjects, and opening up new historiographical possibilities, particularly for the historical representation of women. Some writers, at first eager to broaden the historian's mandate, retreated and regrouped when faced with social history's potential to become women's history; others, empowered by the increasing interest in histories of the private sphere, turned this feminized theory into a distinctly feminine practice. Dogging these historiographical experiments was the novel, which seemed to some a more flexible, immediate, and accessible medium than conventional historical narrative but which to others threatened to break down the barrier between the real and the imaginary, the serious and the trivial, the masculine and the feminine. Although, as I have emphasized throughout, the discussion was uneven, with concerns and questions overlapping, contradicting, and confusing each other, by the end of the century some of its central issues were resolved. Most obviously and importantly, the blurred and permeable border between historical and fictional texts so apparent and controversial in the early nineteenth century became distinct and unyielding. In particular, history became a professional pursuit and was institutionalized, primarily in the universities. Fully legitimated and authoritative historical writing emerged after this only from a formal academic setting; it had clearly defined characteristics and conformed to specific standards of evidence and documentation.[1]

This movement away from amateurism had two chief effects. First, historians thus finally succeeded in Macaulay's project of reclaiming their territory from usurping novelists. History and fiction took strikingly divergent paths after the 1880s, with novelists interrogating, critiquing, and eventually discarding, at least in the self-conscious echelons of high culture, the realist and historicist conventions embraced by academic historians. Realist novels of course continued to be written and read, as did historical novels, sometimes with the highest seriousness; today, however, historical novels generally rank only a small step higher than romance novels in the critical hierarchy. Significantly, most historical novels, like romance novels, cater primarily to a female readership, a phenomenon which may be related to the other principal effect of historiography's institutionalization.

The second important consequence of the entrenchment of history in the academy was that women, condemned to amateur status by their exclusion from most seats of higher learning, once again found themselves outsiders, their exile from history now formal and explicit rather than traditional and thus, in some ways, less definitive. Women's isolation from professional history, and the related lack of attention to women's history, did not change significantly until the 1970s, when agitation for women's political and social equality aroused demands for their historical recognition and a second burst of activity by and about women in history began.[2]

This second outbreak—overtly political, emancipatory, and professional—superficially bears little resemblance to the Victorian phenomenon I have treated in this study. It began, however, in the same way: assembling an array of "women worthies," to use Natalie Davis's phrase, to make the case for women's active and crucial participation in historical experience.[3] And, inevitably, it, too, led to confrontations with the available models for historical change as well as historical representation. Driven by the skepticism of their colleagues about the legitimacy of women's history as a special field to be more theoretically self-conscious than their nineteenth-century predecessors, the twentieth-century pioneers of women's history—Gerda Lerner, Joan Kelly, Natalie Davis, and Elizabeth Fox-Genovese, among others- -soon questioned the adequacy of "herstory" approaches.[4] "The history of notable women," Lerner pointed out in 1975, "is the history of exceptional, even deviant women, and does not describe the experience and history of the mass of women."[5] This critique gained force from the increasing influence of social history, which achieved academic predominance in the twentieth century and provided women's history with models and legitimated its concerns, much as it had in the nineteenth century.[6] Like women's history, Joan Scott explains, "social history challenged the narrative line of political history ('white men make history') by taking as its subject large-scale social processes as they were realized in many dimensions of human experience"; social history's focus on processes such as modernization or the spread of capitalism justified a "focus on groups customarily excluded from political history."[7] Victorian women historians, as we have seen, defended their own work on similar grounds, drawing strength from and appropriating to their own ends the historiographical revisionism of successful and established male historians.

But twentieth-century women's historians soon moved beyond the fuller picture social history enabled and authorized. As they sought to historicize gender identities and recognize variation among women, they ventured into problematic territory largely avoided by nineteenth-century writers. Their primary concern was that inquiring into women as a distinct and coherent category risked reifying gender differences and perpetuating a false sense of homogeneity. As early as 1969, Gerda Lerner suggested what later scholars argued for more explicitly: that gender must to some extent be recognized as a construct, not a fixed or natural identity, and that culture, class, race, and other distinctions disrupt or complicate attempts to generalize about "women's" experience.[8] Elizabeth Fox-Genovese urged that historians subject definitions of gender to historical analysis rather than accept them as givens, and Joan Kelly emphasized the importance of the feminist assertion that "the relation between the sexes is a social and not a natural one." "[C]ategorization by gender," Kelly said, "no longer implies a mothering role and subordination to men, except as a social role and relation recognized as such, as socially constructed and socially imposed."[9] Although the vocabulary differs, these statements resemble Foucauldian and post-structuralist theories of gender as an unstable discursive construct. Nothing could be further from the prevailing assumption in the Victorian texts that "woman" is a stable, enduring, universal category; the clash of such essentialism with historical particularity in *Romola*, however, creates a crisis of historical analysis that points towards the twentieth-century re-imaginings of gender as bound up in, rather than isolated from, historical process and change.

Once they began asking questions about women and treating gender as a historical construct rather than a fixed identity, women's historians found that the whole past had to be reinterpreted. One of the first targets was periodization—"not surprising," Gerda Lerner remarked dryly, "when we consider that the traditional time frame in history has been derived from political history," from which women were so widely excluded.[10] Joan Kelly's famous essay "Did Women Have A Renaissance?" exemplifies the ways women's historians called into question the tidy categorizations previously taken as reliable guides to general historical developments:

> To take the emancipation of women as a vantage point is to discover that events that further the historical development of men, liberating them from natural, social, or ideological constraints, have quite different, even opposite, effects upon women. ... [The] developments [for which the Renaissance is known] affected women adversely, so much so that there was no renaissance for women—at least, not during the Renaissance.[11]

Kelly soon realized that doubting or discarding conventional periodization led to further problems: "what .... did this say about the validity of all previous histories"?[12] Like other women's historians, Kelly came to believe that realizing the goals of women's history meant transforming history entirely, not adding new details to old stories. Natalie Davis in her turn claimed that attention to gender would affect historical understanding of power, social structures, property, and cultural symbols as well as periodization, and Elizabeth Fox-Genovese warned that women's history that only filled in gaps in mainstream historiography would falter in the crucial job of challenging the structures of the discipline as a whole.[13] The failure of nineteenth-century women's history to win a lasting place in, much less revolutionize, mainstream historiography, testifies to the justice of these fears.

A powerful consciousness of the inadequacies and biases of existing histories, combined with a sense of immense possibility for revision and change, thus lay behind Gerda Lerner's bold proclamation

Conclusion 203

that "all history as we now know it . . . is merely pre-history."[14] As this formulation suggests, the leaders of this century's women's history movement in its professional, academic aspect have paid little attention to, and acknowledged few debts to, their nineteenth-century forerunners.[15] No doubt this is due in large part to ignorance: even in their own day the Victorian women historians never achieved much status or recognition, despite their often extensive original research and their treatment of novel and popular subjects, and today their works almost universally languish in obscurity. Moreover, because they clung to Victorian dogmas about woman's nature—because they did not recognize or analyze the historicity of gender—their histories offer little to excite or inspire a twentieth-century feminist seeking models for her own more radical project. The great weakness of nineteenth-century women's history as manifested in the texts I have examined is this imaginative and theoretical failure. The great strength, however, is what these women writers made of the models they had—their variations on the plots most readily available to them. They succeeded in making women visible parts of the historical past; this in itself is no negligible accomplishment. Their most lasting contribution, though, and the one for which they are gradually winning recognition in this century, was their participation in the general reorientation of historical studies towards the everyday and the social. Though largely forgotten by professional history, these women helped lay the foundation for the shift in priorities that made the next burst of women's historiography possible.

And for all the neglect of their work within the academy, there seems to have been a relatively continuous tradition of amateur women's history from the nineteenth century to the present. This tradition, involving especially biographical works of queens or other notable women, is exemplified today by Lady Antonia Fraser, author of numerous historical biographies almost all of which cite nineteenth-century works, most often those of Agnes Strickland. Indeed, a review of my own library revealed that every modern biography I have of a British queen cites Strickland.[16] This discovery suggests new insights as well as new questions. It underlines Strickland's marginality even as it affirms the lasting value of her efforts: in the century and a half since her *Lives* first appeared, not enough substantial work has been done on the queens of England for her volumes to have been supplanted as the classic accounts. Macaulay is no longer consulted as an authority on seventeenth-century English politics—his *History* attracts attention today more as a literary than a historical classic—but then seventeenth-century English politics has remained an important topic for historical investigation and representation. Ironically, then, in one respect at least Strickland has quietly outlasted her more eminent contemporary. Amateur women's history in this century also shares some of the characteristic features of its nineteenth-century beginnings, most notably a desire to bridge the gap between scholarly and popular writing, to humanize the face of history without sacrificing accuracy to interest. Further study of recent historical biographies by and about women will no doubt illuminate further the continuing appeal of this genre as well as the implications and significance of its vexed relationship with "serious" historiography.

The long separation between women and professional narrative historiography has made some women writers suspicious of such histories and inspired them to experiment with the possibilities of fictional representation as an alternative perhaps more compatible with female experience. In her 1988 novel *Ana Historic*, for instance, Daphne Marlatt rejects both the clarity and the constraints of linear history in favor of a variegated text that juxtaposes past and present, personal and objective, fact and fiction, in search of the story of a nineteenth-century woman who emigrates from England to Canada. Through her twentieth-century narrator, she also questions the conventions of historical practice and priorities:

> i learned that history is the real story the city fathers tell of the only important events in the world. a tale of their exploits hacked out against a silent backdrop of trees, of wooden masses. so many claims to fame. so many ordinary men turned into heroes. (where are the city mothers?) the city fathers busy building a town out of so many shacks labelled the Western Terminus of the Transcontinental, Gateway to the East—all these capital letters to convince themselves of its, of their, significance.[17]

Marlatt's vision is ultimately exclusionary: for her, women's history can achieve authenticity only through isolation from masculinity in both life and representation. She shares with the Victorian women a conviction that women differ essentially from men, but she ends up far

Conclusion

from their conception of a female identity complementary to a male one. Although none of the Victorian women writers I have discussed in this study ever imagined prose as unorthodox or ideology as radical as Marlatt's, her experimental novel nonetheless continues the project they began: testing the limitations and possibilities of various forms, various narratives, seeking more complex and more adequate ways to write about women and history.

NOTES

1. See Philippa Levine, *The Amateur and the Professional: Antiquarians, Historians and Archaeologists in Victorian England, 1838-1886* (Cambridge: Cambridge UP, 1986). Levine identifies the founding of the *English Historical Review* in 1886 as the culmination of the trend confirming "the primacy of the professional historian" (p. 164).

2. In *History and Feminism: A Glass Half Full* (New York: Twayne, 1993), Judith P. Zinsser gives a full account of the relationship between feminism and professional history in the twentieth century.

3. Natalie Zemon Davis, "'Women's History' in Transition: The European Case," *Feminist Studies* Vol. 3 No. 3/4 (Spring/Summer 1976), pp. 83-103. The point, Joan Scott explains, "was to give value to an experience that had been ignored (hence devalued) and to insist on female agency in the making of history." *Gender and the Politics of History* (New York: Columbia UP, 1988), p. 18.

4. See Berenice Carroll's introduction to *Liberating Women's History: Theoretical and Critical Essays* (Urbana: U of Illinois P, 1976), p. x.

5. "Placing Women in History: A 1975 Perspective," in Carroll, ed., *Liberating Women's History*, pp. 357-367; p. 357.

6. See Zinsser, especially pp. 48-49; see also Joan Scott, *Gender and the Politics of History*, especially pp. 21-22.

7. *Gender and the Politics of History*, p. 21.

8. Gerda Lerner, "New Approaches to the Study of Women in American History," *Journal of Social History* Vol. 3 (Fall 1969), pp. 53-62, rpt. in Nancy F. Cott, ed., *Theory and Method in Women's History*, 2 Vols. (New York: K. G. Saur, 1992). Vol. 1, pp. 3-12.

9. Fox-Genovese, "Placing Women's History in History," *New Left Review* No. 133 (May-June 1982), pp. 5-29; Kelly, "The Social Relations of the Sexes: Methodological Implications of Women's History," in *Women, History and Theory* (Chicago: U of Chicago P, 1984), pp. 1-18; p. 6.

10. "Placing Women in History: A 1975 Perspective," p. 362.
11. "Did Women Have A Renaissance?" *Women, History and Theory*, pp. 19-50; p. 19.
12. Zinsser, *History and Feminism*, p. 40.
13. Davis, "'Women's History' in Transition"; Fox-Genovese, "Placing Women's History in History." See also Linda Gordon, "What Should Women's Historians Do: Politics, Social Theory, and Women's History," in Cott, ed., *Theory and Method in Women's History*, Vol. 1, pp. 258-65.
14. "Placing Women in History: A 1975 Perspective," p. 366.
15. Some recognition and exploration of a female historical tradition has begun to appear in the recent literature. Daniel Woolf's essay "A Feminine Past? Gender, Genre, and Historical Knowledge in England, 1500-1800," *American Historical Review* Vol. 102 No. 3 (June 1997) is exemplary in this respect. See also Rosemary Mitchell, "The Busy Daughters of Clio: Women Writers of History between 1820 and 1880," forthcoming in the *Women's History Review* (Spring 1998); Bonnie G. Smith, "The Contribution of Women to Modern Historiography in Great Britain, France, and the United States, 1750-1940," *American Historical Review* Vol. 89 No. 3 (1984), pp. 709-32; Natalie Zemon Davis, "Gender and Genre: Women as Historical Writers, 1400-1820," in Patricia Labalme, ed., *Beyond Their Sex: Learned Women of the European Past* (New York: NYU P, 1980), pp. 153-82; Gerda Lerner, *The Creation of Feminist Consciousness: From the Middle Ages to Eighteen-Seventy* (New York: Oxford UP, 1993), especially Chapter 11; or Zinsser, *History and Feminism*, especially pp. 28-34.
16. Antonia Fraser: *The Weaker Vessel: Woman's Lot in Seventeenth-Century England* (London: Methuen, 1984); *Mary Queen of Scots* (London: Panther, 1969); *King Charles II* (London: Weidenfeld & Nicolson, 1979); *Warrior Queens* (New York: Knopf, 1989), which also cites Mrs. Matthew Hall's *Queens Before the Conquest*; and *The Six Wives of Henry VIII* (New York: Knopf, 1992), which also cites Mary Anne Everett Wood's *Letters of Royal and Illustrious Ladies*. Other works consulted are Carolly Erickson, *The First Elizabeth* (New York: Summit Books, 1983); Norah Lofts, *Anne Boleyn* (New York: Coward, McCann & Geoghegan, 1979); Marion Meade, *Eleanor of Aquitaine: A Biography* (New York: Hawthorn Dutton, 1977); and Alison Weir, *The Six Wives of Henry VIII* (New York: Grove Weidenfeld, 1991).
17. Daphne Marlatt, *Ana Historic* (Toronto: Coach House Press, 1988), p. 28.

Bibliography

Anon. "Milliner's Apprentices." *Fraser's Magazine* Vol. 33 (March 1846), pp. 308-16.
Anon. Review of Eliot's *Romola*. *Athenaeum* No. 1863 (July 11 1863), p. 46.
Anon. Review of Eliot's *Romola*. *British Quarterly Review* Vol. 38 (October 1863), pp. 448-65.
Anon. Review of Macaulay's *History*. *North British Review* Vol. 10 (February 1849), pp. 367-424.
Anon. Review of Stone's *Art of Needlework*. *Athenaeum* No. 670 (August 29 1840), pp. 675-76.
Anon. Review of Strickland's *Lives of the Queens of England*. *Dublin Review* Vol. 20 (May 1841), pp. 506-18.
Anon. *Woman's Worth: or, Hints to Raise the Female Character*. London: Stevens & Co., 1847.
[Abraham, G. W.]. Review of Strickland's *Lives of the Queens of Scotland*. *Dublin Review* Vol. 38 (March 1855), pp. 73-97.
Aikin, Lucy. *Memoirs of the Court of Queen Elizabeth*. 6th ed. 2 Vols. London: Longman, Hurst, Rees, et al, 1826.
[Alison, Archibald]. Review of Macaulay's *History of England*. *Blackwood's Magazine* Vol. 65 (April 1849), pp. 383-405.
[Alison, Archibald, Jr.]. Review of Alison's *History of Europe 1815-1852*. *Blackwood's Magazine* Vol. 87 (April 1860), pp. 441-67.
Altick, Richard. *The English Common Reader: A Social History of the Mass Reading Public 1800-1900*. Chicago: U of Chicago P, 1957.
Amyot, Thomas. "A Defence of the Early Antiquity of the Bayeux Tapestry." *Archaeologia* Vol. XIX (1821), pp. 192-206.

Armstrong, Nancy. *Desire and Domestic Fiction: A Political History of the Novel.* Oxford: Oxford UP, 1985.
Auerbach, Nina. *Woman and the Demon: The Life of a Victorian Myth.* Cambridge MA: Harvard UP, 1982.
Bagehot, Walter. *The English Constitution.* London: C. A. Watts & Co., Ltd., 1964.
[———]. Review of Macaulay's *History of England. National Review* Vol. 2 (April 1856), pp. 357-87.
[Bagshawe, H. R.]. Review of Strickland's *Queens of England. Dublin Review* Vol. 12 (May 1842), pp. 518-25.
Ballstadt, Carl. *The Literary History of the Strickland Family.* Unpublished Ph.D. dissertation, University of London, 1965.
Barrett, Dorothea. *Vocation and Desire: George Eliot's Heroines.* London: Routledge, 1989.
Barrett Browning, Elizabeth. *Aurora Leigh.* Chicago: Academy Chicago Publishers, 1979.
Beaty, Jerome. "History By Indirection: The Era of Reform in *Middlemarch.*" *Victorian Studies* Vol. 1 (December 1957), pp. 173-79.
Beer, Gillian. *Arguing with the Past: Essays in Narrative from Woolf to Sydney.* London: Routledge, 1989.
———. *George Eliot.* Bloomington: Indiana UP, 1986.
Blake, Kathleen. "*Middlemarch* and the Woman Question." *Nineteenth-Century Fiction* Vol. 31 No. 3 (December 1976), pp. 285-312.
Bonaparte, Felicia. *The Triptych and the Cross: The Central Myths of George Eliot's Poetic Imagination.* New York: NYU P, 1979.
Booth, Alison. *Greatness Engendered: George Eliot and Virginia Woolf.* Ithaca: Cornell UP, 1992.
Borer, Mary Cathcart. *Willingly to School: A History of Women's Education.* London: Lutterworth, 1975.
[Brewer, J. S.]. "New Sources of English History." *Quarterly Review* Vol. 130 (April 1871), pp. 373-407.
Brooks, Richard A. E. "The Development of the Historical Mind," in Joseph E. Baker, ed., *The Reinterpretation of Victorian Literature.* Princeton: Princeton UP, 1950, pp. 130-152.
Browning, Robert. *The Ring and the Book.* Ed. Richard D. Altick. Harmondsworth: Penguin, 1971.
Bruce, John Collingwood. *The Bayeux Tapestry Elucidated.* London: John Russell Smith, 1856.

Buckley, Jerome Hamilton. *The Triumph of Time: A Study of the Victorian Concepts of Time, History, Progress, and Decadence.* Cambridge MA: Harvard UP, 1966.

Bullen, J. B. "George Eliot's *Romola* as a Positivist Allegory." *Review of English Studies* Vol. 26 No. 104 (November 1975), pp. 425-35.

Burrow, J. W. *A Liberal Descent: Victorian Historians and the English Past.* Cambridge: Cambridge UP, 1981.

Burstyn, Joan N. *Victorian Education and the Ideal of Womanhood.* London: Croom Helm, 1980.

Bush, Mrs. Forbes. *Memoirs of the Queens of France.* 2nd ed. 2 Volumes London: Henry Colburn, 1843.

Carlyle, Thomas. "Boswell's *Life of Johnson.*" *Selected Essays.* N.p.: T. Nelson & Sons, n.d., pp. 165-227.

———. "On History." *A Carlyle Reader.* Ed. G. B. Tennyson. Cambridge: Cambridge UP, 1984, pp. 55-66.

———. *Sartor Resartus.* Ed. Kerry McSweeney and Peter Sabor. London: Oxford UP, 1987.

———. "Sir Walter Scott." *Selected Essays*, pp. 65-125.

Carr, E. H. *What Is History?* 2nd edition. Ed. R. W. Davis. London: MacMillan, 1961.

Carroll, Berenice, ed. *Liberating Women's History: Theoretical and Critical Essays.* Urbana: U of Illinois P, 1976.

Chandler, Alice. *A Dream of Order: The Medieval Ideal in Nineteenth-Century English Literature.* Lincoln: U of Nebraska P, 1970.

Chapman, Raymond. *The Sense of the Past in Victorian Literature.* London: Croom Helm, 1986.

[Cheney, Edward]. Review of Kavanagh's *Woman in France During the Eighteenth Century. Quarterly Review* Vol. 88 (1851), pp. 352-85.

Christ, Carol. *The Finer Optic: The Aesthetics of Particularity in Victorian Poetry.* New Haven: Yale UP, 1975.

———. "'The Hero as Man of Letters': Masculinity and Victorian Nonfiction Prose," in Thaïs Morgan, ed., *Victorian Sages and Cultural Discourse.* New Brunswick, NJ: Rutgers UP, 1990, pp. 19-31.

Clive, John. *Not By Fact Alone: Essays on the Writing and Reading of History.* Boston: Houghton Mifflin, 1989.

Comte, August. *Positive Philosophy.* Translated and abridged by Harriet Martineau. 3 Vols. London: George Bell, 1896.

———. *System of Positve Polity.* Translated by Richard Congreve, Frederic Harrison, et al. 4 Vols. London: Longmans, Green, and Co., 1875-77.

Costello, Louisa Stuart. *Memoirs of Eminent Englishwomen*. 2 Volumes. London: Bentley, 1844.

Cott, Nancy F., ed. *Theory and Method in Women's History*. 2 Volumes. New York: K. G. Saur, 1992.

[Croker, J. W.]. Review of Macaulay's *History of England*. *Quarterly Review* Vol. 84 (March 1849), pp. 549-630.

Crosby, Christina. *The Ends of History: Victorians and the 'Woman Question'*. New York: Routledge, 1991.

Crosland, Mrs. Newton. *Memorable Women: The Story of Their Lives*. Boston: Ticknor & Fields, 1854.

Culler, A. Dwight. *The Victorian Mirror of History*. New Haven: Yale UP, 1985.

Culler, Jonathan. *On Deconstruction: Theory and Criticism After Structuralism*. Ithaca: Cornell UP, 1982.

Dale, Peter Allan. *In Pursuit of a Scientific Culture: Science, Art, and Society in the Victorian Age*. Madison: U of Wisconsin P, 1989.

———. *The Victorian Critic and the Idea of History: Carlyle, Arnold, Pater*. Cambridge MA: Harvard UP, 1977.

Dauphin, Cécile, Anette Farge, et al. "Women's Culture and Women's Power: An Attempt at Historiography." *Journal of Women's History* Vol. 1 No. 1 (Spring 1989), pp. 63-88.

David, Deirdre. *Intellectual Women and Victorian Patriarchy: Harriet Martineau, Elizabeth Barrett Browning, George Eliot*. Ithaca: Cornell UP, 1987.

Davin, Anna. "Redressing the Balance or Transforming the Art? The British Experience," in S. Jay Kleinberg et al., eds., *Retrieving Women's History*, pp. 60-78.

Davis, Natalie Zemon. "Gender and Genre: Women as Historical Writers, 1400-1820," in Labalme, ed., *Beyond Their Sex*, pp. 153-82.

———. "'Women's History' in Transition: The European Case." *Feminist Studies* Vol. 3 No. 3/4 (Spring/Summer 1976), pp. 83-103.

[Donne, W. B.]. Review of Froude's *History of England from the Fall of Wolsey to the Death of Elizabeth*. *Fraser's Magazine* Vol. 54 (July 1856), pp. 31-46.

Donovan, Josephine. *Feminist Theory: The Intellectual Traditions of American Feminism*. New York: Continuum, 1992.

Dubois, Ellen, Gerda Lerner, et al. "Politics and Culture in Women's History." *Feminist Studies* Vol. 6 No. 1 (Spring 1980), pp. 26-64.

Eagleton, Terry. *The Ideology of the Aesthetic.* Cambridge, MA: Basil Blackwell, 1990.

———. *Literary Theory: An Introduction.* Minneapolis: U of Minnesota P, 1983.

Edelstein, T. J. "They Sang 'The Song of the Shirt': The Visual Iconography of the Seamstress." *Victorian Studies* Vol. 23 No. 2 (Winter 1980), pp. 183-210.

Edwards, Owen Dudley. *Macaulay.* New York: St. Martin's, 1988.

Eliot, George. *Adam Bede.* Ed. Stephen Gill. Harmondsworth: Penguin, 1980.

———. *Daniel Deronda.* Ed. Barbara Hardy. Harmondsworth: Penguin, 1967.

———. *The George Eliot Letters.* Ed. Gordon S. Haight. 9 Volumes. New Haven: Yale UP, 1954-1978.

———. *Felix Holt, The Radical.* Ed. Peter Coveney. Harmondsworth: Penguin, 1972.

———. "Margaret Fuller and Mary Wollstonecraft." *Selected Critical Writings,* pp. 180-86.

———. *Middlemarch: A Study of Provincial Life.* Ed. Gordon S. Haight. Boston: Houghton Mifflin, 1956.

———. *Middlemarch: A Study of Provincial Life.* Ed. W. J. Harvey. Harmondsworth: Penguin, 1965.

———. *Romola.* Ed. Andrew Sanders. Harmondsworth: Penguin, 1980.

———. "R. W. Mackay's *The Progress of the Intellect.*" *Selected Critical Writings,* pp. 18-36.

———. Review of George Roberts's *Social History of the People of the Southern Counties of England in Past Centuries. Westminster Review* Vol. 11 (January 1857), pp. 292-93.

———. Review of C. W. Fullom's *History of Woman. Westminster Review* Vol. 8 (July 1855), pp. 301-2.

———. *Scenes of Clerical Life.* Ed. David Coveney. Harmondsworth: Penguin, 1973.

———. *Selected Critical Writings.* Ed. Rosemary Ashton. London: Oxford UP, 1992.

———. "Silly Novels By Lady Novelists." *Selected Critical Writings,* pp. 296-321.

———. "Thomas Carlyle." *Selected Critical Writings,* pp. 187-92.

———. "Woman in France: Madame de Sablé." *Selected Critical Writings,* pp. 37-68.

Elledge, Scott. "The Background and Development in English Criticism of the Theories of Generality and Particularity." *PMLA* Vol. 62 No. 1 (March 1947), pp. 147-82.

Ellis, Sarah Stickney. *The Wives of England, Their Relative Duties, Domestic Influences, & Social Obligations.* London: Fisher, Son & Co., 1843.

———. *The Women of England, Their Social Duties, and Domestic Habits.* London: Fisher, Son & Co., 1839.

Ferris, Ina. *The Achievement of Literary Authority: Gender, History, and the Waverley Novels.* Ithaca: Cornell UP, 1991.

———. "Re-Positioning the Novel: *Waverley* and the Gender of Fiction." *Studies in Romanticism* Vol. 28 No. 2 (Summer 1989), pp. 291-301.

Finch, Anne. "The Introduction." *Norton Anthology of English Literature*, ed. M. H. Abrams et al. 5th edition. 2 Volumes. Vol. 1, pp. 1959-61.

Fleishman, Avrom. *The English Historical Novel: Walter Scott to Virginia Woolf.* Baltimore: Johns Hopkins UP, 1971.

Fox-Genovese, Elizabeth. "Placing Women's History in History." *New Left Review* No. 133 (May-June 1982), pp. 5-29.

[Froude, J. A.]. "Mary Stuart." *Westminster Review* Vol. 1 n.s. (January 1852), pp. 96-142.

Froude, J. A. *The Reign of Elizabeth.* 5 Volumes. London: J. M. Dent, 1911.

Gay, Peter. *The Enlightenment: An Interpretation: The Science of Freedom.* New York: Norton, 1969.

———. *Style in History: Gibbon, Ranke, Macaulay, Burckhardt.* New York: Norton, 1974.

Gilbert, Sandra, and Susan Gubar. *The Madwoman in the Attic: The Woman Writer and the Nineteenth-Century Literary Imagination.* New Haven: Yale UP, 1979.

Gooch, G. P. *History and Historians in the Nineteenth Century.* New York: Peter Smith, 1913.

Gordon, Ann D., Mari Jo Buhle, and Nancy Schrom Dye. "The Problem of Women's History," in Berenice Carroll, ed., *Liberating Women's History: Theoretical and Critical Essays.* Urbana: U of Illinois P, 1976, pp. 75-92

Gordon, Linda S. "What Should Women's Historians Do: Politics, Social Theory, and Women's History," in Cott, ed., *Theory and Method in Women's History*, Vol. 1, pp. 258-65.

Gorham, Deborah. *The Victorian Girl and the Feminine Ideal.* Bloomington: Indiana UP, 1982.

[Greg, W. R.]. "Juvenile and Female Labour." *Edinburgh Review* Vol. 79 (January 1844), pp. 130-56.

[———]. Review of Alison's *History of Europe 1815-1852*. *Edinburgh Review* Vol. 97 (April 1853), pp. 269-314.

Guedella, Philip. *The Queen and Mr. Gladstone*. 2 Volumes. London: Hodder and Stoughton, Ltd., 1933.

Haight, Gordon S. *George Eliot: A Biography*. Oxford: Clarendon, 1968.

Hale, J. R. *The Evolution of British Historiography from Bacon to Napier*. Cleveland: Meridian, 1964.

Hall, Mrs. Matthew. *The Queens Before the Conquest*. 2 Volumes. London: Henry Colburn, 1854.

———. *The Royal Princesses of England, from the Reign of George the First*. London: George Routledge & Sons, 1871.

Harris, J. F. C. *The Early Victorians 1832-1851*. New York: Praeger, 1971.

Harrison, Frederic. "The Future of Woman." *Realities and Ideals, Social, Political, Literary, and Artistic*. New York: Macmillan, 1908, pp. 63-81.

———. "The Realm of Woman." *Realities and Ideals*, pp. 82-101.

Hartshorne, Charles Henry. *English Medieval Embroidery*. London: John Henry Parker, 1848.

Hayden, Ilse. *Symbol and Privilege: The Ritual Context of British Royalty*. Tucson: U of Arizona P, 1987.

Hays, Mary. *Memoirs of Queens, Illustrious and Celebrated*. London: T. & J. Allman, 1821.

Heilbrun, Carolyn. *Reinventing Womanhood*. New York: Norton, 1979.

———. *Writing A Woman's Life*. New York: Ballantine, 1988.

Helsinger, Elizabeth K., Robin Lauterbach Sheets, and William Veeder. *The Woman Question: Society and Literature in Britain and America 1837-1883. Volume 3, Literary Issues*. Chicago: U of Chicago P, 1983.

[Heraud, J. A.?]. "Historical Romance II." *Fraser's Magazine* Vol. 5 (March 1832), pp. 207-17.

Heyck, T. W. *The Transformation of Intellectual Life in Victorian England*. New York: St. Martin's, 1982.

Hill, Georgiana. *A History of English Dress from the Saxon Period to the Present Day*. 2 Volumes. London: Richard Bentley & Sons, 1893.

Holt, Emily Sarah. *Memoirs of Royal Ladies*. 2 Volumes. London: Hurst & Blackett, 1861.

Homans, Margaret. *Bearing the Word: Language and Female Experience in Nineteenth-Century Women's Writing*. Chicago: U of Chicago P, 1986.

———. "'To the Queen's Private Apartments': Royal Portraiture and the Construction of Victoria's Sovereign Obedience." *Victorian Studies* Vol. 37 No. 1 (Autumn 1993), pp. 1-41.

[Hosack, John?]. Review of Strickland's *Queens of Scotland*. *Tait's Edinburgh Magazine* Vol. 18 (April 1851), pp. 238-45.

Houghton, Walter E. *The Victorian Frame of Mind 1830-1870*. New Haven: Yale UP, 1957.

Hume, David. *An Enquiry Concerning Human Understanding*. Ed. Antony Flew. La Salle, IL: Open Court, 1988.

[Hutton, R. H.] Review of *Romola*. *Spectator* No. 1829 (July 18 1863), pp. 2265-7.

Isaacson, Saul. "Carlyle and Macaulay in the Journals: Toward a New Historiography." *Carlyle Annual* Vol. 10 (1989), pp. 21-30.

Jameson, Anna. *Lives of Celebrated Female Sovereigns and Illustrious Women*. Ed. Mary E. Hewitt. Philadelphia: Porter & Coates, 1870. (Orig. pub. 2 Volumes. London: Henry Colburn, 1831.)

Jann, Rosemary. *The Art and Science of Victorian History*. Columbus: Ohio UP, 1985.

[Jephson, John Mounteney]. Review of Palgrave's *History of Normandy and of England*. *Fraser's Magazine* Vol. 56 (July 1857), pp. 16-32.

Jessop, Augustus. "Women as Historians (I)." *Literature* No. 65 (January 14, 1899), pp. 41-42.

———. "Women as Historians (II)." *Literature* No. 66 (January 21, 1899), pp. 67-68.

[Johnstone, Christian]. Review of Stone's *Art of Needlework*. *Tait's Edinburgh Magazine* Vol. VII (November 1840), pp. 715-23.

Kavanagh, Julia. *Woman in France During the Eighteenth Century*. 2 Volumes. London: G. P. Putnam's Sons, 1893. (Orig. pub. London: Smith & Elder, 1850.)

———. *Women of Christianity, Exemplary for Acts of Piety and Charity*. New York: D. Appleton & Co., 1869. (Orig. pub. London, 1851.)

Kelly, Joan. *Women, History and Theory*. Chicago: U of Chicago P, 1984.

[Kemble, J. M.]. Review of Doran's *Queens of the House of Hanover*. *Fraser's Magazine* Vol. 52 (August 1855), pp. 135-49.

[———]. Review of Macaulay's *History of England*. *Fraser's Magazine* Vol. 53 (Feb. 1856), pp. 147-66.

Kenyon, John. *The History Men: The Historical Profession in England Since the Renaissance*. Pittsburgh: U of Pittsburgh P, 1983.

King, Mrs. F. E. *Female Scriptural Characters, Exemplifying Female Virtues.* Boston: Wells & Lilly, 1816.

King, Margaret L. "Book-Lined Cells: Women and Humanism in the Early Italian Renaissance," in Labalme, ed., *Beyond Their Sex*, pp. 66-90.

Kingsley, Charles. Review of Froude's *History of England from the Fall of Wolsey to the Death of Elizabeth. Macmillan's Magazine* Vol. 9 (January 1864), pp. 211-24.

[Kirwan, A.V.?]. Review of Pardoe's *Louis XIV, and the Court of France in the Seventeenth Century. Fraser's Magazine* Vol. 35 (June 1847), pp. 684-99.

Kleinberg, S. Jay, et al. *Retrieving Women's History: Changing Perceptions of the Role of Women in Politics and Society.* Oxford: Berg/Unesco, 1988.

Knoepflmacher, U. C. *Religious Humanism and the Victorian Novel.* Princeton: Princeton UP, 1965.

Labalme, Patricia, ed. *Beyond Their Sex: Learned Women of the European Past.* New York: NYU P, 1980.

Lamb, Mary. "On Needle-work." *British Lady's Magazine* Vol. 1 No. 4 (April 1815), pp. 257-60.

Lambert, Miss. *Hand-Book of Needlework.* Philadelphia: Willis P. Hazard, 1850. (Orig. pub. London, 1843.)

Langland, Elizabeth. *Nobody's Angels: Middle-Class Women and Domestic Ideology in Victorian Culture.* Ithaca: Cornell UP, 1995.

Lawrance, Hannah. *Historical Memoirs of the Queens of England, from the Commencement of the Twelfth Century.* 2 Volumes. London: Edward Moxon, 1838.

———. *The History of Woman in England, and her influence on society and literature from the earliest period.* London: Henry Colburn, 1843.

Lerner, Gerda. *The Creation of Feminist Consciousness: From the Middle Ages to Eighteen-Seventy.* New York: Oxford UP, 1993.

———. "New Approaches to the Study of Women in American History." *Journal of Social History* Vol. 3 (Fall 1969), pp. 53-62. Rpt. in Cott, ed., *Theory and Method in Women's History*, Vol. 1, pp. 3-12.

———. "Placing Women in History: A 1975 Perspective," in Carroll, ed., *Liberating Women's History*, pp. 357-67.

Levey, Santina. *Discovering Embroidery of the Nineteenth Century.* Aylesbury: Shire Publications, 1971.

Levine, George. "*Romola* as Fable," in Barbara Hardy, ed., *Critical Essays on George Eliot.* London: Routledge & Kegan Paul, 1979, pp. 78-98.

Levine, Joseph. *Humanism and History: Origins of Modern English Historiography.* Ithaca: Cornell UP, 1987.

Levine, Philippa. *The Amateur and the Professional: Antiquarians, Historians and Archaeologists in Victorian England, 1838-1886*. Cambridge: Cambridge UP, 1986.

[Lewes, G. H.]. "A Gentle Hint to Writing Women." *Leader* 1 (1850), p. 189, cited in Elizabeth K. Helsinger, Robin Lauterbach Sheets, and William Veeder, *The Woman Question: Society and Literature in Britain and America 1837-1883, Volume 3: Literary Issues* (Chicago: U of Chicago P, 1983), pp. 4-5.

Lewis, Sarah. *Woman's Mission*. Boston: W. Crosby & Co., 1840.

Lieb, Laurie Yager. "'The Works of Women Are Symbolical': Needlework in the Eighteenth Century." *Eighteenth-Century Life* Vol. X, n.s. 2 (May 1986), pp. 28-44.

[Lister, T. H.]. "The Waverley Novels." *Edinburgh Review* Vol. 55 (April 1832), pp. 61-79.

[Lister, T. H.?]. Review of Aikin's *Memoirs of the Court of Charles I*. *Edinburgh Review* Vol. 58 (1834), pp. 398-422.

Macaulay, Thomas Babington. *The History of England from the Accession of James II*. 3 Volumes. London: J. M. Dent & Sons Ltd., 1913. (Orig. pub. 5 Vols., 1848-1861.)

———. "History." *The Lays of Ancient Rome & Miscellaneous Essays and Poems*. London: J. M. Dent & Sons, 1910; rpt. 1963, pp. 1-39.

[———]. Review of Sir James Mackintosh's *History of the Revolution in England in 1688*. *Edinburgh Review* Vol. 61 (July 1835), pp. 265-322.

Macheski, Cecilia. "Penelope's Daughters: Images of Needlework in Eighteenth-Century Literature," in Mary Anne Schofield and Cecilia Macheski, eds., *Fetter'd or Free? British Women Novelists 1670-1815*. Athens, OH: Ohio UP, 1986, pp. 85-100.

Maitzen, Rohan. "'By No Means an Improbable Fiction': *Redgauntlet*'s Novel Historicism." *Studies in the Novel* Vol. 25 No. 2 (Summer 1993), pp. 170-83.

———. "'This Feminine Preserve': Historical Biographies by Victorian Women." *Victorian Studies* Vol. 38 No. 3 (Spring 1995), pp. 371-93.

———. "'When Pit Jumps On Stage': Historiography and Theatricality in Carlyle's *French Revolution*." *Carlyle Annual* Vol. 13 (1992/3), pp. 44-54.

Malthus, Thomas. *An Essay on the Principle of Population*. Ed. Antony Flew. Harmondsworth: Penguin, 1970.

Marlatt, Daphne. *Ana Historic*. Toronto: Coach House Press, 1988.

Martin, Carol A. "George Eliot: Feminist Critic." *Victorian Newsletter* No. 65 (Spring 1984), pp. 22-25.

[May, T. E.]. Review of Froude's *Reign of Elizabeth*. *Edinburgh Review* Vol. 124 (October 1866), pp. 476-511.

[McCarthy, Justin?]. Review of Eliot's *Romola*. *Westminster Review* Vol. 24 (October 1863), pp. 244-52

McCormack, Kathleen. "The Sybil and the Hyena: George Eliot's Wollstonecraftian Feminism." *Dalhousie Review* Vol. 63 No. 4 (Winter 1983-84), pp. 602-14.

McGann, Jerome. *The Beauty of Inflections: Literary Investigations in Historical Method and Theory*. Oxford: Clarendon, 1985.

Meisel, Martin. *Realizations: Narrative, Pictorial, and Theatrical Arts in Nineteenth-Century England*. Princeton: Princeton UP, 1983.

Mermin, Dorothy. *Godiva's Ride: Women of Letters in England, 1830-1880*. Bloomington: Indiana UP, 1993.

Millgate, Jane. *Macaulay*. London: Routledge & Kegan Paul, 1973.

[Milman, H. H.]. Review of Froude's *Reign of Elizabeth*. *Quarterly Review* Vol. 114 No. 228 (October 1863), pp. 510-37.

Mink, Louis O. "Narrative Form as a Cognitive Instrument," in *Historical Understanding*, ed. Brian Fay, Eugene O. Golob, and Richard T. Vann. Ithaca: Cornell UP, 1987, pp. 182-203.

Mitchell, Rosemary. "A Stitch in Time? Women, Needlework, and the Making of History in Victorian Britain." *Journal of Victorian Culture* Vol. 1 No. 2 (Autumn 1996), pp. 185-202.

———. "The Busy Daughters of Clio: Women Writers of History between 1820 and 1880." *Women's History Review* (forthcoming, Spring 1998).

[Moncrieff, James]. Review of Macaulay's *History of England*. *Edinburgh Review* Vol. 90 (July 1849), pp. 249-292.

[———]. Review of Macaulay's *History of England* Vols. 3 & 4. *Edinburgh Review* Vol. 105 (January 1857), pp. 142-81.

[———]. Review of Macaulay's *History of England*. *Edinburgh Review* Vol. 114 (October 1861), pp. 279-317.

Nairn, Tom. *The Enchanted Glass: Britain and its Monarchy*. London: Radius, 1988.

Neff, Wanda F. *Victorian Working Women: An Historical and Literary Study of Women in British Industries and Professions 1832-1850*. London: Frank Cass & Co., 1966.

Oliphant, Margaret. *Autobiography.* Arranged and edited by Mrs. Harry Coghill, foreword by Laurie Langbauer. Chicago: U of Chicago P, 1988.

[———]. "Family History." *Blackwood's Magazine* Vol. 80 (October 1856), pp. 456-71.

[———]. "Modern Light Literature: History." *Blackwood's Magazine* Vol. 78 (October 1855), pp. 437-51.

[———]. "Mr. Froude and Queen Mary." *Blackwood's Magazine* Vol. 107 (January 1870), pp. 105-23.

[———]. Review of Burton's *History of Scotland to 1688. Blackwood's Magazine* Vol. 101 (March 1867), pp. 317-337.

[———]. Review of Trevelyan's *Life and Letters of Lord Macaulay. Blackwood's Magazine* Vol. 119 (May 1876), pp. 614-637.

Ormond, Leonée. "'The spacious times of great Elizabeth': The Victorian Vision of the Elizabethans." *Victorian Poetry* Vol. 25 Nos. 3-4 (Autumn-Winter 1987), pp. 29-46.

Osaki, Amy Boyce. "A 'Truly Feminine Employment': Sewing and the Early Nineteenth-Century Woman." *Winterthur Portfolio* Vol. 23 No. 4 (Winter 1988), pp. 225-41.

[Palgrave, Francis]. Review of Annie Forbes Bush's *Memoirs of the Queens of France. Quarterly Review* Vol. 71 (1843), pp. 411-16.

Parker, Roszika. *The Subversive Stitch: Embroidery and the Making of the Feminine.* London: The Women's Press, 1984.

[Patterson, R. H.]. Review of Alison's *History of Europe 1789-1815* and *History of Europe 1815-1852. Blackwood's Magazine* Vol. 79 (April 1856), pp. 404-421.

[———]. Review of Alison's *History of Europe 1815-1852* (revised edition). *Blackwood's Magazine* Vol. 100 (Oct. 1866), pp. 475-93.

Paxton, Nancy. "Feminism and Positivism in George Eliot's *Romola*," in Rhoda B. Nathan, ed., *Nineteenth-Century Women Writers of the English-Speaking World.* New York: Greenwood, 1986, pp. 143-50.

———. *George Eliot and Herbert Spencer: Feminism, Evolutionism, and the Reconstruction of Gender.* Princeton: Princeton UP, 1991.

Peardon, Thomas Preston. *The Transition in English Historical Writing 1760-1830.* New York: Columbia UP, 1933.

Perkins, David. *Is Literary History Possible?* Baltimore: Johns Hopkins UP, 1992.

Phillips, Mark. "Macaulay, Scott, and the Literary Challenge to Historiography." *Journal of the History of Ideas* Vol. 50 No. 1 (Jan.-Mar. 1989), pp. 117-33.

[Phillipps, C. S. M.]. Review of Alison's *History of Europe 1789-1815*. *Edinburgh Review* Vol. 76 (October 1842), pp. 1-60.

Pinney, Thomas, ed. *Essays of George Eliot*. New York: Columbia UP, 1963.

———, ed. *Selected Letters of Thomas Babington Macaulay*. Cambridge: Cambridge UP, 1982.

[Pollock, W. F.]. Review of Carlyle's *Frederick the Great*. *Quarterly Review* Vol. 105 (April 1859), pp. 275-304.

Poovey, Mary. *Uneven Developments: The Ideological Work of Gender in Mid-Victorian England*. Chicago: U of Chicago P, 1988.

Pope-Hennessy, Dame Una. *Agnes Strickland: Biographer of the Queens of England 1796-1874*. London: Chatto & Windus, 1940.

Purvis, June. *A History of Women's Education in England*. Philadelphia: Open University P, 1991.

Reilly, Jim. *Shadowtime: History and Representation in Hardy, Conrad and George Eliot*. New York: Routledge, 1993.

Rich, Adrienne. *Poems Selected and New 1950-1974*. New York: Norton, 1975.

Rigney, Ann. "Adapting History to the Novel." *New Comparison* Vol. 9 (1989), pp. 127-43.

Roberts, Mary. *Select Female Biography, Comprising Memoirs of Eminent British Ladies*. London: Harvey & Darton, 1829.

Rowbotham, Sheila. *Hidden From History*. New York: Pantheon, 1974.

Ruskin, John. "Of Queens' Gardens." *Sesame and Lilies, The Two Paths, and The King of the Golden River*. London: J. M. Dent & Sons, 1907, pp. 48-79.

[Sandars, T. C.]. Review of Buckle's *History of Civilization in England*. *Fraser's Magazine* Vol. 56 (Oct. 1857), pp. 409-424.

[Sanford, J. L.] Review of Froude's *History of England from the Fall of Wolsey to the Death of Elizabeth*. *National Review* Vol. 3 (July 1856), pp. 107-27.

Schor, Naomi. *Reading in Detail: Aesthetics and the Feminine*. New York: Methuen, 1987.

Scott, Joan Wallach. *Gender and the Politics of History*. New York: Columbia UP, 1988.

Scott, Sir Walter. *Waverley*. Ed. Andrew Hook. Harmondsworth: Penguin, 1972.

Shaw, Harry E. *The Forms of Historical Fiction: Sir Walter Scott and His Successors.* Ithaca: Cornell UP, 1983.

Showalter, Elaine. *A Literature of Their Own: British Women Novelists from Bronte to Lessing.* Princeton: Princeton UP, 1977.

Shuttleworth, Sally. *George Eliot and Nineteenth-Century Science: The Make-Believe of a Beginning.* Cambridge: Cambridge UP, 1984.

Smith, Bonnie G. "The Contribution of Women to Modern Historiography in Great Britain, France, and the United States, 1750-1940." *American Historical Review* Vol. 89 No. 3 (1984), pp. 709-32.

[Smith, Goldwin]. Review of Froude's *History of England from the Fall of Wolsey to the Death of Elizabeth. Edinburgh Review* Vol. 108 (July 1858), pp. 206-252.

Smith, Hilda L. "Female Bonds and the Family: Recent Directions in Women's History," in Paula A. Treichler, Cheris Kramarae, and Beth Stafford, eds., *For Alma Mater: Theory and Practice in Feminist Scholarship.* Chicago: U of Illinois P, 1985, pp. 272-91.

Spacks, Patricia Meyer. *Gossip.* New York: Knopf, 1985.

Spectator No. 611 (March 14, 1840).

——— No. 719 (April 9, 1842).

——— No. 742 (September 17, 1842).

——— No. 885 (June 14, 1845).

——— No. 947 (August 22, 1846).

——— No. 1586 (November 20, 1858).

Stage, Sarah. "Women's History and 'Woman's Sphere': Major Works of the 1970s." *Socialist Review* Nos. 50/51 (March-June 1980), pp. 245-53.

Standley, Arline Reilein. *Auguste Comte.* Boston: Twayne, 1981.

Stimpson, Catharine. "Feminist Criticism," in Stephen Greenblatt and Giles Gunn, eds., *Redrawing the Boundaries.* New York: MLA, 1992, pp. 251-70.

Stodart, M. A. *Female Writers: Thoughts on Their Proper Sphere, and on Their Powers of Usefulness.* London: Seeley and Burnside, 1842.

[Stone, Elizabeth]. *The Art of Needlework, from the Earliest Ages; Including Some Notices of the Ancient Historical Tapestries.* London: Henry Colburn, 1841.

Strickland, Agnes. *Life of Queen Elizabeth.* London: J. M. Dent & Sons, 1906.

———. *Life of Mary, Queen of Scots.* 2 Volumes. London: George Bell & Sons, 1888.

———. *Lives of the Queens of England, from the Norman Conquest.* 12 Volumes. Philadelphia: Lea & Blanchard, 1848. (Orig. pub. 12 Volumes. London: Henry Colburn, 1840-1848.)

———. *Lives of the Queens of England, from the Norman Conquest.* Philadelphia: George Barrie & Sons, 1902.

———. *Lives of the Queens of Scotland and English Princesses Connected with the Regal Succession of Great Britain.* 8 Volumes. New York: Harper & Bros., 1851.

———. *Lives of the Queens of Scotland and English Princesses Connected with the Regal Succession of Great Britain.* London: Blackwood, 1852.

———, ed. *Letters of Mary, Queen of Scots.* London: Henry Colburn, 1843.

Strickland, Jane Margaret. *Life of Agnes Strickland.* London: William Blackwood & Sons, 1887.

Thirsk, Joan. "The History Women," in *Chattel, Servant, or Citizen: Women's Status in Church, State and Society,* eds. M. O'Dowd and S. Wichert. Belfast: Institute of Irish Studies, the Queen's University, 1995, pp. 1-11.

Thompson, Dorothy. *Queen Victoria: Gender and Power.* London: Virago, 1990.

Walkley, Christina. *The Ghost in the Looking Glass: The Victorian Seamstress.* London: Peter Owen, 1986.

Wallace, Anne D. "'Nor in Fading Silks Compose': Sewing, Walking, and Poetic Labour in *Aurora Leigh.*" *ELH* Vol 64 No. 1 (Spring 1997), pp. 223-56.

Wardle, Patricia. *Guide to English Embroidery.* London: HM Stationer's Office, 1970.

Warren, Mrs., and Mrs. Pullan. *Treasures in Needlework; Comprising Instructions in Knitting, Netting, Crochet, Point Lace, Tatting, Braiding, and Embroidery; Illustrated with Useful and Ornamental Designs, Patterns, etc.* London: Ward & Lock, 1855.

Watt, Ian. *The Rise of the Novel.* Berkeley: U of California P, 1957.

Weimann, Robert. "Past Significance and Present Meaning in Literary History," in Ralph Cohen, ed., *New Directions in Literary History.* Baltimore: Johns Hopkins UP, 1974, pp. 43-61.

Welsh, Alexander. *George Eliot and Blackmail.* Cambridge, MA: Harvard UP, 1985.

Winnett, Susan. "Coming Unstrung: Women, Men, Narrative, and Principles of Pleasure." *PMLA* Vol. 105 No. 3 (May 1990), pp. 505-18.

Wood, Mary Anne Everett. *Letters of Royal and Illustrious Ladies of Great Britain, from the Commencement of the Twelfth Century to the Close of the Reign of Queen Mary.* London: Henry Colburn, 1846.

Woolf, Daniel. "A Feminine Past? Gender, Genre, and Historical Knowledge in England, 1500-1800." *American Historical Review* Vol. 102 No. 3 (June 1997), pp. 645-679.

Wright, T. R. *The Religion of Humanity: The Impact of Comtean Positivism on Victorian Britain.* Cambridge: Cambridge UP, 1986.

Young, G. M. *Victorian England: Portrait of an Age.* New York: Oxford UP, 1964.

Zinsser, Judith P. *History and Feminism: A Glass Half Full.* New York: Twayne, 1993.

Index

Abraham, G. W.
  reviews by, 10
Aikin, Lucy, 8, 36
Alison, Archibald
  reviews by, 4, 14, 106
  reviews of, 6, 10, 13, 74
Alison, Archibald, Jr.
  reviews by, 13
Armstrong, Nancy, 157

Balfour, Clara Lucas
  reviews of, 122-123
Bagehot, Walter, 156-157
  reviews by, 14
Bagshawe, H. R.
  reviews by, 74
Barrett, Dorothea, 152
Barrett Browning, Elizabeth. *See* Browning, Elizabeth Barrett
Bayeux Tapestry, 61
  controversy over, 81-82
  in Stone's *Art of Needlework*, 92
  in Strickland's *Lives of the Queens of England*, 80-83
Beer, Gillian, xiii

Benger, Elizabeth Ogilvy, 8
biography, 35-36
Boleyn, Anne, 78-79
Bonaparte, Felicia, 128
Booth, Alison, 121, 129
Braddon, Mary Elizabeth, 181
Browning, Elizabeth Barrett, 69-70
Bruce, John Collingwood, 61, 82
Buckle, T. E.
  reviews of, 10
Bullen, J. B., 127
Burrow, J. W., 6
Burton, John Hill
  reviews of, 25, 74
Bush, Annie Forbes, 8
  reviews of, 49, 82

Carlyle, Thomas, 86-87, 108, 136
  reviews of, 15
  on Scott, 9
  and social history, 18, 20
  and women's history, 39
Carr, E. H., xi, 14, 80, 88
Chandler, Alice, 66
Cheney, Edward
  reviews by, 49

Christ, Carol, 7, 15
Clark, Esther Lewis, 63
Colburn, Henry, 48
Comte, Auguste, 126-129
Costello, Louisa, 44, 47
Croker, J. W.
  reviews by, 22, 74, 76
Crosby, Christina, 6
Crosland, Mrs. Newton
  reviews of, 122-123

David, Deirdre, 121, 129
Davis, Natalie, 23, 44, 200, 202
Donne, W. B.
  reviews by, 13
Doran, Dr.
  reviews of, 7-8, 10, 36, 50

Eagleton, Terry, 30n52
Eliot, George, 5. See also separate entries for *Middlemarch* and *Romola*
  Adam Bede, 124-125, 139-141
  and Carlyle, 108
  Daniel Deronda, 141
  Felix Holt, 69
  and femininity, 138-139
  and feminism, 130, 137
  The Mill on the Floss, 124-125
  review of C. W. Fullom's *History of Woman*, 124
  Scenes of Clerical Life, 139-141
  "Silly Novels by Lady Novelists," 138
  and social history, 107-108
  and the 'Woman Question,' 137-138
  and woman's influence, 139-141
  and women historians, 122-123
  and women's history, 123-125, 157
Elizabeth I, xvi-xvii, 44, 161-196
  Armada speech, 195
  and femininity, 166-167, 188-189
  Froude's portrayal of, 164-172, 191-196
  and marriage, 167-170
  and maternity, 170
  and needlework, 77, 84, 188-189
  and 'queenly ideal,' 190
  and religion, 193-195
  Strickland's *Life*, 164-172, 188-191
  Victorian perceptions of, 163-164
Ellis, Sarah Stickney, 40

facts, historical. *See* historical facts.
Fedele, Cassandra, 125-126
feminism, xii
  cultural feminism, 52
  and women's history, 53, 200
Ferris, Ina, 7
fiction
  historical, 200
  and history, 3, 5-6, 9, 199-200
  and social history, 19
  and women's history, 54-55, 158
Finch, Anne, 62

Index

Fleishman, Avrom, 117
Fox-Genovese, Elizabeth, 200, 201, 202
Fraser, Lady Antonia, 203
Freer, Martha Walker, 8
   reviews of, 17
French Revolution, 4, 11
Froude, J. A.
   Reign of Elizabeth, xvi-xvii, 164-172, 181-187, 191-196. *See also* Elizabeth I and Mary, Queen of Scots
   reviews by, 122-123
   reviews of, 3, 13, 15, 17, 24
Fuller, Margaret, 52

Gooch, G. P., 6
gossip
   and fiction, 52, 54
   and women's culture, 51-52
   and women's history, 50-54
Grainger, R. D., 95
Greg, W. R., 97
   reviews by, 6
Green, Mary Ann Everett, 9. *See also* Wood, Mary Ann Everett

Hall, Mrs. Matthew, 9, 41, 44, 47, 50
Harrison, Frederic, 127
Hartshorne, Charles Henry, 66, 73
Hayden, Ilse, 157
Hays, Mary, 36, 44, 45, 53, 55, 143
Heilbrun, Carolyn, xii, 53, 125
Hill, Georgiana, 34
historical facts, xi, 14, 80

history
   accessibility of, 11
   affect in, 9-10
   details in, 12-18. *See also* women and details
   dignity of, 10, 14, 21
   Enlightenment theories of, 19, 111
   feminization of, xiii, 12, 75
   and fiction, 3, 5-6, 9, 199-200
   and narrative form, xii, xiii, 162
   and needlework, xiv-xv, 62, 74-98
   professionalization of, 199-200
   and Romanticism, 19, 112
   Victorians and, 4
history, social. *See* social history
Holt, Emily Sarah, 55
Homans, Margaret, 155, 157
Hood, Thomas, 95
Howard, Katharine, 45
Hume, David, 111
Hutton, R. H.
   reviews by, 120

Jameson, Anna, 34, 44, 45, 54, 143
Jann, Rosemary, 6
Jephson, John Mounteney
   reviews by, 9
Johnstone, Christian
   reviews by, 72, 73, 75, 90, 93-94

Katharine of Aragon, 78
Kavanagh, Julia, 8, 41
Kelly, Joan, 200, 201, 202

Kemble, J. M.
  reviews by, 7-8, 10, 13
Kenyon, John, 6
Kingsley, Charles
  reviews by, 3, 24
Kirwan, A. V.
  reviews by, 50

Lamb, Mary, 67
Lawrance, Hannah, 8, 34, 36, 37, 54, 90
Lerner, Gerda, 200, 201, 202
Levine, George, 103, 121
Levine, Joseph M., 6
Lewes, G. H., 68
Lewis, Sarah, 40, 46
Lister, T. H.
  reviews by, 19
literacy, 11
literary history, xiii

Macaulay, Thomas Babington, 3, 5, 11, 16-17, 46, 86, 203-204
  History of England, 12, 20-23, 108; Chapter 3 of, 21-22, 110; details in, 14
  reviews by, 10
  reviews of *History of England*, 4, 10, 12, 13, 14, 22, 74, 76, 106
  and social history, 20
  and women readers, 50
  and women's history, 39-40
Mackintosh, Sir James
  reviews of, 10
Malthus, Thomas, 18-19
Marlatt, Daphne, 204-205

Marsh, Anne, 34
Martineau, Harriet, 33
Mary, Queen of Scots, xvi-xvii, 41, 43, 161-196
  and female community, 179-180
  as feminine ideal, 174-176
  and femininity, 166-167, 173, 182
  Froude's portrayal of, 164-172, 181-187
  and marriage, 167-170
  and maternity, 170-171
  and melodrama, 185
  and needlework, 84, 176-178
  and 'queenly ideal,' 174-176, 180-181
  Strickland's *Life*, 164-181
  Victorian perceptions of, xvii, 163-164, 186-187
May, T. E.
  reviews by, 15, 17
McGann, Jerome, xiii
memoirs. *See* biography
Mermin, Dorothy, xiii, 130
Middlemarch, 70, 88, 135-158. *See also* Eliot, George
  Dorothea's character, 137, 141-142, 151-152
  Dorothea and ideals of womanhood, 142-143, 150-151
  Dorothea and queenliness, 143-144
  Dorothea and woman's influence, 144-147
  historical details in, 152

and 'queenly ideal,' 137, 143-147, 154
and social history, 20, 40, 136-157
and woman's nature, 148-149
and the 'Woman Question,' 135
and women's history, xvi, 135-136, 157
Mink, Louis O., xii, xiii
Mitchell, Rosemary, 55n1, 98n1
Moncrieff, James
reviews by, 10, 12, 13, 22
Morgan, Lady Sydney, 90

narrative form. *See* history and narrative form
needlework
across cultures, 89-90
and female community, 73, 79-80, 88-89, 93, 96
and femininity, 63, 97
and history. *See* history and needlework
as metaphor, 74-77
opponents of, 67
professional, 94-97
and social class, xv, 62, 64, 71-73, 94-97
and social history, 80, 87-88
and social status, 64-65
in Stone's *Art of Needlework*. *See* Stone, Elizabeth
in Strickland's *Lives of the Queens of England*. *See* Strickland, Agnes
as supplement, 76
in Victorian literature, 69, 96

and Victorian medievalism, 65-67
and women writers, 68-69
and women's culture, 71-74
and women's history. *See* women's history and needlework
and women's roles, 65
novel. *See* fiction

Oliphant, Margaret, 68
reviews by, 11, 24, 25-26, 36, 74
Ogborne, Elizabeth, 34
Ormond, Leonée, 164

Palgrave, Francis
reviews by, 49, 82
reviews of, 9
Palliser, Fanny, 34
Pardoe, Julia
reviews of, 50, 122-123
Patterson, R. H.
reviews by, 13, 74
Paxton, Nancy, 128
Peardon, Thomas Preston, 6
Phillipps, C. S. M.
reviews by, 10
Positivism. *See* Comte, Auguste

Queen Victoria. *See* Victoria (Queen of England)

Roberts, Mary, 47
Romola, 103-131, 201. *See also* Eliot, George
characterization in, 114
GE's comments on, 117, 121
historical details in, 104-106

and narrative possibilities,
   125-126, 130-131
and Positivism, 126-129
reviews of, 106, 120-121
Romola's character, 104, 110-111, 117-122
Romola as Madonna, 119-120, 129
Romola and public life, 120
Romola and queenliness, 118
Savonarola's character, 116-117
and social history, 103
and theories of history, 111-113
Tito's character, 115-116
and women's education, 107
and women's history, xv, 103-104, 109-110, 129-131
Ruskin, John, xvi, 154-155

Sandars, T. C.
   reviews by, 10
Sanford, J. L.
   reviews by, 15
Schor, Naomi, 16
Scott, Joan, 52, 201
Scott, Sir Walter, 5, 7, 19, 74
   and theories of history, 112-113
   Waverley, 9, 112-113
separate spheres ideology, 168
Shaw, Harry E., 113
Shuttleworth, Sally, 117, 128
Smith, Goldwin
   reviews by, 13
social history, 18
   and fiction, 19
   and needlework. *See* needlework and social history
   and politics, 11-12, 22-23
   and women's history, 23-24, 38
Stone, Elizabeth, 34, 37
   The Art of Needlework, xiv-xv, 71, 73, 75, 83-93; and social history, 85-87; and women's history, 85-87; and women historians, 90; form of, 91; Bayeux Tapestry, 92
   reviews of *The Art of Needlework*, 67, 70, 72, 73, 75, 90, 93-94
Strickland, Agnes, 8, 25, 36, 37, 43, 44, 45, 48, 49, 54, 90
   importance of, 203-204
   Life of Elizabeth, 164-172, 188-191. *See also* Elizabeth I
   Life of Mary, Queen of Scots, xvi-xvii, 164-181. *See also* Mary, Queen of Scots
   Lives of the Queens of England, 52; needlework in, xiv-xv, 77-83; Bayeux Tapestry, 80-83
   and needlework, xv, 49, 69, 77
   reviews of, 10, 17, 25, 50, 51, 74, 81, 122-123
Strickland, Jane Margaret, 69
Stuart, Mary. *See* Mary, Queen of Scots
Syme, Ebenezer
   reviews by, 122-123

Index

Tennyson, Alfred, 177
Thirsk, Joan, 55*n*1
Thompson, Dorothy, 155, 157
Tudor, Elizabeth. *See* Elizabeth I

Victoria (Queen of England), xvi, 155-157

Welsh, Alexander, xiii
Winnett, Susan, 130
women
  and details, 16
  and fiction, 5, 9
  and gossip, 51
  and history, xii
  and influence, 40
  and needlework, 63-64
  roles of, 42-43
  and writing, 62
women historians
  audience, 48
  and biography, 35-36
  and 'general history,' 37, 76, 82
  and propriety, 50
  and 'queenly ideal,' 154
  reviews of, 17
  and social history, 38, 82-83
  in Stone's *Art of Needlework*, 90
  twentieth-century, 200-203
  Victorian, xiv, 8, 33-55, 201
  and women's roles, 43
women readers
  and fiction, 49
  and 'general history,' 50
  and propriety, 49
  and women's history, 48
women writers, 12
  and needlework, 68-69
women's history, xii
  amateur, 200, 203-204
  audience for, 48
  and constructions of gender, 201-202
  developing tradition of, 42
  and feminism, 53, 200
  and fiction, 54-55, 158
  and gender ideology, 40-42
  and gossip, 50-54
  and influence, 40-42
  and narrative form, 53
  and needlework, 76
  and periodization, 202
  and politics, 23, 200
  and Positivism, 129-131
  and propriety, 49
  and role models, 46-47
  and social history, 23-24, 38, 87, 201
  theories of, xiv, 40, 200-202
  twentieth-century, 200-203
  and women's culture, 52
Wood, Mary Ann Everett, 36. *See also* Green, Mary Ann Everett
Woolf, Daniel, 206*n*15
Wright, T. R., 128

For Product Safety Concerns and Information please contact our EU
representative GPSR@taylorandfrancis.com
Taylor & Francis Verlag GmbH, Kaufingerstraße 24, 80331 München, Germany

www.ingramcontent.com/pod-product-compliance
Lightning Source LLC
Chambersburg PA
CBHW050556170426
43201CB00011B/1714